CASSEROLE & ONE-POT

THE **COMPLETE** COOKBOOK

CASSEROLE & ONE-POT

TASTY RECIPES FOR EVERY DAY

Edited by Helen Aitkin

BARNES & NOBLE

NEW YORK

Contents

Soups	7
Casseroles	39
Curries	91
Stews	133
On the side	215
Index	252

You will find the following cookery ratings on the recipes in this book:

A single pot symbol indicates a recipe that is simple and generally straightforward to make—perfect for beginners.

Two symbols indicate the need for just a little more care and a little more time.

Three symbols indicate special recipes that need more investment in time, care and patience—but the results are worth it.

Soups

CHICKEN LAKSA

**Preparation time: 30 minutes +
  minutes soaking**
Total cooking time: 35 minutes
Serves 4–6

1½ tablespoons coriander seeds
1 tablespoon cumin seeds
1 teaspoon ground turmeric
1 onion, roughly chopped
1 tablespoon roughly chopped fresh ginger
3 cloves garlic, peeled
3 stems lemon grass (white part only), sliced
6 candlenuts or macadamias (see NOTES)
4–6 small fresh red chillies
2–3 teaspoons shrimp paste, roasted
    (see NOTES)
1 litre chicken stock
¼ cup (60 ml/2 fl oz) oil
400 g (13 oz) chicken thigh fillets, cut into
    2 cm (¾ inch) pieces
3 cups (750 ml/24 fl oz) coconut milk
4 fresh kaffir lime leaves
2½ tablespoons lime juice
2 tablespoons fish sauce
2 tablespoons grated palm sugar or soft
    brown sugar
250 g (8 oz) dried rice vermicelli
1 cup (90 g/3 oz) bean sprouts
4 fried tofu puffs, julienned
¼ cup (15 g/½ oz) roughly chopped fresh
    Vietnamese mint
⅔ cup (20 g/¾ oz) fresh coriander leaves
lime wedges, to serve

1 Dry-fry the coriander and cumin seeds in a
frying pan over medium heat for 1–2 minutes, or
until fragrant, tossing constantly to prevent them
burning. Grind finely in a mortar and pestle or
a spice grinder.

2 Place all the spices, onion, ginger, garlic,
lemon grass, candlenuts, red chillies and
shrimp paste in a food processor or blender.
Add about ½ cup (125 ml/4 fl oz) of the stock
and blend to a fine paste.

3 Heat the oil in a wok or large saucepan
over low heat and gently cook the paste for
3–5 minutes, stirring constantly to prevent it
burning or sticking to the bottom. Add the
remaining stock and bring to the boil over high
heat. Reduce the heat to medium and simmer
for 15 minutes, or until reduced slightly. Add
the chicken and simmer for 4–5 minutes, or
until cooked through.

4 Add the coconut milk, lime leaves, lime
juice, fish sauce and palm sugar, and simmer
for 5 minutes over medium–low heat. Do not
bring to the boil or cover with a lid, as the
coconut milk will split.

5 Meanwhile, place the vermicelli in a
heatproof bowl, cover with boiling water and
soak for 6–7 minutes, or until softened. Drain
and divide among large serving bowls with the
bean sprouts. Ladle the hot soup over the top
and garnish with some tofu strips, mint and
coriander leaves. Serve with a wedge of lime.

NUTRITION PER SERVE (6)
Protein 22 g; Fat 43 g; Carbohydrate 40 g;
Dietary Fibre 5 g; Cholesterol 58 mg;
2620 kJ (625 cal)

NOTES: Raw candlenuts are slightly toxic so
must be cooked before use.
To roast the shrimp paste, wrap the paste in foil
and place under a hot grill for 1 minute.

To avoid stains, wear rubber gloves to grate the cooled beetroot.

Allow the meat to cool, then cut it into dice using a sharp knife.

HOT BEEF BORSCHT

Preparation time: 30 minutes
Total cooking time: 2 hours 50 minutes
Serves 4–6

500 g (1 lb) gravy beef, cut into large pieces
500 g (1 lb) fresh beetroot
1 onion, finely chopped
1 carrot, cut into short strips
1 parsnip, cut into short strips
1 cup (75 g/2¹/₂ oz) finely shredded cabbage
sour cream and chopped fresh chives,
    to serve

1 Put the beef and 1 litre water in a large, heavy-based saucepan, and bring slowly to the boil. Reduce the heat, cover and simmer for 1 hour. Skim the surface as required.

2 Cut the stems from the beetroot, wash well and place in a large, heavy-based saucepan with 1 litre water. Bring to the boil, then reduce the heat and simmer for 40 minutes, or until tender. Drain, reserving 1 cup (250 ml/8 fl oz) of the liquid. Cool, then peel and grate the beetroot.

3 Remove the meat from the stock, cool and dice. Skim any fat from the surface of the stock. Return the meat to the stock and add the onion, carrot, parsnip, beetroot and reserved liquid. Bring to the boil, reduce the heat, cover and simmer for 45 minutes.

4 Stir in the cabbage and simmer for a further 15 minutes. Season to taste. Serve with the sour cream and chives.

NUTRITION PER SERVE (6)
Protein 20 g; Fat 10 g; Carbohydrate 10 g; Dietary Fibre 5 g; Cholesterol 80 mg; 940 kJ (225 cal)

Halve the tomatoes and scoop out the seeds with a teaspoon.

Brown the shanks in 2 batches, remove with tongs and drain on paper towels.

LAMB HOTPOT

Preparation time: 40 minutes +
1 hour refrigeration
Total cooking time: 2 hours
Serves 4

2 tablespoons olive oil
8 lamb shanks
2 onions, sliced
4 cloves garlic, finely chopped
3 bay leaves, torn in half
1–2 teaspoons hot paprika
2 teaspoons sweet paprika
1 tablespoon plain flour
$^1/_4$ cup (60 g/2 oz) tomato paste
1.5 litres vegetable stock
4 potatoes, chopped
4 carrots, sliced
3 celery sticks, thickly sliced
3 tomatoes, seeded and chopped

1 To make the lamb stock, heat 1 tablespoon of the oil in a large, heavy-based saucepan over medium heat. Brown the shanks well in two batches, then drain on paper towels.

2 Add the remaining oil to the pan and cook the onion, garlic and bay leaves over low heat for 10 minutes, stirring regularly. Add the paprikas and flour and cook, stirring, for 2 minutes. Gradually add the combined tomato paste and vegetable stock. Bring to the boil, stirring continuously, and return the shanks to the pan. Reduce the heat to low and simmer, covered, for $1^1/_2$ hours, stirring occasionally.

3 Remove and discard the bay leaves. Remove the shanks, allow to cool slightly and then cut the meat from the bone. Discard the bone. Cut the meat into pieces and refrigerate. Refrigerate the stock for about 1 hour, or until fat forms on the surface and can be spooned off.

4 Return the meat to the stock along with the potato, carrot and celery, and bring to the boil. Reduce the heat and simmer for 15 minutes. Season, and add the chopped tomato to serve.

NUTRITION PER SERVE
Protein 70 g; Fat 15 g; Carbohydrate 30 g; Dietary Fibre 8 g; Cholesterol 170 mg; 2200 kJ (525 cal)

Once the shiitake mushrooms have been soaked, thinly slice the caps.

ROAST DUCK AND NOODLE BROTH

**Preparation time: 25 minutes +
    25 minutes soaking**
Total cooking time: 10 minutes
Serves 4–6

3 dried shiitake mushrooms
1 Chinese roast duck (1.5 kg/3 lb)
2 cups (500 ml/16 fl oz) chicken stock
2 tablespoons light soy sauce
1 tablespoon Chinese rice wine
2 teaspoons sugar
400 g (13 oz) fresh flat rice noodles
2 tablespoons oil
3 spring onions, thinly sliced
1 teaspoon finely chopped fresh ginger
400 g (13 oz) bok choy, leaves separated
1/4 teaspoon sesame oil

1 Soak the mushrooms in 1 cup (250 ml/ 8 fl oz) boiling water for 20 minutes. Drain, reserving the liquid and squeezing the excess liquid from the mushrooms. Discard the stems and thinly slice the caps.
2 Remove the skin and flesh from the duck. Discard the fat and carcass. Finely slice the duck meat and the skin (you should have about 400 g/13 oz of duck meat).
3 Place the chicken stock, soy sauce, rice wine, sugar and the reserved mushroom liquid in a saucepan over medium heat. Bring to a simmer and cook for 5 minutes.
4 Meanwhile, place the rice noodles in a heatproof bowl, cover with boiling water and soak briefly. Gently separate the noodles with your hands and drain well. Divide evenly among large soup bowls.

5 Heat the oil in a wok over high heat. Add the spring onion, ginger and mushrooms, and cook for several seconds. Transfer to the broth with the bok choy and duck meat, and simmer for 1 minute, or until the duck has warmed through and the bok choy has wilted. Ladle the soup on the noodles and drizzle sesame oil on each serving. Serve immediately.

NUTRITION PER SERVE (6)
Protein 17 g; Fat 24 g; Carbohydrate 31 g; Dietary Fibre 2 g; Cholesterol 77 mg; 1695 kJ (405 cal)

Place all the meatball ingredients in a bowl and combine with your hands.

Once the pork balls have been shaped, add them to the wok one by one.

CHINESE PORK AND NOODLE SOUP

Preparation time: 25 minutes + overnight refrigeration + 1 hour refrigeration
Total cooking time: 4 hours
Serves 4–6

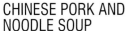

STOCK
1.5 kg (3 lb) chicken bones (chicken necks, backs, wings), washed
3 cloves garlic, sliced
2 slices fresh ginger, 1 cm (1/2 inch) thick
4 spring onions, white part only

150 g (5 oz) Chinese cabbage, shredded
1 tablespoon peanut oil
2 teaspoons sesame oil
4 cloves garlic, crushed
1 tablespoon grated fresh ginger
300 g (10 oz) pork mince
1 egg white
1/4 teaspoon ground white pepper

2 tablespoons light soy sauce
1 tablespoon Chinese rice wine
1 1/2 tablespoons cornflour
1/2 cup (15 g/1/2 oz) fresh coriander leaves, finely chopped
6 spring onions, thinly sliced
200 g (6 1/2 oz) fresh thin egg noodles

1 To make the stock, place the bones and 3.5 litres water in a large saucepan and bring to a simmer—do not boil. Cook for 30 minutes, removing any scum that rises to the surface. Add the garlic, ginger and spring onion, and cook, partially covered, at a low simmer for 3 hours. Strain through a fine sieve, then cool. Cover and refrigerate overnight. Remove the layer of fat from the surface once it has solidified.

2 Bring a large saucepan of water to the boil and cook the cabbage for 2 minutes, or until soft. Drain, cool and squeeze out the excess water.

3 Heat the peanut oil and 1 teaspoon of the sesame oil in a small frying pan, and cook the garlic and ginger for 1 minute, or until the garlic just starts to brown. Allow to cool.

4 Combine the mince, cabbage, garlic mixture, egg white, white pepper, soy sauce, rice wine, cornflour, half the coriander and half the spring onion. Cover and refrigerate for 1 hour. Shape tablespoons of the mixture into balls.

5 Bring 1.5 litres of the stock (freeze the leftover stock) to the boil in a wok over high heat. Reduce the heat to medium and simmer for 1–2 minutes. Add the pork balls and cook, covered, for 8–10 minutes, or until they rise to the surface and are cooked through.

6 Bring a large saucepan of water to the boil. Cook the noodles for 1 minute, then drain and rinse. Divide among serving bowls and ladle the soup and balls on top. Garnish with the remaining spring onion, coriander and sesame oil.

NUTRITION PER SERVE (6)
Protein 17 g; Fat 9.5 g; Carbohydrate 23 g; Dietary Fibre 2 g; Cholesterol 35 mg; 1030 kJ (245 cal)

Cook the pancetta, onion, garlic, celery and carrot for 5 minutes.

Purée 1 cup (250 ml/8 fl oz) of the bean mixture in a food processor.

PASTA AND BEAN SOUP

**Preparation time: 15 minutes + overnight
  soaking + 10 minutes resting**
Total cooking time: 1 hour 45 minutes
Serves 4

200 g (6½ oz) dried borlotti beans
¼ cup (60 ml/2 fl oz) olive oil
90 g (3 oz) piece pancetta, finely diced
1 onion, finely chopped
2 cloves garlic, crushed
1 celery stick, thinly sliced
1 carrot, diced
1 bay leaf
1 sprig fresh rosemary
1 sprig fresh flat-leaf parsley
400 g (13 oz) can diced tomatoes, drained
1.6 litres vegetable stock
2 tablespoons finely chopped fresh
  flat-leaf parsley
150 g (5 oz) ditalini or other small
  dried pasta

extra virgin olive oil, to serve
grated fresh Parmesan, to serve

1 Place the beans in a large bowl, cover with cold water and leave to soak overnight. Drain and rinse.
2 Heat the oil in a large saucepan, add the pancetta, onion, garlic, celery and carrot, and cook over medium heat for 5 minutes, or until golden. Season with pepper. Add the bay leaf, rosemary, parsley, tomato, stock and beans, and bring to the boil. Reduce the heat and simmer for 1½ hours, or until the beans are tender. Add more boiling water if necessary to maintain the liquid level.
3 Discard the bay leaf, rosemary and parsley sprigs. Scoop out 1 cup (250 ml/8 fl oz) of the bean mixture and purée in a food processor or blender. Return to the pan, season with salt and ground black pepper, and add the parsley and pasta. Simmer for 6 minutes, or until the pasta is al dente. Remove from the heat and set aside for 10 minutes. Serve drizzled with extra virgin olive oil and sprinkled with Parmesan.

NUTRITION PER SERVE
Protein 13 g; Fat 20 g; Carbohydrate 38 g; Dietary Fibre 7.5 g; Cholesterol 12 mg; 1643 kJ (393 cal)

NOTE: If you prefer, you can use three 400 g (13 oz) cans drained borlotti beans. Simmer with the other vegetables for 30 minutes.

Cook the processed onion, garlic, parsley and pancetta mixture.

Simmer the soup until the pasta and vegetables are al dente.

MINESTRONE

**Preparation time: 25 minutes +
  overnight soaking**
Total cooking time: 2 hours
Serves 6

125 g (4 oz) dried borlotti beans
1 large onion, roughly chopped
2 cloves garlic
1/4 cup (7 g/ 1/4 oz) roughly chopped fresh
  flat-leaf parsley
60 g (2 oz) pancetta, chopped
1/4 cup (60 ml/2 fl oz) olive oil
1 celery stick, halved lengthways, cut into
  1 cm (1/2 inch) slices
1 carrot, halved lengthways, cut into
  1 cm (1/2 inch) slices
1 potato, diced
2 teaspoons tomato paste
400 g (13 oz) can diced tomatoes
6 fresh basil leaves, roughly torn
2 litres chicken or vegetable stock

2 thin zucchini, cut into 1.5 cm
  (5/8 inch) slices
3/4 cup (115 g/4 oz) shelled peas
60 g (2 oz) green beans, cut into 4 cm
  (1 1/2 inch) lengths
80 g (2 3/4 oz) silverbeet leaves, shredded
75 g (2 1/2 oz) ditalini or small pasta

PESTO
1 cup (30 g/1 oz) loosely packed fresh
  basil leaves
20 g (3/4 oz) lightly toasted pine nuts
2 cloves garlic
100 ml (3 1/2 fl oz) olive oil
1/4 cup (25 g/3/4 oz) grated fresh Parmesan

1 Put the beans in a large bowl, cover with water and soak overnight. Drain and rinse under cold water.
2 Place the onion, garlic, parsley and pancetta in a food processor and process until finely chopped. Heat the oil in a saucepan, add the pancetta mixture and cook over low heat, stirring occasionally, for 8–10 minutes.

3 Add the celery, carrot and potato, and cook for 5 minutes, then stir in the tomato paste, tomato, basil and borlotti beans. Season with black pepper. Add the stock and bring slowly to the boil. Cover and simmer, stirring occasionally, for 1 1/2 hours.
4 Season, and add the zucchini, peas, green beans, silverbeet and pasta. Simmer for 8–10 minutes, or until the vegetables and pasta are al dente.
5 To make the pesto, combine the basil, pine nuts and garlic with a pinch of salt in a food processor. Process until finely chopped. With the motor running, slowly add the olive oil. Transfer to a bowl and stir in the Parmesan and ground black pepper to taste. Serve the soup in bowls with the pesto on top.

NUTRITION PER SERVE
Protein 9 g; Fat 30 g; Carbohydrate 20 g; Dietary Fibre 5.3 g; Cholesterol 9 mg; 1593 kJ (380 cal)

Remove the lime rind with a vegetable peeler, and cut it into long, thin strips.

Chop the chilli, onion, garlic, ginger, lemon grass and coriander until smooth.

CHICKEN AND COCONUT MILK SOUP

**Preparation time: 30 minutes +
   5 minutes soaking**
Total cooking time: 15 minutes
Serves 8

150 g (5 oz) dried rice vermicelli
1 lime
4 small fresh red chillies, seeded
   and chopped
1 medium onion, chopped
2 cloves garlic, crushed
4 thin slices fresh ginger, finely chopped
2 stems lemon grass (white part only),
   chopped
1 tablespoon chopped fresh coriander
1 tablespoon peanut oil
3 cups (750 ml/24 fl oz) chicken stock
2¾ cups (685 ml/22 fl oz) coconut milk
500 g (1 lb) chicken tenderloins, cut into
   thin strips

4 spring onions, chopped
150 g (5 oz) fried tofu puffs, sliced
1 cup (90 g/3 oz) bean sprouts
3 teaspoons soft brown sugar

1 Soak the vermicelli in boiling water for 5 minutes. Drain, cut into short lengths and set aside.
2 Remove the lime rind with a vegetable peeler and cut it into strips.
3 Place the chilli, onion, garlic, ginger, lemon grass and coriander into a food processor and process in short bursts for 20 seconds, or until smooth.
4 Heat the oil in a large heavy-based saucepan over medium heat. Add the chilli mixture and cook, stirring frequently, for 3 minutes, or until fragrant. Add the stock, coconut milk and lime rind, and bring to the boil. Add the chicken and cook, stirring, for 4 minutes, or until tender.

5 Add the spring onion, tofu, bean sprouts and brown sugar, and season with salt. Stir over medium heat for 3 minutes, or until the spring onion is tender. Divide the noodles among bowls and pour the soup over the top. Garnish with chilli and coriander.

NUTRITION PER SERVE
Protein 20 g; Fat 25 g; Carbohydrate 19 g; Dietary Fibre 3.5 g; Cholesterol 44 mg; 1555 kJ (370 cal)

Once the mixture has thickened, return the browned chicken thighs to the pan.

Add the basmati rice to the soup during the last 15 minutes of cooking.

MULLIGATAWNY

Preparation time: 20 minutes
Total cooking time: 1 hour 15 minutes
Serves 4

30 g (1 oz) butter
375 g (12 oz) chicken thigh cutlets, skin and fat removed
1 large onion, finely chopped
1 apple, peeled, cored and diced
1 tablespoon curry paste
2 tablespoons plain flour
3 cups (750 ml/24 fl oz) chicken stock
1/4 cup (50 g/1 3/4 oz) basmati rice
1 tablespoon chutney
1 tablespoon lemon juice
1/4 cup (60 ml/2 fl oz) cream

1 Heat the butter in a large heavy-based saucepan. Cook the chicken for 5 minutes, or until browned, then remove and set aside. Add the onion, apple and curry paste to the pan. Cook for 5 minutes, or until the onion is soft. Stir in the flour and cook for 2 minutes, then add half the stock. Stir until the mixture boils and thickens.

2 Return the chicken to the pan with the remaining stock. Stir until boiling, then reduce the heat, cover and simmer for 1 hour. Add the rice for the last 15 minutes of cooking.

3 Remove the chicken from the pan. Remove the meat from the bones, dice finely and return to the pan. Add the chutney, lemon juice and cream, and season to taste.

NUTRITION PER SERVE
Protein 25 g; Fat 16 g; Carbohydrate 25 g;
Dietary Fibre 2 g; Cholesterol 28 mg;
1396 kJ (333 cal)

Cut the ends off the enoki mushrooms, then separate the stems.

HOT AND SOUR SOUP

**Preparation time: 40 minutes + overnight refrigeration +
10 minutes standing**
Total cooking time: 4 hours
Serves 6

STOCK
1.5 kg (3 lb) chicken bones (chicken necks, backs, wings), washed
2 slices fresh ginger, 1 cm (½ inch) thick
4 spring onions, white part only

200 g (6½ oz) chicken breast fillet, cut into 2 cm (¾ inch) pieces
2 tablespoons garlic and red chilli paste
¼ cup (60 ml/2 fl oz) light soy sauce
¾ teaspoon ground white pepper
115 g (4 oz) baby corn, quartered lengthways
⅓ cup (80 ml/2¾ fl oz) Chinese black vinegar

4 fresh shiitake mushrooms, stems removed, caps thinly sliced
100 g (3½ oz) enoki mushrooms, trimmed and separated
65 g (2¼ oz) fresh black wood fungus, cut into 1 cm (½ inch) strips
200 g (6½ oz) fresh Shanghai noodles
200 g (6½ oz) firm tofu, cut into 2.5 cm (1 inch) cubes
¼ cup (30 g/1 oz) cornflour
3 eggs, lightly beaten
1 teaspoon sesame oil
2 spring onions, thinly sliced on the diagonal

1 To make the stock, place the bones and 3.5 litres water in a large saucepan and simmer—do not boil. Cook for 30 minutes, removing any scum as it rises to the surface. Add the ginger and spring onion, and cook, partially covered, at a low simmer for 3 hours. Strain through a fine sieve and allow to cool. Cover and refrigerate overnight. Remove the layer of fat from the surface.

2 Bring 2 litres of the stock to the boil in a large saucepan over high heat (freeze any remaining stock). Reduce the heat to medium, add the chicken, garlic and chilli paste, soy sauce and white pepper, and stir to combine. Simmer, covered, for 10 minutes, or until the chicken is cooked. Add the corn, vinegar, mushrooms, wood fungus, noodles and tofu. Season with salt, and gently simmer for 5 minutes—do not stir.

3 Combine the cornflour and ¼ cup (60 ml/2 fl oz) water. Slowly stir into the soup until combined and slightly thickened. Return to a simmer, then pour the egg over the surface in a very thin stream. Turn off the heat, stand for 10 minutes, then stir in the sesame oil. Garnish with the spring onion.

NUTRITION PER SERVE
Protein 23 g; Fat 9.5 g; Carbohydrate 31 g; Dietary Fibre 3.5 g; Cholesterol 128 mg; 1265 kJ (300 cal)

Thinly slice the partially frozen steak across the grain.

BEEF PHO

**Preparation time: 15 minutes +
    40 minutes freezing
Total cooking time: 30 minutes
Serves 4**

400 g (13 oz) rump steak, trimmed
1 litre beef stock
$\frac{1}{2}$ onion
1 star anise
1 cinnamon stick
1 tablespoon fish sauce
pinch ground white pepper
200 g (6½ oz) fresh thin round
    rice noodles
2 spring onions, thinly sliced
30 fresh Vietnamese mint leaves
1 cup (90 g/3 oz) bean sprouts
1 small white onion, thinly sliced
1 small fresh red chilli, thinly sliced

1 Wrap the meat in plastic wrap and freeze for 30–40 minutes, or until partially frozen. Thinly slice the meat across the grain.
2 Place the stock in a large heavy-based saucepan with the onion half, star anise, cinnamon stick, fish sauce, white pepper and 2 cups (500 ml/16 fl oz) water, and bring to the boil over high heat. Reduce the heat to medium–low and simmer, covered, for 20 minutes. Discard the onion, star anise and cinnamon stick.
3 Meanwhile, cover the noodles with boiling water and gently separate. Drain and refresh with cold water. Divide the noodles and spring onion among the serving bowls. Top with equal amounts of beef, mint, bean sprouts, onion slices and chilli. Ladle the simmering broth into the bowls, and serve.

NUTRITION PER SERVE
Protein 28 g; Fat 5.5 g; Carbohydrate 24 g; Dietary Fibre 2 g; Cholesterol 64 mg; 1100 kJ (265 cal)

NOTE: It is important that the broth is kept hot as the heat will cook the slices of beef.

BOUILLABAISSE

**Preparation time: 30 minutes +
5 minutes soaking
Total cooking time: 1 hour 15 minutes
Serves 6**

¹/₄ cup (60 ml/2 fl oz) olive oil
1 large onion, chopped
2 leeks, sliced
4 cloves garlic, crushed
500 g (1 lb) ripe tomatoes, peeled and
    roughly chopped
1–2 tablespoons tomato paste
6 sprigs fresh flat-leaf parsley
2 bay leaves
2 sprigs fresh thyme
1 sprig fresh fennel
¹/₄ teaspoon saffron threads
2 kg (4 lb) seafood trimmings (fish heads,
    bones, shellfish remains)
1 tablespoon Pernod or Ricard
4 potatoes, cut into 1.5 cm (⁵/₈ inch) slices
1.5 kg (3 lb) fish fillets and steaks, such as
    blue-eye, bream, red fish and snapper, cut
    into large chunks (see NOTE)
2 tablespoons chopped fresh flat-leaf parsley

TOASTS
¹/₂ baguette, cut into twelve 1.5 cm
    (⁵/₈ inch) slices
2 large cloves garlic, halved

ROUILLE
3 slices day-old Italian white bread,
    crusts removed
1 red capsicum, seeded and quartered
1 small fresh red chilli, seeded and chopped
3 cloves garlic, crushed
1 tablespoon chopped fresh basil leaves
¹/₃ cup (80 ml/2³/₄ fl oz) olive oil

1 Heat the oil in a large saucepan over low heat. Cook the onion and leek for 5 minutes without browning. Add the garlic, chopped tomato and 1 tablespoon of the tomato paste. Simmer for 5 minutes. Stir in 2 litres cold water, then add the parsley, bay leaves, thyme, fennel, saffron and seafood trimmings. Bring to the boil, then reduce the heat and simmer for 30–40 minutes.

2 Strain the stock into a large saucepan, pressing out the juices. Set aside ¹/₄ cup (60 ml/2 fl oz) stock. Add the Pernod to the saucepan and stir in extra tomato paste if needed to enrich the color. Season with salt and freshly ground black pepper. Bring to the boil and add the potato, then reduce the heat and simmer for 5 minutes.

3 Add the blue-eye and bream, cook for 2–3 minutes, then add the red fish and snapper, and cook for 5–6 minutes, or until cooked.

4 To make the toasts, toast the bread until golden on both sides. While still warm, rub with the garlic.

5 To make the rouille, soak the bread in enough cold water to cover, for 5 minutes. Cook the capsicum, skin-side up, under a hot grill until the skin blackens and blisters. Place in a plastic bag and leave to cool, then peel away the skin. Roughly chop the flesh. Squeeze the bread dry and place in a food processor with the capsicum, chilli, garlic and basil. Process to a smooth paste. With the motor running, gradually add the oil until the consistency resembles mayonnaise. Thin the sauce with 1–2 tablespoons of the reserved fish stock, and season to taste.

6 To serve, place 2 pieces of toast in the base of six soup bowls. Spoon in the soup and fish pieces and scatter some parsley over the top. Serve with the rouille.

NUTRITION PER SERVE
Protein 60 g; Fat 30 g; Carbohydrate 40 g; Dietary Fibre 5.5 g; Cholesterol 175 mg; 2838 kJ (678 cal)

NOTE: It is important to try to use at least four different varieties of fish, choosing a range of textures and flavors. Rascasse, where available, is traditional, but cod, bass, John dory, halibut, monkfish, turbot, hake and red mullet are also used. Shellfish such as lobster, scallops or mussels can be used.

Simmer the onion, leek, garlic, tomato and tomato paste for 5 minutes.

Cook the firmer-fleshed fish pieces slightly longer than the delicate pieces.

Rub the halved garlic cloves over the toasted bread slices.

Simmer the chicken breast fillets for 10 minutes, or until cooked.

Simmer the rice in the strained stock until the rice is tender.

AVGOLEMONO WITH CHICKEN

Preparation time: 30 minutes
Total cooking time: 30 minutes
Serves 4

1 onion, halved
2 cloves
1 carrot, cut into chunks
1 bay leaf
500 g (1 lb) chicken breast fillets
$1/3$ cup (75 g/$2^1/2$ oz) short-grain rice
3 eggs, separated
$1/4$ cup (60 ml/2 fl oz) lemon juice
2 tablespoons chopped fresh flat-leaf parsley
4 thin lemon slices, to garnish

1 Stud the onion halves with the cloves and place in a large saucepan with 1.5 litres water. Add the carrot, bay leaf and chicken. Season with salt and freshly ground black pepper. Slowly bring to the boil, then reduce the heat and simmer for 10 minutes, or until the chicken is cooked.

2 Strain the stock into a clean saucepan, reserving the chicken and discarding the vegetables. Add the rice to the stock, bring to the boil, then reduce the heat and simmer for 15 minutes, or until tender. Tear the chicken into shreds.

3 Whisk the egg whites until stiff peaks form, then beat in the yolks. Slowly beat in the lemon juice. Gently stir in 150 ml (5 fl oz) of the hot (not boiling) soup and beat thoroughly. Add the egg mixture to the soup and stir gently over low heat until thickened slightly. It should still be quite thin. Do not let it boil or the eggs may scramble. Add the shredded chicken, and season.

4 Set aside for 3–4 minutes to allow the flavors to develop, then sprinkle with the parsley. Garnish with the lemon slices and serve immediately.

NUTRITION PER SERVE
Protein 35 g; Fat 6.5 g; Carbohydrate 18 g; Dietary Fibre 1.5 g; Cholesterol 198 mg; 1145 kJ (274 cal)

Skim any fat from the surface of the stock before adding the lentils.

Stir the silverbeet into the onion mixture and cook until wilted.

LENTIL AND SILVERBEET SOUP

Preparation time: 20 minutes + overnight refrigeration
Total cooking time: 3 hours 20 minutes
Serves 6

CHICKEN STOCK

1 kg (2 lb) chicken bones (chicken necks, backs, wings), washed
1 small onion, roughly chopped
1 bay leaf
3–4 sprigs fresh flat-leaf parsley
1–2 sprigs fresh oregano or thyme

1½ cups (280 g/9 oz) brown lentils, washed
850 g (1 lb 12 oz) silverbeet
¼ cup (60 ml/2 fl oz) olive oil
1 large onion, finely chopped
4 cloves garlic, crushed
½ cup (25 g/¾ oz) finely chopped fresh coriander leaves

⅓ cup (80 ml/2¾ fl oz) lemon juice
lemon wedges, to serve

1 To make the stock, place all the ingredients in a large saucepan, add 3 litres water and bring to the boil. Skim any scum from the surface. Reduce the heat and simmer for 2 hours. Strain the stock, discarding the bones, onion and herbs. Chill overnight. (You will need 1 litre.)
2 Skim any fat from the stock. Place the lentils in a large saucepan and add the stock and 1 litre water. Bring to the boil, then reduce the heat and simmer, covered, for 1 hour.
3 Meanwhile, remove the stems from the silverbeet and shred the leaves. Heat the oil in a saucepan over medium heat and cook the onion for 2–3 minutes, or until transparent. Add the garlic and cook for 1 minute. Add the silverbeet and toss for 2–3 minutes, or until wilted. Stir the mixture into the lentils. Add the coriander and lemon juice, season, and simmer, covered, for 15–20 minutes. Serve with the lemon wedges.

NUTRITION PER SERVE
Protein 52 g; Fat 15 g; Carbohydrate 20 g; Dietary Fibre 11 g; Cholesterol 83 mg; 1782 kJ (425 cal)

Cut the barbecued pork into thin slices, using a small sharp knife.

Remove the kernels from the corn cobs by cutting down the cob with a knife.

PORK, CORN AND NOODLE SOUP

Preparation time: 15 minutes
Total cooking time: 30 minutes
Serves 4

2 small fresh corn cobs
200 g (6½ oz) dried ramen noodles
2 teaspoons peanut oil
1 teaspoon grated fresh ginger
1.5 litres chicken stock
2 tablespoons mirin
200 g (6 oz) piece Chinese barbecued pork
   (char sui), thinly sliced
3 spring onions, sliced on the diagonal
20 g (¾ oz) unsalted butter

1 Remove the corn kernels from the cob using a sharp knife.
2 Cook the ramen noodles in a large saucepan of boiling water for 4 minutes, or until tender. Drain, then rinse in cold water.
3 Heat the oil in a large saucepan over high heat. Stir-fry the ginger for 1 minute. Add the chicken stock and mirin and bring to the boil. Reduce the heat and simmer for 8 minutes.
4 Add the pork slices and cook for 5 minutes, then add the corn kernels and two-thirds of the spring onion, and cook for a further 4–5 minutes, or until the corn is tender.
5 Separate the noodles by running them under hot water, then divide them among four deep bowls. Ladle on the soup, then place 1 teaspoon butter on each serving. Garnish with the remaining spring onion and serve immediately.

NUTRITION PER SERVE
Protein 23 g; Fat 10.5 g; Carbohydrate 42 g;
Dietary Fibre 3 g; Cholesterol 77 mg;
1510 kJ (360 cal)

NOTE: This soup is traditionally served with the butter on top. However, for a healthier option, it is also quite delicious without the butter.

Remove the seeds from the peeled tomato with a teaspoon.

Gently simmer the fish pieces in the soup until they are cooked.

VIETNAMESE FISH AND NOODLE SOUP

**Preparation time: 30 minutes +
5 minutes soaking**
Total cooking time: 25 minutes
Serves 4

1 teaspoon shrimp paste
150 g (5 oz) mung bean vermicelli
2 tablespoons peanut oil
6 cloves garlic, finely chopped
1 small onion, thinly sliced
2 long fresh red chillies, chopped
2 stems lemon grass (white part only),
   thinly sliced
1.25 litres chicken stock
$^1/_4$ cup (60 ml/2 fl oz) fish sauce
1 tablespoon rice vinegar
4 ripe tomatoes, peeled, seeded
   and chopped
500 g (1 lb) firm white fish fillets (snapper or
   blue-eye), cut into 3 cm (1 $^1/_4$ inch) pieces

$^1/_2$ cup (10 g/ $^1/_4$ oz) fresh Vietnamese
   mint, torn
$^1/_2$ cup (15 g/$^1/_2$ oz) fresh coriander leaves
1 cup (90 g/3 oz) bean sprouts
1 tablespoon fresh Vietnamese mint, extra
1 tablespoon fresh coriander leaves, extra
2 long fresh red chillies, extra, sliced
lemon wedges, to serve

1 Wrap the shrimp paste in foil and place it under a hot grill for 1 minute. Remove and set aside until needed.

2 Soak the vermicelli in boiling water for 3–4 minutes. Rinse under cold water, drain and then cut into 15 cm (6 inch) lengths.

3 Heat the oil in a heavy-based saucepan over medium heat. Add the garlic and cook for 1 minute, or until golden. Add the onion, chilli, lemon grass and shrimp paste, and cook, stirring, for a further minute. Pour in the stock, fish sauce and rice vinegar, then add the tomato. Bring to the boil, then reduce the heat to medium and simmer for 10 minutes. Add the fish and simmer gently for 3 minutes, or until cooked. Stir in the mint and coriander leaves.

4 Divide the noodles and bean sprouts among four serving bowls and ladle the soup on top. Top with the extra mint, coriander leaves and chilli. Serve with lemon wedges.

NUTRITION PER SERVE
Protein 33 g; Fat 13 g; Carbohydrate 21 g;
Dietary Fibre 5.5 g; Cholesterol 74 mg;
1405 kJ (335 cal)

Stir and toss the prawn heads, shells and tails until the heads turn bright orange.

Process the chilli, onion, garlic, ginger, lemon grass, spices and stock.

PRAWN LAKSA

Preparation time: 45 minutes
Total cooking time: 50 minutes
Serves 4

1 kg (2 lb) raw medium prawns
1/3 cup (80 ml/2¾ fl oz) oil
2–6 small fresh red chillies, seeded
1 onion, roughly chopped
3 cloves garlic, halved
2 cm x 2 cm (¾ inch x ¾ inch) piece fresh
   ginger or galangal, chopped
3 stems lemon grass (white part only),
   chopped
1 teaspoon ground turmeric
1 tablespoon ground coriander
2 teaspoons shrimp paste
2½ cups (625 ml/20 fl oz) coconut cream
2 teaspoons grated palm sugar or soft
   brown sugar
4 fresh kaffir lime leaves, crushed
1–2 tablespoons fish sauce

200 g (6½ oz) packet fish balls
190 g (6½ oz) packet fried
   tofu puffs
250 g (8 oz) dried rice vermicelli
125 g (4 oz) bean sprouts
1/3 cup (20 g/¾ oz) chopped fresh mint
2 teaspoons fresh coriander leaves

1 Peel the prawns and gently pull out the dark vein from each prawn back, starting at the head end. Reserve the heads, shells and tails. Cover and refrigerate the prawn meat.

2 Heat 2 tablespoons of the oil in a wok or large saucepan and add the prawn shells and heads. Stir over medium heat for 10 minutes, or until orange, then add 1 litre water. Bring to the boil, then reduce the heat and simmer for 15 minutes. Strain the stock through a fine sieve, discarding the shells. Clean the pan.

3 Finely chop the chillies (use 2 for mild flavor, increase for hot), onion, garlic, ginger and lemon grass with the turmeric, coriander and 1/4 cup (60 ml/2 fl oz) of the prawn stock in a food processor.

4 Heat the remaining oil in the pan, add the chilli mixture and shrimp paste, and stir over medium heat for 3 minutes, or until fragrant. Pour in the remaining stock and simmer for 10 minutes. Add the coconut cream, sugar, lime leaves and fish sauce, and simmer for 5 minutes. Add the prawns and simmer for 2 minutes, or until firm and light pink. Add the fish balls and tofu puffs, and simmer gently until just heated through.

5 Soak the rice vermicelli in a bowl of boiling water for 2 minutes, then drain and divide it among serving bowls. Top with the bean sprouts and ladle the soup over the top. Sprinkle with the mint and coriander.

NUTRITION PER SERVE
Protein 58 g; Fat 58 g; Carbohydrate 71 g;
Dietary Fibre 9 g; Cholesterol 514 mg;
4331 kJ (1031 cal)

Stir the chopped coriander into the simmering chickpea mixture.

Add the milk to the dumpling mixture and mix with a flat-bladed knife.

CHICKPEA AND HERB DUMPLING SOUP

Preparation time: 30 minutes
Total cooking time: 35 minutes
Serves 4

1 tablespoon oil
1 onion, chopped
2 cloves garlic, crushed
2 teaspoons ground cumin
1 teaspoon ground coriander
1/4 teaspoon chilli powder
2 x 300 g (10 oz) cans chickpeas, drained
3 1/2 cups (875 ml/28 fl oz) vegetable stock
2 x 425 g (14 oz) cans chopped tomatoes
1 tablespoon chopped fresh coriander leaves
1 cup (125 g/4 oz) self-raising flour
25 g (3/4 oz) butter, chopped
2 tablespoons grated fresh Parmesan

2 tablespoons mixed chopped fresh
    herbs (chives, flat-leaf parsley and
    coriander leaves)
1/4 cup (60 ml/2 fl oz) milk

1 Heat the oil in a large saucepan and cook the onion over medium heat for 2–3 minutes, or until soft. Add the garlic, cumin, ground coriander and chilli, and cook for 1 minute, or until fragrant. Add the chickpeas, stock and tomato. Bring to the boil, then reduce the heat and simmer, covered, for 10 minutes. Stir in the coriander.

2 To make the dumplings, sift the flour into a bowl and add the chopped butter. Rub the butter into the flour with your fingertips until it resembles fine breadcrumbs. Stir in the cheese and mixed fresh herbs. Make a well in the centre, add the milk and mix with a flat-bladed knife until just combined. Bring the dough together into a rough ball, divide into eight portions and roll into small balls.

3 Add the dumplings to the soup, cover and simmer for 20 minutes, or until a skewer comes out clean when inserted into the centre of the dumplings.

NUTRITION PER SERVE

Protein 17 g; Fat 16 g; Carbohydrate 50 g;
Dietary Fibre 12 g; Cholesterol 23 mg;
1767 kJ (422 cal)

Cut the ginger into julienne strips (thin strips the size and shape of matchsticks).

After soaking the mushrooms, drain and thinly slice them.

SOBA NOODLE AND VEGETABLE SOUP

**Preparation time: 15 minutes +
    5 minutes soaking**
Total cooking time: 10 minutes
Serves 4

250 g (8 oz) soba noodles
2 dried shiitake mushrooms
2 litres vegetable stock
120 g (4 oz) snow peas, cut into thin strips
2 small carrots, cut into thin 5 cm
    (2 inch) strips
2 cloves garlic, finely chopped
6 spring onions, cut into 5 cm (2 inch)
    lengths and thinly sliced lengthways
3 cm (1 ¼ inch) piece fresh ginger, julienned
⅓ cup (80 ml/2¾ fl oz) soy sauce
¼ cup (60 ml/2 fl oz) mirin or sake
1 cup (90 g/3 oz) bean sprouts

1 Cook the noodles according to the packet instructions, then drain.
2 Soak the mushrooms in ½ cup (125 ml/ 4 fl oz) boiling water until soft. Drain, reserving the liquid. Discard the stems and slice the caps.
3 Combine the vegetable stock, mushrooms, reserved liquid, snow peas, carrot, garlic, spring onion and ginger in a large saucepan. Bring slowly to the boil, then reduce the heat to low and simmer for 5 minutes, or until the vegetables are tender. Add the soy sauce, mirin and bean sprouts. Cook for a further 3 minutes.
4 Divide the noodles among four large serving bowls. Ladle the hot liquid and vegetables over the top and garnish with coriander.

NUTRITION PER SERVE
Protein 13 g; Fat 1.5 g; Carbohydrate 30 g;
Dietary Fibre 6 g; Cholesterol 11 mg;
1124 kJ (270 cal)

Using a sharp knife, cut the peeled pumpkin into large cubes.

Add the vegetables and beans, and simmer until the vegetables are cooked.

CHUNKY VEGETABLE SOUP

Preparation time: 20 minutes +
overnight soaking
Total cooking time: 1 hour 5 minutes
Serves 6

¹/₂ cup (100 g/3¹/₂ oz) dried red kidney beans
or borlotti beans
1 tablespoon olive oil
1 leek, halved lengthways, chopped
1 small onion, diced
2 carrots, chopped
2 celery sticks, chopped
1 large zucchini, chopped
1 tablespoon tomato paste
1 litre vegetable stock
400 g (13 oz) pumpkin, cut into 2 cm
(³/₄ inch) cubes
2 potatoes, cut into 2 cm (³/₄ inch) cubes
¹/₄ cup (7 g/ ¹/₄ oz) chopped fresh
flat-leaf parsley

1 Put the beans in a large bowl, cover with cold water and soak overnight. Rinse, then transfer to a saucepan, cover with cold water and cook for 45 minutes, or until just tender. Drain.

2 Meanwhile, heat the oil in a large saucepan. Add the leek and onion, and cook over medium heat for 2–3 minutes without browning, or until they start to soften. Add the carrot, celery and zucchini, and cook for 3–4 minutes. Add the tomato paste and stir for a further 1 minute. Pour in the stock and 1.25 litres water, and bring to the boil. Reduce the heat to low and simmer for 20 minutes.

3 Add the pumpkin, potato, parsley and red kidney beans, and simmer for a further 20 minutes, or until the vegetables are tender and the beans are cooked. Season to taste. Serve immediately with crusty wholemeal or wholegrain bread.

NUTRITION PER SERVE
Protein 7.5 g; Fat 4 g; Carbohydrate 19 g;
Dietary Fibre 7 g; Cholesterol 0 mg;
600 kJ (143 cal)

NOTE: To save time, use a 420 g (14 oz) can of red kidney beans instead of dried beans.

Using a sharp knife, chop the carrots, potatoes and celery.

Add the drained barley to the cooked vegetables and stir in.

BARLEY SOUP WITH GOLDEN PARSNIPS

Preparation time: 30 minutes +
overnight soaking
Total cooking time: 2 hours 20 minutes
Serves 6

200 g (6½ oz) pearl barley
1 tablespoon oil
2 onions, chopped
2 cloves garlic, finely chopped
2 carrots, chopped
2 potatoes, chopped
2 celery sticks, chopped
2 bay leaves, torn in half
2 litres chicken stock
½ cup (125 ml/4 fl oz) milk
40 g (1 ¼ oz) butter
3 parsnips, cubed
1 teaspoon soft brown sugar
chopped fresh parsley, to serve

1 Soak the barley in water overnight. Drain. Place in a saucepan with 2 litres water. Bring to the boil, then reduce the heat and simmer, partially covered, for 1¼ hours, or until tender. Drain the barley.

2 Heat the oil in a large saucepan, add the onion, garlic, carrot, potato and celery, and cook for 3 minutes. Stir well and cook, covered, for 15 minutes over low heat, stirring occasionally.

3 Add the barley, bay leaves, stock, milk, 2 teaspoons of salt and 1 teaspoon of pepper. Bring to the boil, then reduce the heat and simmer the soup, partially covered, for 35 minutes. If the soup is too thick, add about 1 cup (250 ml/8 fl oz) cold water, a little at a time, until the soup reaches your preferred consistency.

4 While the soup is simmering, melt the butter in a frying pan, add the parsnip and toss in the butter. Sprinkle with the sugar and cook until golden brown and tender. Serve the parsnip on top of the soup and sprinkle with the parsley.

NUTRITION PER SERVE
Protein 7 g; Fat 10 g; Carbohydrate 40 g; Dietary Fibre 8 g; Cholesterol 20 mg; 1190 kJ (285 cal)

Simmer the haddock in a frying pan until it flakes easily when lifted with a fork.

Lay the fish on paper towels to drain well, then flake into small pieces.

SMOKED HADDOCK CHOWDER

Preparation time: 20 minutes
Total cooking time: 35 minutes
Serves 4–6

500 g (1 lb) smoked haddock
1 potato, diced
1 celery stick, diced
1 onion, finely chopped
50 g (1¾ oz) butter
1 rasher bacon, rind removed, finely
   chopped
2 tablespoons plain flour
½ teaspoon dry mustard
½ teaspoon Worcestershire sauce
1 cup (250 ml/8 fl oz) milk
½ cup (30 g/1 oz) chopped fresh parsley
¼ cup (60 ml/2 fl oz) cream (optional)

1 To make the fish stock, put the fish in a frying pan, cover with water and bring to the boil. Reduce the heat and simmer for 8 minutes, or until the fish flakes easily. Drain, reserving the fish stock, then peel, bone and flake the fish.

2 Put the potato, celery and onion in a medium saucepan, and pour over enough of the reserved fish stock to cover the vegetables. Bring to the boil, then reduce the heat and simmer for 8 minutes, or until the vegetables are tender.

3 Melt the butter in a large saucepan, add the bacon and cook, stirring, for 3 minutes. Add the flour, mustard and Worcestershire sauce, and stir until combined. Cook for 1 minute. Remove from the heat and gradually pour in the milk, stirring continuously until smooth. Return to the heat and stir for 5 minutes, until the mixture comes to the boil and has thickened. Stir in the vegetables and remaining stock, then add the parsley and fish. Simmer over low heat for 5 minutes, or until heated through. Taste for seasoning, and serve with some cream, if desired.

NUTRITION PER SERVE (6)
Protein 20 g; Fat 10 g; Carbohydrate 8 g;
Dietary Fibre 1 g; Cholesterol 90 mg;
970 kJ (230 cal)

NOTE: Chowder is a thick, hearty soup, made with seafood, fish, vegetables or chicken.

Cook the chicken and noodles in the stock until the noodles are warmed through.

Cook the bok choy for 2 minutes, or until the leaves have wilted.

ASIAN CHICKEN NOODLE SOUP

Preparation time: 10 minutes
Total cooking time: 10 minutes
Serves 4

85 g (3 oz) fresh egg noodles
1.25 litres chicken stock
1 tablespoon mirin
2 tablespoons soy sauce
3 cm (1 ¼ inch) piece fresh ginger, julienned
2 chicken breast fillets, thinly sliced
2 bunches baby bok choy, leaves separated
fresh coriander leaves, to garnish

1 Soak the noodles in boiling water for 1 minute, then drain and set aside. In a large saucepan, heat the stock to simmering, and add the mirin, soy sauce, ginger, chicken and noodles. Cook for 5 minutes, or until the chicken is tender and the noodles are warmed through. Remove any scum from the surface of the soup.

2 Add the bok choy and cook for a further 2 minutes, or until the bok choy leaves have wilted. Serve in deep bowls, garnished with fresh coriander leaves. Serve with sweet chilli sauce, if desired.

NUTRITION PER SERVE
Protein 30 g; Fat 3 g; Carbohydrate 15 g; Dietary Fibre 1 g; Cholesterol 65 mg; 915 kJ (220 cal)

NOTE: Mirin is a sweet rice wine used for cooking. Sweet sherry, with a little sugar added, can be used instead.

Simmer the chicken for 20–25 minutes, or until cooked through.

Once the cooked chicken has cooled, cut it into thin slices.

CANJA (PORTUGUESE CHICKEN BROTH WITH RICE)

Preparation time: 15 minutes
Total cooking time: 1 hour
Serves 6

2.5 litres chicken stock
1 onion, cut into thin wedges
1 teaspoon grated lemon rind
1 sprig fresh mint
500 g (1 lb) potatoes, chopped
1 tablespoon olive oil
2 chicken breast fillets
1 cup (200 g/6½ oz) long-grain rice
2 tablespoons lemon juice
fresh shredded mint, to garnish

1 Combine the chicken stock, onion, lemon rind, mint sprig, potato and olive oil in a large saucepan. Slowly bring to the boil, then reduce the heat, add the chicken breasts and simmer gently for 20–25 minutes, or until the chicken is cooked through.

2 Remove the chicken breasts and discard the mint sprig. Cool the chicken, then cut it into thin slices.

3 Meanwhile, add the rice to the pan and simmer for 25–30 minutes, or until the rice is tender. Return the sliced chicken to the pan, add the lemon juice and stir for 1–2 minutes, or until the chicken is warmed through. Season, and serve garnished with mint.

NUTRITION PER SERVE
Protein 20 g; Fat 5 g; Carbohydrate 38 g; Dietary Fibre 2 g; Cholesterol 37 mg; 1197 kJ (286 cal)

NOTE: Rice and potato absorb liquid on standing, so serve immediately.

EIGHT-TREASURE NOODLE SOUP

**Preparation time: 20 minutes +
20 minutes soaking**
Total cooking time: 20 minutes
Serves 4

10 g (¼ oz) dried shiitake mushrooms
375 g (12 oz) fresh thick egg noodles
1.2 litres chicken stock
¼ cup (60 ml/2 fl oz) light soy sauce
2 teaspoons Chinese rice wine
200 g (6½ oz) chicken breast fillet, cut into
   1 cm (½ inch) strips on the diagonal
200 g (6½ oz) Chinese barbecued pork
   (char sui), cut into 5 mm (¼ inch) slices
¼ onion, finely chopped
1 carrot, cut into 1 cm (½ inch) slices on the
   diagonal
120 g (4 oz) snow peas, cut in half on the
   diagonal
4 spring onions, thinly sliced

1 Soak the mushrooms in boiling water for 20 minutes, or until soft. Drain and squeeze out any excess liquid. Discard the stems and thinly slice the caps.

2 Bring a large saucepan of water to the boil and cook the noodles for 1 minute, or until cooked through. Drain, then rinse with cold water. Divide evenly among four deep warmed serving bowls.

3 Meanwhile, bring the chicken stock to the boil in a large saucepan over high heat. Reduce the heat to medium and stir in the soy sauce and rice wine. Simmer for 2 minutes. Add the chicken and pork and cook for 2 minutes, or until the chicken is cooked and the pork is heated through. Add the onion, carrot, snow peas, mushrooms and half the spring onion, and cook for 1 minute, or until the carrot is tender.

4 Divide the vegetables and meat among the serving bowls and ladle on the hot broth. Garnish with the remaining spring onion.

NUTRITION PER SERVE
Protein 42 g; Fat 7 g; Carbohydrate 61 g; Dietary Fibre 4 g; Cholesterol 109 mg; 1995 kJ (475 cal)

Place the cucumber over a small bowl and remove the seeds with a spoon.

FISH BALL AND NOODLE SOUP

Preparation time: 20 minutes
Total cooking time: 15 minutes
Serves 4–6

500 g (1 lb) firm white fish fillets, skin and
    bones removed (ling or perch)
2 tablespoons rice flour
200 g (6¹/₂ oz) dried somen noodles
2¹/₂ teaspoons dashi powder
2 tablespoons light soy sauce
1 tablespoon mirin
200 g (6¹/₂ oz) Chinese cabbage, shredded
2 spring onions, thinly sliced on the diagonal
¹/₂ Lebanese cucumber, unpeeled, seeded
    and cut into 5 cm (2 inch) strips

1 Place the fish in a food processor and process until smooth. Combine the rice flour and ¹/₃ cup (80 ml/2³/₄ fl oz) water in a small bowl, and stir until smooth, then add to the fish and process for a further 5 seconds. Using 2 teaspoons of mixture at a time, shape into balls with wet hands.
2 Cook the somen noodles in a large saucepan of boiling water for 2 minutes, or until tender, then drain.
3 Bring 2 litres water to the boil in a large saucepan. Reduce the heat to low, add the dashi powder and stir until dissolved. Bring the stock to the boil over high heat and add the soy sauce, mirin and salt to taste. Add the fish balls, reduce the heat to medium and simmer for 3 minutes, or until the balls rise to the surface and they are cooked through. Add the cabbage, increase the heat to high and return to the boil. Stir in the noodles and cook for 1 minute, or until warmed through.
4 To serve, divide the noodles and fish balls among serving bowls, then ladle the liquid on top. Garnish with the spring onion and cucumber.

NUTRITION PER SERVE (6)
Protein 22 g; Fat 2.5 g; Carbohydrate 27 g; Dietary Fibre 2 g; Cholesterol 49 mg; 930 kJ (220 cal)

Cook the chopped onion in a large saucepan until softened.

Add the spices to the onion and eggplant mixture, and stir until fragrant.

SPICED LENTIL SOUP

**Preparation time: 10 minutes +
    20 minutes standing**
Total cooking time: 50 minutes
Serves 4

1 eggplant
¼ cup (60 ml/2 fl oz) olive oil
1 onion, finely chopped
2 teaspoons brown mustard seeds
2 teaspoons ground cumin
1 teaspoon garam masala
¼ teaspoon cayenne pepper (optional)
2 large carrots, cut into cubes
1 celery stick, diced
400 g (13 oz) can crushed tomatoes
1 cup (110 g/3½ oz) Puy lentils
1 litre chicken stock
¾ cup (35 g/1 ¼ oz) roughly chopped fresh
    coriander leaves
½ cup (125 g/4 oz) plain yoghurt

1 Cut the eggplant into cubes, place in a colander, sprinkle with salt and leave for 20 minutes. Rinse well and pat dry with paper towels.
2 Heat the oil in a large saucepan over medium heat. Add the onion and cook for 5 minutes, or until softened. Add the eggplant, stir to coat in oil and cook for 3 minutes, or until softened.
3 Add all the spices and cook, stirring, for 1 minute, or until fragrant and the mustard seeds begin to pop. Add the carrot and celery and cook for 1 minute. Stir in the tomato, lentils and stock and bring to the boil. Reduce the heat and simmer for 40 minutes, or until the lentils are tender and the liquid is reduced to a thick stew-like soup. Season to taste with salt and cracked black pepper.
4 Stir the coriander into the soup just before serving. Ladle the soup into four warmed bowls and serve with a dollop of the yoghurt on top.

NUTRITION PER SERVE
Protein 11 g; Fat 16 g; Carbohydrate 20 g; Dietary Fibre 8.5 g; Cholesterol 5 mg; 1148 kJ (274 cal)

Chop the dried wakame into fine pieces with a sharp knife.

MISO WITH RAMEN

**Preparation time: 15 minutes +
15 minutes soaking
Total cooking time: 15 minutes
Serves 4**

1 teaspoon finely chopped dried wakame
180 g (6 oz) fresh ramen noodles
100 g (3¹/₂ oz) silken firm tofu, cut into
   1.5 cm (⁵/₈ inch) cubes
2 spring onions, thinly sliced on the diagonal
1³/₄ teaspoons dashi powder
2–3 tablespoons red miso
   (see NOTE)
2 teaspoons mirin
2 teaspoon Japanese soy sauce

1 Soak the wakame in a bowl of tepid water for 15 minutes. Drain and set aside.

2 Cook the noodles in a large saucepan of boiling salted water for 2 minutes, or until cooked through. Drain and rinse, then divide among warmed serving bowls. Place the tofu and spring onion on top.

3 Meanwhile, bring 1.25 litres water to the boil in a large saucepan. Reduce the heat to low and add the dashi powder, stirring for 30 seconds, or until dissolved.

4 In a bowl, combine the miso with 1 cup (250 ml/8 fl oz) of the dashi stock, whisking until smooth. Return the miso mixture to the pan of stock and stir until combined—be careful not to boil the broth as this will diminish the flavor of the miso. Add the mirin, soy sauce and wakame, and gently heat for 1 minute, then stir to combine. Ladle the broth over the noodles, tofu and spring onion, and serve immediately.

NUTRITION PER SERVE
Protein 9 g; Fat 3 g; Carbohydrate 28 g; Dietary Fibre 2.5 g; Cholesterol 6 mg; 735 kJ (175 cal)

NOTE: Shiro (white) miso can be used instead of red miso, however the flavor will not be as strong—adjust to taste.

Soak the red kidney beans and black beans in separate bowls overnight.

Add the tomato, stock, capsicum, corn and tomato paste.

MEXICAN BEAN CHOWDER

Preparation time: 20 minutes +
  overnight soaking
Total cooking time: 1 hour 15 minutes
Serves 6

³/₄ cup (155 g/5 oz) dried red kidney beans
³/₄ cup (165 g/5¹/₂ oz) dried Mexican black
  beans (see NOTE)
1 tablespoon oil
1 onion, chopped
2 cloves garlic, crushed
¹/₂–1 teaspoon chilli powder
1 tablespoon ground cumin
2 teaspoons ground coriander
2 x 400 g (13 oz) cans chopped tomatoes
3 cups (750 ml/24 fl oz) vegetable stock
1 red capsicum, chopped
1 green capsicum, chopped
440 g (14 oz) can corn kernels

2 tablespoons tomato paste
grated Cheddar, to serve
sour cream, to serve

1 Soak the kidney beans and black beans in separate bowls in plenty of cold water overnight. Drain. Place in a large saucepan, cover with water and bring to the boil. Reduce the heat and simmer for 45 minutes, or until tender. Drain.
2 Heat the oil in a large saucepan, add the onion and cook over medium heat until soft. Add the garlic, chilli powder, cumin and coriander, and cook for 1 minute. Stir in the tomato, stock, capsicum, corn and tomato paste. Cook, covered, for 25–30 minutes. Add the beans during the last 10 minutes of cooking. Stir occasionally.
3 Serve topped with the grated Cheddar and a spoonful of sour cream.

NUTRITION PER SERVE
Protein 20 g; Fat 7 g; Carbohydrate 40 g; Dietary Fibre 20 g; Cholesterol 3 mg; 1250 kJ (300 cal)

NOTE: Mexican black beans are also known as black turtle beans.

Peel and cut the potatoes into strips and then into small cubes.

Remove the bay leaf from the chowder with a pair of tongs.

CLAM CHOWDER

Preparation time: 25 minutes
Total cooking time: 45 minutes
Serves 4

30 g (1 oz) butter
2 rashers bacon, finely chopped
1 large onion, finely chopped
4 potatoes, cut into small cubes
2 cups (500 ml/16 fl oz) fish stock
1 bay leaf
1/2 cup (125 ml/4 fl oz) milk
4 x 105 g (31/2 oz) cans baby clams, drained
    and chopped
1/4 cup (15 g/1/2 oz) finely chopped
    fresh parsley
1 cup (250 ml/8 fl oz) cream

1 Heat the butter in a large saucepan. Cook the bacon and onion for 2–3 minutes, or until softened. Stir in the potato. Cook for a further 2–3 minutes, then gradually pour on the stock. Add the bay leaf.

2 Bring the mixture to the boil, then reduce the heat and simmer, covered, for 20 minutes, or until the potato is cooked. Simmer for 10 minutes, or until the soup is reduced and slightly thickened. Discard the bay leaf.

3 Add the milk, chopped clams, parsley and cream. Stir to reheat, but do not allow the soup to boil. Season with salt and freshly ground black pepper.

NUTRITION PER SERVE
Protein 20 g; Fat 40 g; Carbohydrate 20 g;
Dietary Fibre 3 g; Cholesterol 250 mg;
2090 kJ (500 cal)

Casseroles

NAVARIN OF LAMB

Preparation time: 25 minutes
Total cooking time: 1 hour 35 minutes
Serves 4

8 lamb noisettes (see NOTES)
seasoned plain flour
2 tablespoons oil
2 celery sticks, sliced diagonally into
   2 cm (³⁄₄ inch) lengths
12 baby carrots, peeled (see NOTES)
12 new potatoes
6 sprigs fresh thyme
¹⁄₄ cup (15 g/¹⁄₂ oz) chopped fresh parsley
2 onions, chopped
2 cloves garlic, crushed
¹⁄₃ cup (40 g/1 ¹⁄₄ oz) plain flour
2¹⁄₂ cups (625 ml/21 fl oz) chicken stock
1 cup (250 ml/8 fl oz) red wine
¹⁄₄ cup (60 g/2 oz) tomato paste
chopped fresh parsley, extra, to garnish

1 Toss the lamb in the seasoned flour, shaking off the excess. Preheat the oven to moderate 180°C (350°F/Gas 4).

2 Heat the oil in a heavy-based saucepan. In batches, brown the lamb well on both sides over medium–high heat. Remove from the heat, drain well on paper towels, then transfer to a greased, 3 litre casserole dish. Top with the celery, carrots, potatoes, thyme and parsley.

3 Cook the onion and garlic in the same heavy-based pan, stirring over medium heat for 5–10 minutes, or until the onion is soft.

4 Add the flour and stir for 1 minute, or until the onion is coated. Add the remaining ingredients and stir until the sauce boils and thickens. Pour the sauce over the lamb and vegetables. Bake, covered, for 1¹⁄₄ hours, or until the lamb is tender. Carefully remove the string from the lamb, and sprinkle with extra parsley to serve.

NUTRITION PER SERVE

Protein 40 g; Fat 60 g; Carbohydrate 60 g; Dietary Fibre 10 g; Cholesterol 120 mg; 4050 kJ (970 cal)

NOTES: A noisette is a round slice of meat, cut from a boned loin and tied with string to hold its shape. For this recipe you could also use a boned leg of lamb, cut into 3 cm (1¹⁄₄ inch) cubes.

If baby carrots are not available, use four sliced carrots instead.

Add the lightly floured lamb to the hot oil and brown well all over.

Add the stock, wine and tomato paste to the softened onion mixture.

Add the drained cannellini beans to the onion mixture in the pan.

Add the wine and stock to the bean mixture, and cook for 2 hours.

TUNA AND WHITE BEAN CASSEROLE

Preparation time: 40 minutes +
overnight soaking
Total cooking time: 3 hours
Serves 6

2 cups (400 g/13 oz) dried cannellini beans
¼ cup (60 ml/2 fl oz) olive oil
2 red onions, chopped
2 cloves garlic, crushed
1 teaspoon ground coriander
1 teaspoon finely grated lemon rind
2 teaspoons chopped fresh thyme
2 cups (500 ml/16 fl oz) white wine
2 cups (500 ml/16 fl oz) fish stock
475 g (15 oz) can tuna in brine, drained
1 bunch fresh basil, leaves only
4 large ripe tomatoes, cut into 1 cm
    (½ inch) slices

TOPPING
½ cup (40 g/1 ¼ oz) fresh breadcrumbs
1 clove garlic, crushed
½ cup (30 g/1 oz) finely chopped fresh
    parsley
30 g (1 oz) butter, melted

1 Soak the beans in water overnight, then drain.
2 Heat the oil in a large, heavy-based saucepan. Add the onion, garlic, coriander, rind and thyme. Cook over medium heat for 10–15 minutes, or until the onion is softened. Add the beans and cook for 10 minutes.
3 Add the wine and stock. Cover and cook over low heat for 2 hours, until the beans are tender but not mashed.
4 Preheat the oven to hot 210°C (415°F/ Gas 6–7). Transfer the bean mixture to a large casserole dish. Top with the tuna and basil leaves. Arrange the tomato slices over the basil.
5 To make the topping, combine the breadcrumbs, garlic and parsley. Sprinkle over the tomato. Drizzle with the butter. Bake for 30 minutes, or until golden. Serve with crusty bread.

NUTRITION PER SERVE
Protein 32 g; Fat 16 g; Carbohydrate 36 g; Dietary Fibre 16 g; Cholesterol 41 mg; 1920 kJ (459 cal)

Once the shells have been cleaned, prise them open and remove the mussels.

SEAFOOD MORNAY CASEROLE

Preparation time: 25 minutes
Total cooking time: 40 minutes
Serves 4–6

400 g (13 oz) mussels
3 medium white fish fillets, cut into
   3 cm (1 1/4 inch) cubes
250 g (8 oz) raw medium prawns, peeled
   and deveined
200 g (6 1/2 oz) scallops, trimmed
1 small onion, halved
2 bay leaves
1/2 lemon, sliced
1/2 cup (125 ml/4 fl oz) white wine

SAUCE
45 g (1 1/2 oz) butter
1 celery stick, chopped
1 large carrot, finely chopped
1 1/2 tablespoons plain flour
1 1/2 cups (375 ml/12 fl oz) milk
125 g (4 oz) Gruyère cheese, grated
1 cup (130 g/4 1/2 oz) frozen peas

TOPPING
1 cup (80 g/2 3/4 oz) fresh breadcrumbs
1/2 cup (45 g/1 1/2 oz) flaked almonds
2 teaspoons finely grated lemon rind
1/2 teaspoon freshly ground black pepper
60 g (2 oz) butter, chopped

1 Preheat the oven to moderate 180°C
(350°F/Gas 4). Discard any open mussels,
then remove the beards from the rest of the
mussels and wash away any grit. Prise open the
shells and remove the mussels. Place the fish,
prawns, scallops and mussels in a saucepan.
Cover with cold water and add the onion, bay
leaves, lemon and wine. Bring slowly to the boil.
Cover, then reduce the heat to low and simmer
for 3–4 minutes. Remove the seafood from the
cooking liquid and place it in a lightly greased
casserole dish.

2 To make the sauce, heat the butter in a
saucepan. Cook the celery and carrot for
1 minute, then add the flour. Stir over low heat
for 2 minutes, or until the mixture is lightly
golden. Add the milk gradually, stirring until
smooth. Stir constantly over medium heat for
3 minutes, or until the mixture boils and thickens.
Boil for 1 minute, then remove from the heat and
cool the sauce to room temperature.
3 Stir the cheese and peas into the sauce, then
pour it over the seafood. Mix gently to combine.
4 To make the topping, combine the
breadcrumbs, almonds, rind and pepper in a
bowl. Spread evenly over the top of the seafood
mixture. Dot with the butter. Bake for 20 minutes,
or until the seafood is heated through and the
top is golden brown.

NUTRITION PER SERVE (6)
Protein 42 g; Fat 31 g; Carbohydrate 18 g;
Dietary Fibre 3 g; Cholesterol 177 mg;
2165 kJ (515 cal)

NOTE: Any combination of cooked seafood can
be used in this recipe. The cooking liquid can
replace half the milk, if desired.

Cut the pork belly across the grain into slices, then into pieces.

Return all the browned pork pieces to the casserole dish.

CARAMEL PORK WITH SHANGHAI NOODLES

Preparation time: 15 minutes
Total cooking time: 2 hours 30 minutes
Serves 4

500 g (1 lb) Shanghai noodles
700 g (1 lb 7 oz) boneless pork belly
2 teaspoons peanut oil
150 g (5 oz) caster sugar
5 cloves garlic, crushed
5 slices fresh ginger, 5 mm (¼ inch) thick
2 stems lemon grass (white part only), bruised
1 teaspoon white pepper
2 cups (500 ml/16 fl oz) chicken stock
70 ml (2 ¼ fl oz) fish sauce
100 g (3½ oz) canned bamboo shoots, drained well
4 spring onions, cut into 3 cm (1 ¼ inch) pieces

1 tablespoon lime juice
1 tablespoon chopped fresh coriander leaves (optional)

1 Cook the Shanghai noodles in a large saucepan of boiling water for 4–5 minutes, or until tender. Rinse, drain and cut the noodles into 10 cm (4 inch) lengths.
2 Preheat the oven to moderate 180°C (350°F/Gas 4). Cut the pork belly across the grain into 1 cm (½ inch) thick slices, then cut each slice into 2 cm (¾ inch) pieces. Heat the oil in a 4 litre clay pot or flameproof casserole dish over medium–high heat. Cook the pork in two batches for about 5 minutes, or until it starts to brown all over. Remove the pork and drain the fat.
3 Add the sugar and 2 tablespoons water to the casserole dish, stirring until the sugar has dissolved and scraping up any sediment that may have stuck to the bottom. Increase the heat to high and cook for 2–3 minutes without stirring until dark golden, being careful not to burn—you should just be able to smell the caramel.

4 Return the pork to the casserole dish, then stir in the garlic, ginger, lemon grass, white pepper, stock, 2 tablespoons of the fish sauce and 1½ cups (375 ml/12 fl oz) water. Bake, covered, for 1 hour, then remove the lid and cook for 1 hour, or until the pork is very tender. Carefully remove the ginger and lemon grass.
5 Add the noodles to the casserole dish with the bamboo shoots, spring onion, lime juice and the remaining fish sauce, and stir to combine. Return the dish to the oven for a further 10 minutes to heat through. Stir in the chopped coriander, if desired, and serve immediately with steamed Asian greens.

NUTRITION PER SERVE
Protein 49 g; Fat 7.5 g; Carbohydrate 73 g; Dietary Fibre 4 g; Cholesterol 166 mg; 2305 kJ (550 cal)

Brown the chicken pieces, in batches, until they are browned all over.

Gradually add the stock to the flour mixture, then stir until the sauce boils and thickens.

CHICKEN, LEEK AND SWEET POTATO ONE-POT

Preparation time: 15 minutes
Total cooking time: 1 hour 40 minutes
Serves 4

600 g (1 ¼ lb) orange sweet potato
2 tablespoons olive oil
1.5 kg (3 lb) chicken pieces
1 leek, cut into 2 cm (¾ inch) slices
2 cloves garlic, crushed
2 tablespoons plain flour
2 cups (500 ml/16 fl oz) chicken stock
2 tablespoons fresh thyme

1 Preheat the oven to hot 220°C (425°F/Gas 7). Peel the sweet potato and cut it into chunks. Heat 1 tablespoon of the oil in a large flameproof casserole dish. Cook the chicken in batches for 3–4 minutes, or until browned. Set aside. Add the remaining oil and cook the leek and garlic for 2 minutes, or until soft.
2 Add the flour to the dish and cook, stirring, for about 1 minute to brown the flour. Gradually add the stock, stirring until the sauce boils and thickens. Remove from the heat. Return the chicken to the pan.
3 Add the sweet potato and half the thyme. Bake, covered, for 1½ hours, or until the chicken is cooked through and the sweet potato is tender. Season, and scatter with the remaining thyme. Serve with steamed rice.

NUTRITION PER SERVE
Protein 80 g; Fat 25 g; Carbohydrate 25 g; Dietary Fibre 4 g; Cholesterol 260 mg; 2778 kJ (665 cal)

Cook the macaroni in a large saucepan of boiling water until just tender.

Add the fish, thyme and mushrooms to the pan, and cook until the fish is tender.

FISH AND MACARONI CASSEROLE

Preparation time: 20 minutes
Total cooking time: 50 minutes
Serves 4

1 cup (155 g/5 oz) macaroni
30 g (1 oz) butter
1 onion, chopped
500 g (1 lb) white fish fillets, cut into
    2 cm (³/₄ inch) cubes
1 tablespoon chopped fresh thyme
100 g (3¹/₂ oz) butter mushrooms, sliced
¹/₂ teaspoon hot English mustard
1 tablespoon plain flour
1 cup (250 ml/8 fl oz) chicken stock
¹/₂ cup (125 ml/4 fl oz) cream
¹/₂ cup (125 g/4 oz) sour cream
1 cup (80 g/2³/₄ oz) fresh breadcrumbs
1 cup (125 g/4 oz) grated Cheddar
¹/₂ cup (50 g/1³/₄ oz) grated fresh Parmesan
2 tablespoons chopped fresh parsley

1 Preheat the oven to moderate 180°C (350°F/Gas 4). Cook the macaroni in a large saucepan of rapidly boiling water until just tender. Drain and set aside.
2 Heat the butter in a heavy-based saucepan over medium heat. Cook the onion for 3 minutes, or until golden. Add the fish, thyme and mushrooms. Cook for 5 minutes, or until the fish is tender. Remove from the pan and keep warm.
3 Stir the mustard and flour into the pan. Add the stock and cream gradually. Stir constantly over medium heat for 3 minutes, or until the mixture boils and thickens. Boil for 1 minute, then remove from the heat. Stir in the sour cream.
4 Transfer the mixture to a large bowl, and stir in the macaroni, fish and mushrooms. Spoon into a large ovenproof dish. Combine the breadcrumbs, cheese and parsley. Sprinkle over the macaroni mixture. Bake for 30 minutes, or until golden. Serve with a green salad.

NUTRITION PER SERVE
Protein 49 g; Fat 50 g; Carbohydrate 46 g; Dietary Fibre 3.5 g; Cholesterol 217 mg; 3465 kJ (830 cal)

HINT: If you prefer, you can use a drained can of tuna instead of the fresh fish.

When the oil is hot, brown the lamb over high heat in batches.

Add the onion, celery and carrot to the pan, and cook until soft and golden.

LAMB WITH BORLOTTI BEANS

Preparation time: 20 minutes + overnight soaking
Total cooking time: 2 hours
Serves 6

1 cup (200 g/6½ oz) dried borlotti beans
1 tablespoon olive oil
12 lamb loin chops
1 onion, finely chopped
1 celery stick, chopped
1 carrot, chopped
3 cloves garlic, finely chopped
½ teaspoon dried chilli flakes
1 teaspoon cumin seeds
2 cups (500 ml/16 fl oz) lamb or
   chicken stock
2 bay leaves
¼ cup (60 ml/2 fl oz) lemon juice
⅓ cup (20 g/¾ oz) chopped fresh parsley
1 tablespoon shredded fresh mint

1 Soak the beans overnight in cold water. Drain, rinse well and set aside.

2 Preheat the oven to moderate 180°C (350°F/Gas 4). Heat the oil in a large heavy-based saucepan. Brown the lamb over high heat in batches, then transfer to a casserole dish.

3 Add the onion, celery and carrot to the pan, and cook over low heat for 10 minutes, or until soft and golden. Add the garlic, chilli and cumin seeds, and cook for 1 minute, then transfer to the casserole dish.

4 Add the stock, beans and bay leaves. Cover tightly and bake for 1½–1¾ hours, or until the lamb is very tender and the beans are cooked. Season with salt and freshly cracked black pepper. Stir in the lemon juice, parsley and mint just before serving.

NUTRITION PER SERVE
Protein 30 g; Fat 8 g; Carbohydrate 20 g; Dietary Fibre 5 g; Cholesterol 65 mg; 1185 kJ (280 cal)

BEEF CASSEROLE WITH CARAWAY DUMPLINGS

Preparation time: 1 hour
Total cooking time: 1 hour 15 minutes
Serves 6

1.5 kg (3 lb) round or topside steak, trimmed
    and cut into 3 cm (1 ¼ inch) cubes
½ cup (60 g/2 oz) plain flour
¼ teaspoon ground black pepper
⅓ cup (80 ml/2¾ fl oz) olive oil
1 clove garlic, crushed
2 onions, sliced
1 teaspoon ground sweet paprika
½ teaspoon ground cinnamon
⅓ cup (80 ml/ 2¾ fl oz) red wine
½ cup (125 ml/4 fl oz) beef stock
½ teaspoon dried mixed herbs
⅔ cup (160 g/5½ oz) tomato pasta sauce
3 large red capsicums

DUMPLINGS
1½ cups (185 g/6 oz) self-raising flour
65 g (2 ¼ oz) butter
½ cup (125 ml/4 fl oz) milk
1 teaspoon caraway seeds
1 tablespoon milk, extra

1 Preheat the oven to moderate 180°C (350°F/Gas 4). Toss the meat lightly in the combined flour and pepper, and shake off any excess.

2 Heat 2 tablespoons of the oil in a heavy-based saucepan. Cook the meat quickly in small batches over medium–high heat until well browned. Drain on paper towels.

3 Heat the remaining oil in the pan. Cook the garlic and onion over medium heat, stirring, for 2 minutes, or until soft.

4 Return the meat to the pan with the spices, wine, stock, mixed herbs and tomato pasta sauce. Bring to the boil, then remove from the heat and transfer to a deep casserole dish. Bake, covered, for 45 minutes. Remove from the oven and remove the lid. Increase the oven to very hot 240°C (475°F/Gas 9).

5 Halve the capsicums lengthways and remove the seeds. Grill, skin-side up, under a hot grill for 10 minutes, or until the skin blackens and blisters. Remove from the grill and allow to cool. Carefully peel off the skins. Cut the capsicum into 2 cm (¾ inch) wide strips. Arrange the roasted capsicum over the meat.

6 To make the dumplings, process the flour and butter in a food processor for 10 seconds, or until fine and crumbly. Add the milk all at once and process for 10 seconds, or until a soft dough is formed. Turn the dough onto a lightly floured surface. Add the caraway seeds and knead for 1 minute, or until smooth. Press the dough out to a 1 cm (½ inch) round. Cut 4 cm (1½ inch) rounds using a fluted cutter. Top the casserole with the dumplings and brush with the extra milk. Return the casserole to the oven, uncovered, for 15 minutes, or until the dumplings are puffed and golden.

NUTRITION PER SERVE
Protein 61 g; Fat 31 g; Carbohydrate 40 g; Dietary Fibre 2.5 g; Cholesterol 176 mg; 2880 kJ (685 cal)

Use a large, sharp knife to trim the steak and cut it into cubes.

Cook the meat quickly in small batches in the hot oil until browned.

Cook the garlic and onion over medium heat, stirring, until soft.

Return the meat to the pan with the spices, wine, stock, mixed herbs and tomato pasta sauce.

Finely chop the white part of the lemon grass stems, and shred the lime leaves.

Heat half the peanut oil and brown the lightly floured fish over medium heat.

FISH AND LEMON GRASS CASSEROLE

Preparation time: 15 minutes
Total cooking time: 40 minutes
Serves 4

4 fish cutlets (200 g/6¹/₂ oz each)
seasoned plain flour
2–3 tablespoons peanut oil
2 onions, sliced
2 stems lemon grass (white part only), finely chopped
4 kaffir lime leaves, shredded
1 teaspoon ground cumin
1 teaspoon ground coriander
1 teaspoon finely chopped fresh red chilli
³/₄ cup (185 ml/6 fl oz) chicken stock
1¹/₂ cups (375 ml/12 fl oz) coconut milk
¹/₄ cup (15 g/¹/₂ oz) chopped fresh coriander
2 teaspoons fish sauce

1 Preheat the oven to moderate 180°C (350°F/Gas 4). Toss the fish lightly in the flour. Heat half the oil in a large heavy-based frying pan and cook the fish over medium heat until lightly browned on both sides. Transfer to a shallow ovenproof dish.

2 Heat the remaining oil in the pan. Cook the onion and lemon grass, stirring, for 5 minutes, or until the onion softens. Add the lime leaves, ground spices and chilli, and stir for 2 minutes, or until fragrant.

3 Add the stock and coconut milk to the onion mixture, and bring to the boil. Pour over the fish, then cover and bake for 30 minutes, or until the fish is tender.

4 Transfer the fish to a serving plate. Stir the chopped coriander and the fish sauce into the remaining sauce, and season to taste with salt and freshly ground pepper. Pour the sauce over the fish to serve.

NUTRITION PER SERVE
Protein 35 g; Fat 40 g; Carbohydrate 6 g; Dietary Fibre 1 g; Cholesterol 105 mg; 2040 kJ (490 cal)

NOTE: Kaffir lime leaves are glossy and dark green, with double leaves and a floral citrus smell. They can be frozen.

Add the onion, garlic, cinnamon stick, ginger, saffron and cold water to the lamb.

Add the quince, ground cinnamon and honey to the cooking liquid.

TAGINE OF LAMB WITH QUINCE AND LEMON

Preparation time: 25 minutes
Total cooking time: 2 hours 10 minutes
Serves 4

1.5 kg (3 lb) boned shoulder of lamb, cut
    into 12 even pieces
1 onion, finely chopped
2 cloves garlic, crushed
1 cinnamon stick
1 teaspoon ground ginger
$1/2$ teaspoon saffron threads
1 large quince, peeled, seeded and cut into
    12 pieces
1 teaspoon ground cinnamon
$1/4$ cup (90 g/3 oz) honey
$1/2$ preserved lemon
chopped fresh parsley, to serve

1 Trim the lamb of excess fat and place in a large saucepan. Add the onion, garlic, cinnamon stick, ginger and saffron, and enough cold water to cover. Slowly bring to the boil, stirring occasionally. Reduce the heat, cover and simmer for 45 minutes. Transfer the meat to a large casserole dish and set aside.

2 Add the quince, ground cinnamon and honey to the cooking liquid, and simmer for 15 minutes, or until the quince is tender. Discard the cinnamon stick; remove the quince and add to the meat, reserving the liquid.

3 Preheat the oven to moderate 180°C (350°F/Gas 4). Boil the cooking liquid for 30 minutes, or until reduced by half, then pour over the meat and quince. Remove and discard the flesh from the lemon. Slice the rind thinly, then add to the meat. Cover and bake for 40 minutes, or until the meat is tender. Sprinkle with parsley to serve.

NUTRITION PER SERVE
Protein 80 g; Fat 15 g; Carbohydrate 20 g; Dietary Fibre 3 g; Cholesterol 250 mg; 2160 kJ (515 cal)

HINT: As you work, place the peeled quince in water with a little lemon juice to prevent discoloring.

Place the soaked haricot beans in a large saucepan with the beef stock.

Add the onion, carrot and garlic to the frying pan, and brown well.

CASSOULET

**Preparation time: 20 minutes +
   overnight soaking**
Total cooking time: 4 hours
Serves 6

500 g (1 lb) dried haricot beans
1.5 litres beef stock
2 tablespoons oil
500 g (1 lb) pork spareribs, trimmed
250 g (8 oz) diced lamb
250 g (8 oz) garlic or spiced sausage
125 g (4 oz) piece bacon, cut into cubes
2 onions, chopped
2 carrots, chopped
2 cloves garlic, crushed
1 bay leaf
1 sprig fresh parsley
1 sprig fresh thyme
6 black peppercorns
2 cups (160 g/5½ oz) fresh breadcrumbs
60 g (2 oz) butter, chilled and grated

1 Soak the beans overnight in water.
2 Drain the beans and place in a large saucepan with the stock. Bring slowly to the boil, then reduce the heat and simmer for 1 hour, or until tender. Drain the beans, reserving the liquid.
3 Heat the oil in a frying pan. Brown the pork, lamb, sausage and bacon in several batches. Remove and drain on paper towels. Add the onion, carrot and garlic to the pan, and brown well.
4 Preheat the oven to warm 160°C (315°F/ Gas 2–3). Layer the meats, beans and vegetables in a large casserole dish. Tie the herbs and peppercorns together in a small piece of muslin, and add to the dish. Pour over the liquid from the beans, cover and bake for 2 hours.
5 Remove and discard the herb bag. Combine the breadcrumbs and butter, and sprinkle over the top of the casserole. Return to the oven for 30 minutes, or until the crust is golden and crisp.

NUTRITION PER SERVE
Protein 55 g; Fat 36 g; Carbohydrate 56 g; Dietary Fibre 19 g; Cholesterol 123 mg; 3140 kJ (750 cal)

Drain the blanched shallots, then carefully peel off the skin.

Brown the meat in batches in the hot oil over medium–high heat.

BEEF, POTATO AND CAPSICUM CASSEROLE

Preparation time: 35 minutes
Total cooking time: 2 hours 20 minutes
Serves 4–6

300 g (10 oz) French shallots
2 tablespoons olive oil
1 kg (2 lb) gravy beef, cut into 4 cm (1½ inch) cubes
4 cloves garlic, crushed
3 teaspoons paprika
1 teaspoon fennel seeds
½ teaspoon ground cumin
1 tablespoon plain flour
½ cup (125 ml/4 fl oz) red wine
2 tablespoons brandy
½ teaspoon dried thyme
½ teaspoon dried oregano
1 bay leaf
1½ cups (375 ml/12 fl oz) beef stock
1 tablespoon honey

400 g (13 oz) potatoes, cut into large chunks
2 red capsicums, chopped
½ cup (125 g/4 oz) sour cream
chopped fresh chives, to serve

1 Preheat the oven to moderate 180°C (350°F/Gas 4). Place the shallots in a bowl, cover with boiling water and leave for 30 seconds. Drain and peel.

2 Heat the oil in a large, heavy-based saucepan, then brown the meat in batches over medium–high heat, and transfer to a large casserole dish.

3 Add the shallots to the pan and cook over medium heat until soft and golden. Add the garlic, paprika, fennel seeds and cumin; cook until fragrant.

4 Add the flour, cook for 30 seconds, then remove from the heat. Stir in the red wine and brandy. Return to the heat and add the thyme, oregano, bay leaf and stock. Stir until the mixture bubbles, then add to the meat.

5 Cover and bake for 1½ hours, then add the honey, potato and capsicum. Cook, uncovered, for 30 minutes, or until the potato is tender. Season to taste. Serve with a dollop of sour cream and a sprinkling of chives.

NUTRITION PER SERVE (6)

Protein 40 g; Fat 20 g; Carbohydrate 30 g; Dietary Fibre 3 g; Cholesterol 140 mg; 1790 kJ (430 cal)

Tie up the turkey with string, at regular intervals, to help retain its shape during cooking.

Pour the stock and wine over the turkey and onion wedges.

TURKEY POT ROAST

Preparation time: 20 minutes
Total cooking time: 1 hour 15 minutes
Serves 6

1 kg (2 lb) frozen turkey breast roll
2 tablespoons oil
20 g (³/₄ oz) butter
1 onion, cut into wedges
¹/₂ cup (125 ml/4 fl oz) chicken stock
¹/₂ cup (125 ml/4 fl oz) white wine
300 g (10 oz) orange sweet potato, cut into
    3 cm (1 ¹/₄ inch) pieces
2 zucchini, cut into 2 cm (³/₄ inch) slices
¹/₂ cup (160 g/5¹/₂ oz) redcurrant jelly
1 tablespoon cornflour

1 Preheat the oven to moderate 180°C (350°F/Gas 4). Thaw the turkey according to the instructions on the label. Remove the elasticized string from the turkey and tie up securely with string, at regular intervals, to retain its shape.
2 Heat the oil and butter in a frying pan over high heat, and brown the turkey all over. Transfer the turkey to a 2 litre casserole dish. Place the onion wedges around the turkey, and pour over the stock and wine. Cover and bake for 40 minutes. Add the sweet potato and bake for 10 minutes. Add the zucchini and bake for a further 20 minutes.
3 Transfer the turkey and vegetables to a plate and keep warm. Strain the liquid into a small saucepan. Stir in the redcurrant jelly. Combine the cornflour and 1 tablespoon water, and stir until smooth. Add gradually to the pan, stirring until the mixture boils and thickens. Slice the turkey and serve with the vegetables and sauce.

NUTRITION PER SERVE

Protein 46 g; Fat 12 g; Carbohydrate 21 g; Dietary Fibre 1.5 g; Cholesterol 104 mg; 1630 kJ (390 cal)

Add the tomato pasta sauce and frozen peas to the pan, and cook for 3 minutes.

Cook the pasta in a large saucepan of boiling water until al dente.

PASTA AND VEGETABLE CASEROLE

Preparation time: 20 minutes
Total cooking time: 50 minutes
Serves 4

2 tablespoons olive oil
1 large onion, finely chopped
1 clove garlic, crushed
3 zucchini, sliced
4 button mushrooms, sliced
2 cups (500 g/1 lb) tomato pasta sauce
1 cup (155 g/5 oz) frozen peas
1¹/₂ cups (265 g/8 oz) pasta (penne or spiralli)
¹/₃ cup (35 g/1 ¹/₄ oz) grated fresh Parmesan

1 Preheat the oven to slow 150°C (300°F/Gas 2). Heat half the oil in a frying pan over low heat. Cook the onion and garlic for 4 minutes, or until the onion is soft. Add the zucchini and mushrooms, and cook for 3 minutes. Add the pasta sauce and peas, and cook for 3 minutes. Season to taste. Remove from the heat.
2 Cook the pasta with the remaining oil in a large saucepan of boiling water for 10–12 minutes, or until al dente. Drain, and add to the vegetables.
3 Spoon the mixture into a casserole dish. Sprinkle with the Parmesan and bake, covered, for 20–30 minutes.

NUTRITION PER SERVE
Protein 17 g; Fat 12 g; Carbohydrate 66 g; Dietary Fibre 9 g; Cholesterol 7 mg; 1820 kJ (435 cal)

LAMB SHANKS IN TOMATO SAUCE ON POLENTA

Preparation time: 10 minutes
Total cooking time: 2 hours 30 minutes
Serves 4

2 tablespoons olive oil
1 large red onion, sliced
4 French-trimmed lamb shanks
   (about 250 g/8 oz each)
2 cloves garlic, crushed
400 g (13 oz) can peeled, chopped tomatoes
1/2 cup (125 ml/4 fl oz) red wine
2 teaspoons chopped fresh rosemary
1 cup (150 g/5 oz) instant polenta
50 g (1³/₄ oz) butter
1/2 cup (50 g/1³/₄ oz) grated fresh Parmesan

1 Preheat the oven to warm 160°C (315°F/Gas 2–3). Heat the oil in a 4 litre flameproof casserole dish over medium heat and sauté the onion for 3–4 minutes, or until softening and becoming transparent. Add the lamb shanks and cook for 2–3 minutes, or until lightly browned. Add the garlic, tomato and wine, then bring to the boil and cook for 3–4 minutes. Stir in the rosemary. Season with 1/4 teaspoon each of salt and pepper.

2 Cover and bake for 2 hours. Remove the lid, return to the oven and simmer for a further 15 minutes, or until the lamb just starts to fall off the bone. Check periodically that the sauce is not too dry, adding water if needed.

3 About 20 minutes before serving, bring 1 litre water to the boil in a saucepan. Add the polenta in a thin stream, whisking continuously, then reduce the heat to very low. Simmer for 8–10 minutes, or until thick and coming away from the side of the pan. Stir in the butter and Parmesan. To serve, spoon the polenta onto serving plates, top with the shanks and tomato sauce.

NUTRITION PER SERVE
Protein 39 g; Fat 36.5 g; Carbohydrate 31 g; Dietary Fibre 3 g; Cholesterol 137 mg; 2615 kJ (625 cal)

Leave a long tail of string on the bouquet garni for easy removal.

Cook the beef in batches in a large saucepan until well browned all over.

BEEF CARBONNADE

Preparation time: 15 minutes
Total cooking time: 3 hours 25 minutes
Serves 4

1 leek, green part only
1 bay leaf
1 sprig fresh thyme
1 sprig celery leaves
4 sprigs fresh parsley
40 g (1 ¼ oz) butter
1 tablespoon oil
1 kg (2 lb) chuck or stewing steak, cubed
2 onions, sliced
2 cloves garlic, crushed
2 tablespoons plain flour
1½ cups (375 ml/12 fl oz) brown ale or stout
1 long bread stick
2 teaspoons French mustard
2 teaspoons butter, extra, softened

1 To make a bouquet garni, wrap the green part of the leek loosely around the bay leaf, thyme sprig, celery leaves and parsley, then tie together with string. Leave a long tail on the string for easy removal.

2 Preheat the oven to moderate 180°C (350°F/Gas 4). Heat the butter and oil in a large saucepan, and cook the beef in batches for 3–4 minutes, or until well browned. Remove from the pan. Reduce the heat and cook the onion and garlic for 4 minutes, or until translucent. Sprinkle in the flour, stir well, then cook for 1 minute. Combine the beer with 1½ cups (375 ml/12 fl oz) water, and pour into the pan. Stir well, scraping the pan to incorporate ingredients that are stuck to the base of the pan. Bring to the boil and return the meat to the pan. Add the bouquet garni and return to the boil. Transfer to a 2.5 litre casserole dish, cover well with foil and bake for 2½ hours.

3 Cut the bread into 2 cm (¾ inch) slices and spread with the combined mustard and extra butter. Remove the casserole from the oven, take out the bouquet garni and skim off any fat. Put

the bread slices on the surface of the casserole, mustard-side up, and press down gently to cover with juice. Return to the oven and cook, uncovered, for another 30–40 minutes, or until the bread becomes crusty. Serve with steamed green vegetables.

NUTRITION PER SERVE

Protein 60 g; Fat 25 g; Carbohydrate 30 g; Dietary Fibre 3.5 g; Cholesterol 195 mg; 2455 kJ (585 cal)

Remove the cores from the kidneys and then cut the kidneys into quarters.

Cover the base with potato slices, then add the chops and kidneys.

LANCASHIRE HOTPOT

Preparation time: 20 minutes
Total cooking time: 2 hours
Serves 8

8 lamb forequarter chops
4 lamb's kidneys
1/4 cup (30 g/1 oz) plain flour
50 g (1¾ oz) butter
4 potatoes, thinly sliced
2 large brown onions, sliced
1 large carrot, chopped
1¾ cups (440 ml/14 fl oz) beef or vegetable
   stock
2 teaspoons chopped fresh thyme
1 bay leaf
melted butter, extra

1 Preheat the oven to warm 160°C (315°F/Gas 2–3), and grease a large casserole dish. Trim the chops of excess fat and sinew, then remove the cores from the kidneys and cut into quarters. Toss the chops and kidneys in the flour, shaking off and reserving the excess. Heat the butter in a frying pan and brown the chops quickly on both sides. Remove the chops from the pan and brown the kidneys.

2 Layer half the potato slices in the base of the casserole and top with the chops and kidneys.

3 Add the onion and carrot to the pan, and cook until the carrot begins to brown. Layer on top of the chops and kidneys. Sprinkle the reserved flour over the base of the pan and fry, stirring, until dark brown. Gradually pour in the stock and bring to the boil, stirring. Season well, and add the thyme and bay leaf. Reduce the heat and simmer for 10 minutes. Pour into the casserole dish.

4 Layer the remaining potato over the meat and vegetables. Cover and bake for 1¼ hours. Increase the oven temperature to moderate 180°C (350°F/Gas 4), brush the potato with the extra melted butter and cook, uncovered, for 20 minutes, or until the potato is brown.

NUTRITION PER SERVE
Protein 38 g; Fat 11 g; Carbohydrate 13 g; Dietary Fibre 2 g; Cholesterol 175 mg; 1285 kJ (305 cal)

Place the drained beans in a large saucepan, add the ham hock and cover with cold water.

Trim the ham of all fat, skin and sinew, then roughly chop the meat.

BOSTON BAKED BEANS

Preparation time: 25 minutes +
6–8 hours soaking
Total cooking time: 1 hour 35 minutes
Serves 4–6

1³/₄ cups (350 g/11 oz) dried cannellini
  beans (see NOTES)
1 whole ham hock
2 onions, chopped
2 tablespoons tomato paste
1 tablespoon Worcestershire sauce
1 tablespoon molasses
1 teaspoon French mustard
¹/₄ cup (45 g/1¹/₂ oz) soft brown sugar
¹/₂ cup (125 ml/4 fl oz) tomato juice

1 Cover the beans with cold water and soak for 6–8 hours, or overnight.

2 Drain the beans, rinse them well and place in a large saucepan. Add the ham hock and cover with cold water. Bring to the boil, then reduce the heat and simmer, covered, for 25 minutes, or until the beans are tender. Preheat the oven to warm 160°C (315°F/Gas 2–3).

3 Remove the ham hock from the pan and set aside to cool. Drain the beans, reserving 1 cup (250 ml/8 fl oz) of the cooking liquid. Trim the ham of all skin, fat and sinew, then roughly chop the meat and discard the bone.

4 Transfer the meat and beans to a 2 litre casserole dish. Add the reserved liquid and all remaining ingredients. Mix gently, then cover and bake for 1 hour. Serve with hot buttered toast.

NUTRITION PER SERVE (6)
Protein 28 g; Fat 5 g; Carbohydrate 30 g; Dietary Fibre 2 g; Cholesterol 60 mg; 1090 kJ (260 cal)

NOTES: Any type of dried bean can be used in this recipe.

  To quick-soak beans, place them in a pan, add hot water to cover, bring slowly to the boil, then remove from the heat. Leave to soak for 1 hour before draining and using.

Peel and devein the prawns, and cut the fish into bite-size pieces.

Scrub the mussels, remove the beards, then place in a saucepan of simmering water.

SEAFOOD CASSEROLE WITH FETA AND OLIVES

Preparation time: 20 minutes
Total cooking time: 35 minutes
Serves 4

500 g (1 lb) fresh mussels
2 tablespoons olive oil
1 large onion, sliced
2 x 400 g (13 oz) cans tomatoes, chopped
2 strips lemon rind
1 tablespoon chopped fresh lemon thyme
⅓ cup (80 ml/2¾ fl oz) dry vermouth or
     white wine
1 teaspoon sugar
12 raw king prawns, peeled and deveined,
     tails intact
750 g (1½ lb) firm white fish fillets,
     cut into bite-size pieces
12 black olives
125 g (4 oz) feta cheese, cubed

1 Discard any open mussels. Scrub the rest of the mussels and remove the beards. Place the mussels in a saucepan of simmering water. As soon as the shells open, place the mussels in a bowl of cold water, discarding any unopened ones. Open them up and leave on their half shells, discarding the other half.

2 Preheat the oven to moderate 180°C (350°F/Gas 4). Heat the oil in a large, heavy-based saucepan and cook the onion over low heat for 5 minutes, or until soft but not brown. Add the tomato, lemon rind, lemon thyme, vermouth and sugar. Bring to the boil, and season to taste. Reduce the heat, cover and simmer for 10 minutes.

3 Place the seafood in a shallow ovenproof dish and cover with the hot sauce. Bake, covered, for 10 minutes. Add the olives and feta, covering the seafood with the sauce. Bake for 10 minutes, or until heated through. Serve immediately.

NUTRITION PER SERVE
Protein 70 g; Fat 25 g; Carbohydrate 10 g; Dietary Fibre 4 g; Cholesterol 313 mg; 2430 kJ (580 cal)

Cook the fish in the simmering milk until it flakes easily when tested.

Stir the flour into the onion and garlic, and cook until golden.

CREAMY FISH CASSEROLE

Preparation time: 10 minutes
Total cooking time: 1 hour
Serves 4

2 large potatoes, chopped
$^1/_4$ cup (60 ml/2 fl oz) milk or cream
1 egg
60 g (2 oz) butter
$^1/_2$ cup (60 g/2 oz) grated Cheddar
800 g (1 lb 10 oz) white fish fillets, cut into large chunks
1$^1/_2$ cups (375 ml/12 fl oz) milk, extra
1 onion, finely chopped
1 clove garlic, crushed
2 tablespoons plain flour
2 tablespoons lemon juice
2 teaspoons lemon rind
1 tablespoon chopped fresh dill

1 Preheat the oven to moderate 180°C (350°F/Gas 4). Boil or steam the potato for 8 minutes, or until tender. Drain and mash with the milk or cream, egg and half the butter. Mix in half the cheese, then set aside.

2 Put the fish in a shallow frying pan and cover with the extra milk. Bring to the boil, then reduce the heat and simmer for 2–3 minutes, or until the fish flakes easily. Drain the fish well, reserving the milk, and put in a 1.5 litre ovenproof dish.

3 Melt the remaining butter over medium heat in a saucepan and cook the onion and garlic for 2 minutes. Stir in the flour and cook for 1 minute, or until golden. Remove from the heat and gradually stir in the reserved milk. Return to the heat and stir constantly until the sauce boils and thickens. Reduce the heat and simmer for 2 minutes. Add the lemon juice, rind and dill, and season. Mix with the fish, cover with potato and sprinkle with the remaining cheese. Bake for 35 minutes, or until golden.

NUTRITION PER SERVE

Protein 54 g; Fat 29 g; Carbohydrate 24 g; Dietary Fibre 2.5 g; Cholesterol 253 mg; 2390 kJ (570 cal)

NOTE: You could use ling, perch, hake or snapper.

Form the mince mixture into eight large balls using wet hands.

LION'S HEAD MEATBALLS

Preparation time: 20 minutes + overnight refrigeration +
20 minutes soaking
Total cooking time: 4 hours 45 minutes
Serves 4

CHICKEN STOCK
1.5 kg (3 lb) chicken bones (chicken necks, backs, wings), washed
2 slices fresh ginger, cut into 1 cm (1/2 inch) thick slices
4 spring onions

6 dried Chinese mushrooms
100 g (3 1/2 oz) mung bean vermicelli
600 g (1 1/4 lb) pork mince
1 egg white
4 cloves garlic, finely chopped
1 tablespoon finely grated fresh ginger
1 tablespoon cornflour
1 1/2 tablespoons Chinese rice wine

6 spring onions, thinly sliced
2 tablespoons peanut oil
1/4 cup (60 ml/2 fl oz) light soy sauce
1 teaspoon sugar
400 g (13 oz) bok choy, halved lengthways, leaves separated

1   To make the stock, place the bones and 3.5 litres water in a large saucepan and bring to a simmer—do not let it boil. Remove the scum from the surface and continue doing so over the next 30 minutes. Add the ginger and spring onions, and cook, partially covered, keeping at a low simmer for 3 hours. Strain through a fine sieve. Cool. Cover and refrigerate overnight. Remove the layer of fat from the surface once it has solidified.

2   Soak the Chinese mushrooms in 1 cup (250 ml/8 fl oz) boiling water for 20 minutes. Drain. Discard the stems and thinly slice the caps. Meanwhile, place the vermicelli in a heatproof bowl, cover with boiling water and soak for 3–4 minutes, or until soft. Drain and rinse. Preheat the oven to hot 220°C (425°F/Gas 7).

3   Place the mince, egg white, garlic, ginger, cornflour, rice wine, two-thirds of the spring onion and salt, to taste, in a food processor. Using the pulse button, process until smooth and well combined. Divide the mixture into eight portions and shape into large balls with wet hands.

4   Place 2 cups (500 ml/16 fl oz) of the stock (freeze any remaining stock) in a large saucepan and bring to the boil over high heat, then remove from the heat and keep warm.

5   Heat the oil in a wok over high heat. Fry the meatballs in batches for 2 minutes each side, or until golden, but not cooked through. Drain.

6   Place the meatballs, mushrooms, soy sauce and sugar in a 2.5 litre ovenproof clay pot or casserole dish, and cover with the hot stock. Bake, covered, for 45 minutes. Add the bok choy and noodles and bake, covered, for another 10 minutes. Sprinkle with the remaining spring onion, and serve.

NUTRITION PER SERVE
Protein 35 g; Fat 20 g; Carbohydrate 22 g; Dietary Fibre 4 g; Cholesterol 97 mg; 1720 kJ (410 cal)

HINT: To save time, use 2 cups (500 ml/16 fl oz) purchased stock instead of making your own.

EGGPLANT PARMIGIANA

Preparation time: 30 minutes
Total cooking time: 1 hour 15 minutes
Serves 6–8

¼ cup (60 ml/2 fl oz) olive oil
1 onion, diced
2 cloves garlic, crushed
1.25 kg (2 lb 8 oz) tomatoes, peeled and
    chopped
oil, for shallow-frying
1 kg (2 lb) eggplants, very thinly sliced
250 g (8 oz) bocconcini, sliced
1½ cups (185 g/6 oz) finely grated Cheddar
1 cup (50 g/1⅔ oz) fresh basil leaves
½ cup (50 g/1¾ oz) grated fresh Parmesan

1 Heat the oil in a large frying pan over medium heat. Cook the onion until soft. Add the garlic and cook for 1 minute. Add the tomato and simmer for 15 minutes. Season with salt. Preheat the oven to moderately hot 200°C (400°F/Gas 6).
2 Shallow-fry the eggplant in batches for 3–4 minutes, or until golden brown. Drain on paper towels.
3 Place one-third of the eggplant slices in a 1.75 litre ovenproof dish. Top with half the bocconcini and half the Cheddar. Repeat the layers, finishing with a layer of eggplant.
4 Pour over the tomato mixture. Scatter with torn basil leaves, then Parmesan. Bake for 40 minutes.

NUTRITION PER SERVE (8)
Protein 17 g; Fat 25 g; Carbohydrate 7 g; Dietary Fibre 5 g; Cholesterol 40 mg; 1340 kJ (320 cal)

VARIATION: If you prefer not to fry the eggplant, brush it lightly with oil and brown lightly under a hot grill.

Fry the onion and garlic in the oil, then add the chopped tomato.

Shallow-fry the eggplant in batches, then drain on paper towels.

Add the garlic and spices to the fried onion, and cook for 1 minute.

Cut the trimmed artichokes in half lengthways and place them in the lemon-water.

BEEF AND ARTICHOKE CASSEROLE

Preparation time: 30 minutes
Total cooking time: 2 hours 15 minutes
Serves 4–6

2 tablespoons olive oil
1 kg (2 lb) stewing beef, cut into large cubes
2 red onions, sliced
4 cloves garlic, crushed
1 teaspoon cumin seeds
2 teaspoons ground cumin
1 teaspoon ground coriander
2 teaspoons sweet paprika
1 tablespoon plain flour
2 cups (500 ml/16 fl oz) beef stock
1 teaspoon grated lemon rind
1 tablespoon soft brown sugar
1 tablespoon tomato paste
¼ cup (60 ml/2 fl oz) lemon juice
4 globe artichokes
½ cup (90 g/3 oz) small black olives

1 Preheat the oven to moderate 180°C (350°F/Gas 4). Heat half the oil in a large heavy-based frying pan. Brown the meat in batches over medium–high heat, then transfer to a large casserole dish.
2 Add the remaining oil to the pan and cook the onion over medium heat for 5 minutes, or until soft. Add the garlic, cumin seeds, cumin, coriander and paprika, and cook for 1 minute.
3 Add the flour, cook for 30 seconds, then remove from the heat. Add the stock, return to the heat and stir until the mixture bubbles. Add to the meat with the rind, sugar and tomato paste. Cover tightly and bake for 1½ hours.
4 Meanwhile, add the lemon juice to a bowl of water. Cut the top third from each artichoke, trim the stem to 5 cm (2 inches) and cut away the dark outer leaves. Cut the artichokes in half lengthways. Remove the prickly lavender-topped leaves in the centre and scoop out the hairy choke. Drop the artichokes into the lemon-water until ready to use.

5 Drain the artichokes and add to the casserole, covering them in the liquid. Cover and bake for 30 minutes, or until tender. For a thicker gravy, cook uncovered for 15 minutes more. Season, and stir in the olives to serve.

NUTRITION PER SERVE (6)
Protein 40 g; Fat 12 g; Carbohydrate 8 g; Dietary Fibre 2 g; Cholesterol 112 mg; 1212 kJ (290 cal)

NOTE: Tiny black olives have a great flavor and are sold in delicatessens.

Add the leek and peeled shallots to the pan, and gently fry until soft and golden.

Remove the pan from the heat and stir in the stock, scraping up any brown sediment.

VEAL, LEMON AND CASEROLE

VEAL, LEMON AND CAPER CASSEROLE

Preparation time: 30 minutes
Total cooking time: 2 hours
Serves 4–6

1 tablespoon olive oil
50 g (1¾ oz) butter
1 kg (2 lb) stewing veal, cut into 4 cm
    (1½ inch) chunks
300 g (10 oz) French shallots
3 leeks, cut into large chunks
2 cloves garlic, crushed
1 tablespoon plain flour
2 cups (500 ml/16 fl oz) chicken stock
1 teaspoon grated lemon rind
⅓ cup (80 ml/2¾ fl oz) lemon juice
2 bay leaves
2 tablespoons capers, drained and well
    rinsed
chopped fresh parsley, to serve
caperberries, to garnish

1 Preheat the oven to moderate 180°C (350°F/Gas 4). Heat the oil and half the butter in a large, heavy-based frying pan. Brown the veal in batches over medium–high heat, then transfer to a large casserole dish.

2 Blanch the shallots in boiling water for 30 seconds, then peel and add to the pan with the leek. Gently cook for 5 minutes, or until soft and golden. Add the garlic, cook for 1 minute, then transfer to the casserole dish.

3 Melt the remaining butter in the pan, add the flour and cook for 30 seconds. Remove from the heat, add the stock and stir until well combined. Return to the heat and cook, stirring, until the sauce begins to bubble.

4 Pour the sauce into the casserole dish and stir in the lemon rind, lemon juice and bay leaves. Cover and bake for 1–1½ hours, or until the veal is tender. During the last 20 minutes of cooking, remove the lid to allow the sauces to reduce a little.

5 To serve, stir in the capers and season with salt and freshly cracked black pepper. Sprinkle with parsley and garnish with caperberries.

NUTRITION PER SERVE (6)
Protein 40 g; Fat 13 g; Carbohydrate 5 g; Dietary Fibre 2 g; Cholesterol 160 mg; 1300 kJ (300 cal)

NOTES: Caperberries are sold in jars of brine or vinegar in speciality stores.

If possible, use tiny capers in this dish as they have a superb flavor, but regular capers can be used instead.Add the leek and peeled shallots to the pan, and gently fry until soft and golden.

Cook the whole onions in the casserole dish until they are browned.

Return the cooked bacon and chicken pieces to the casserole dish.

CHICKEN AND RED WINE CASSEROLE

Preparation time: 15 minutes
Total cooking time: 1 hour 50 minutes
Serves 4–6

30 g (1 oz) butter
125 g (4 oz) bacon, roughly chopped
1.5 kg (3 lb) skinless chicken pieces
350 g (11 oz) baby onions
2 tablespoons plain flour
3 cups (750 ml/24 fl oz) red wine
250 g (8 oz) mushrooms, sliced
1 tablespoon fresh thyme leaves, to garnish

1 Preheat the oven to moderate 180°C (350°F/Gas 4). Melt the butter in a large flameproof casserole dish over medium heat. Add the bacon and cook until golden, then remove. Add the chicken pieces and cook, in batches, for 4–5 minutes, or until browned. Remove. Add the onions and cook for 2–3 minutes, or until browned, then remove from the dish.

2 Stir the flour in to the dish, then remove from the heat and slowly pour in the red wine, while stirring. Return to the heat, bring to the boil and return the bacon and chicken to the dish. Cover and bake for 1 hour. Return the onions to the dish and add the mushrooms. Cook for a further 30 minutes. Season to taste with salt and freshly ground black pepper, and garnish with the thyme. Serve with mashed potato, if desired.

NUTRITION PER SERVE (6)
Protein 65 g; Fat 11 g; Carbohydrate 11 g; Dietary Fibre 2 g; Cholesterol 150 mg; 2040 kJ (487 cal)

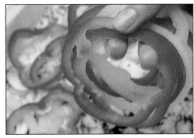

Scatter the garlic, parsley, onion, chilli and capsicum on top of the potato.

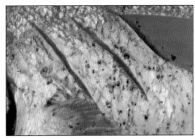

Make three or four diagonal slashes on each side of the stuffed fish.

WHOLE FISH CASSEROLE

**Preparation time: 30 minutes +
    2 hours marinating**
Total cooking time: 1 hour 35 minutes
Serves 4–6

1.25 kg (2½ lb) whole red bream or red
    snapper, cleaned
1 lemon
¼ cup (60 ml/2 fl oz) olive oil
800 g (1 lb 10 oz) potatoes, thinly sliced
3 cloves garlic, thinly sliced
¼ cup (15 g/½ oz) finely chopped
    fresh parsley
1 small red onion, thinly sliced
1 small dried chilli, seeded and finely
    chopped
1 red capsicum, cut into thin rings
1 yellow capsicum, cut into thin rings
2 bay leaves
3–4 sprigs fresh thyme
¼ cup (60 ml/2 fl oz) dry sherry

1 Cut off and discard the fins from the fish and place it in a large non-metallic dish. Cut 2 thin slices from one end of the lemon and reserve. Squeeze the juice from the rest of the lemon inside the fish. Add 2 tablespoons of the oil. Refrigerate, covered, for 2 hours.
2 Preheat the oven to moderately hot 190°C (375°F/Gas 5) and lightly oil a shallow earthenware baking dish large enough to hold the whole fish. Spread half the potato on the base and scatter the garlic, parsley, onion, chilli and capsicum on top. Season with salt and pepper. Cover with the rest of the potato. Pour in ⅓ cup (80 ml/2¾ fl oz) water and sprinkle the remaining olive oil over the top. Cover with foil and bake for 1 hour.
3 Increase the oven temperature to hot 220°C (425°F/Gas 7). Season the fish inside and out with salt and pepper, and place the bay leaves and thyme inside the cavity. Make three or four diagonal slashes on each side. Cut the reserved lemon slices in half and fit these into the slashes on one side of the fish, to resemble fins. Nestle the fish into the potatoes with the lemon on top.

Bake, uncovered, for 30 minutes, or until the fish is cooked through and the potato is golden and crusty.
4 Pour the dry sherry over the fish and return to the oven for 3 minutes. Serve straight from the dish.

NUTRITION PER SERVE (6)
Protein 39 g; Fat 12 g; Carbohydrate 20 g; Dietary Fibre 3 g; Cholesterol 104 mg; 1462 kJ (349 cal)

CREAMY POTATO CASSEROLE

Preparation time: 20 minutes
Total cooking time: 40 minutes
Serves 4–6

750 g (1½ lb) waxy or all-purpose potatoes
    (see NOTES)
1 onion
1 cup (125 g/4 oz) grated Cheddar
1½ cups (375 ml/12 fl oz) cream
2 teaspoons chicken stock powder

1 Preheat the oven to moderate 180°C (350°F/Gas 4). Peel the potatoes and thinly slice them. Peel the onion and slice it into rings.
2 Arrange a layer of overlapping potato slices in the base of a large casserole dish. Top the potato slices with a layer of the onion rings. Divide the grated cheese in half and set aside one half to use as a topping. Sprinkle a little of the remaining grated cheese over the onion rings. Continue layering in this order until all the potato and the onion have been used, finishing with a little of the grated cheese.

3 Pour the cream into a small jug, add the chicken stock powder and whisk gently until the mixture is thoroughly combined. Carefully pour the mixture over the layered potato and onion slices, and sprinkle the top with the reserved grated cheese. Bake the casserole, uncovered, for 40 minutes, or until the potato is tender, the cheese has melted and the top is golden brown.

NUTRITION PER SERVE (6)
Protein 9 g; Fat 35 g; Carbohydrate 15 g; Dietary Fibre 2 g; Cholesterol 100 mg; 1635 kJ (390 cal)

NOTES: If you prefer, you can use different types of stock, including vegetable, to vary the flavor.
    Waxy or all-purpose potatoes are best to use in this recipe because they hold their shape better when slow-cooked.
    If you have a mandolin, use it to cut the potatoes into slices. If not, make sure you use a very sharp knife. Peel the skin very thinly.

Sprinkle a little of the grated cheese over each layer of onion rings.

Pour the cream and chicken stock powder mixture over the potato and onion.

Use a large sharp knife to cut the chicken breasts into cubes.

Add the chicken to the pan and cook in batches until browned.

CHICKEN AND BROCCOLI CASSEROLE

Preparation time: 20 minutes
Total cooking time: 1 hour
Serves 6

30 g (1 oz) butter
4 chicken breast fillets, cut into 3 cm
    (1 1/4 inch) cubes
6 spring onions, sliced
2 cloves garlic, crushed
2 tablespoons plain flour
1 1/2 cups (375 ml/12 fl oz) chicken stock
2 teaspoons Dijon mustard
280 g (9 oz) broccoli, cut into florets
1 kg (2 lb) potatoes, quartered
2 tablespoons milk
60 g (2 oz) butter, extra
2 eggs
1/3 cup (30 g/1 oz) flaked toasted almonds
fresh chives, to garnish

1 Preheat the oven to moderate 180°C (350°F/Gas 4). Heat half the butter in a large frying pan and cook the chicken in batches until browned and cooked through. Remove from the pan. In the same pan, melt the remaining butter and cook the spring onion and garlic for 2 minutes. Stir in the flour and mix well. Pour in the stock and cook, stirring, until the mixture boils and thickens. Add the mustard and then stir in the chicken. Season well with salt and pepper.

2 Meanwhile, steam or microwave the broccoli until just tender, taking care not to overcook it. Refresh the broccoli in iced water and drain well.

3 Boil the potato in salted water for 15–20 minutes, or until tender. Drain and mash well with the milk, extra butter and eggs. Put the broccoli in a 2.5 litre ovenproof dish and pour in the chicken mixture. Pipe or spoon the mashed potato over the top. Sprinkle with the almonds and bake for 25 minutes, or until the top is browned and cooked through. Cut the chives into short lengths and scatter over the top before serving.

NUTRITION PER SERVE
Protein 25 g; Fat 20 g; Carbohydrate 25 g; Dietary Fibre 5.5 g; Cholesterol 135 mg; 1610 kJ (385 cal)

Remove any excess fat from the lamb, then cut it into large pieces.

Heat the oil, then add the lamb and toss until it is browned all over.

LAMB AND BEAN CASSEROLE

Preparation time: 25 minutes + overnight soaking
Total cooking time: 2 hours 15 minutes
Serves 6

1½ cups (300 g/10 oz) borlotti beans or red kidney beans
1 kg (2 lb) boned leg of lamb
1½ tablespoons olive oil
2 rashers bacon, rind removed, chopped
1 large onion, chopped
2 cloves garlic, crushed
1 large carrot, chopped
2 cups (500 ml/16 fl oz) dry red wine
1 tablespoon tomato paste
1½ cups (375 ml/12 fl oz) beef stock
2 large sprigs fresh rosemary
2 sprigs fresh thyme

1 Put the beans in a bowl and cover with plenty of water. Leave to soak overnight, then drain well.
2 Preheat the oven to warm 160°C (315°F/Gas 2–3). Trim any excess fat from the lamb and cut the lamb into 3 cm (1¼ inch) pieces.
3 Heat 1 tablespoon of the oil in a large flameproof casserole dish. Add half the meat and toss over medium–high heat for 2 minutes, or until browned. Remove from the casserole and repeat with the remaining lamb. Remove from the casserole.
4 Heat the remaining olive oil in the casserole and add the bacon and onion. Cook over medium heat for 3 minutes, or until the onion is translucent. Add the garlic and carrot, and cook for 1 minute, or until the mixture is aromatic.

5 Return the meat and any juices to the casserole, increase the heat to high and add the wine. Bring to the boil and cook for 2 minutes. Add the beans, tomato paste, stock, rosemary and thyme, return to the boil, then cover and bake for 2 hours, or until the meat is tender. Stir occasionally during cooking. Skim off any excess fat, remove the sprigs of herbs, and season. Serve with bread.

NUTRITION PER SERVE
Protein 50 g; Fat 10 g; Carbohydrate 48 g; Dietary Fibre 9 g; Cholesterol 117 mg; 2367 kJ (565 cal)

Discard any excess fat and sinew from the steak, and cut the steak into cubes.

When the onion is golden, add the garlic, cumin, thyme and bay leaves.

BEEF AND VEGETABLE CASSEROLE

Preparation time: 40 minutes
Total cooking time: 1 hour 40 minutes
Serves 6

cooking oil spray
500 g (1 lb) lean round steak, cut into 2 cm (³/₄ inch) cubes
1 onion, sliced
3 cloves garlic, crushed
2 teaspoons ground cumin
1 teaspoon dried thyme leaves
2 bay leaves
400 g (13 oz) can chopped tomatoes
500 g (1 lb) potatoes, chopped
2 large carrots, thickly sliced
4 zucchini, thickly sliced
250 g (8 oz) mushrooms, halved
250 g (8 oz) yellow squash, halved
2 tablespoons tomato paste
¹/₂ cup (125 ml/4 fl oz) red wine
¹/₃ cup (20 g/³/₄ oz) chopped fresh parsley

1 Preheat the oven to moderate 180°C (350°F/Gas 4). Spray a deep non-stick frying pan with cooking oil spray and fry the steak in batches until it is browned all over. Remove the meat from the pan. Spray the pan again, add the onion slices and cook until lightly golden. Add the crushed garlic, cumin, thyme and bay leaves, and stir for 1 minute.

2 Return the meat and any juices to the frying pan, tossing to coat the meat with the spices. Add 1¹/₂ cups (375 ml/12 fl oz) water and the chopped tomato, scraping the bottom of the pan. Simmer for 10 minutes, or until thickened. Transfer the mixture to a large casserole dish with the potato, carrot, zucchini, mushrooms, squash, tomato paste and wine.

3 Bake, covered, for 1 hour. Stir well, then uncover and bake for 20 minutes. Season, remove the bay leaves and stir in the parsley.

NUTRITION PER SERVE
Protein 25 g; Fat 4 g; Carbohydrate 20 g; Dietary Fibre 6.5 g; Cholesterol 50 mg; 930 kJ (220 cal)

Cut the cucumbers in half lengthways, then use a teaspoon to scoop out the seeds.

Cook the meatballs in batches, then drain on paper towels.

SWEET AND SOUR MEATBALLS

Preparation time: 20 minutes
Total cooking time: 1 hour 20 minutes
Serves 4–6

1 kg (2 lb) lean beef mince
1 cup (80 g/2¾ oz) fresh breadcrumbs
1 egg, lightly beaten
1 tablespoon Worcestershire sauce
1 tablespoon chilli sauce
1 tablespoon chopped fresh parsley
2 tablespoons oil
1 large cucumber, halved, seeded and
    julienned
1 large carrot, julienned
1 red capsicum, julienned
440 g (14 oz) can pineapple pieces, drained

SAUCE
2 tablespoons soft brown sugar
⅓ cup (80 ml/2¾ fl oz) white vinegar
2 tablespoons barbecue sauce
2 tablespoons tomato sauce
2 cups (500 ml/16 fl oz) pineapple juice
1 tablespoon cornflour

1 Preheat the oven to warm 160°C (315°F/Gas 2–3). Combine the beef, breadcrumbs, egg, sauces and parsley in a large bowl. Using your hands, mix well. Roll 2 teaspoons of the mixture into balls.

2 Heat the oil in a heavy-based frying pan. Cook the meatballs in small batches over medium heat for 3 minutes, or until well browned. Drain on paper towels.

3 To make the sauce, place the sugar, vinegar, sauces and juice in a medium saucepan. Cook over medium heat until the sugar has dissolved. Bring to the boil, then remove from the heat. Blend the cornflour with 2 tablespoons water. Add to the pan, and stir over medium heat for 3 minutes, or until the sauce boils and thickens.

Place the meatballs, cucumber, carrot, capsicum and pineapple in a casserole dish. Pour the sauce over the top. Bake for 1 hour. Serve with rice.

NUTRITION PER SERVE (6)
Protein 38 g; Fat 19 g; Carbohydrate 41 g; Dietary Fibre 2.5 g; Cholesterol 117 mg; 2015 kJ (480 cal)

Score a cross in the base of the tomatoes, soak in boiling water for 30 seconds, then drain and peel.

Cut the tomatoes in half and remove the seeds with a teaspoon.

TOMATO CHICKEN CASSEROLE

Preparation time: 45 minutes
Total cooking time: 1 hour 20 minutes
Serves 4

1.5 kg (3 lb) chicken pieces
40 g (1 ¼ oz) butter
1 tablespoon oil
1 large onion, chopped
2 cloves garlic, chopped
1 small green capsicum, chopped
150 g (5 oz) mushrooms, thickly sliced
1 tablespoon plain flour
1 cup (250 ml/8 fl oz) white wine
1 tablespoon white wine vinegar
4 tomatoes, peeled, seeded and chopped
2 tablespoons tomato paste
½ cup (90 g/3 oz) small black olives
⅓ cup (20 g/¾ oz) chopped fresh parsley

1 Preheat the oven to moderate 180°C (350°F/Gas 4). Remove the excess fat from the chicken pieces and pat dry with paper towels. Heat 2 teaspoons of the butter and 2 teaspoons of the oil in a large flameproof casserole dish. Cook half the chicken over high heat until browned all over, then set aside. Heat another 2 teaspoons of the butter and the remaining oil, and cook the remaining chicken. Set aside.

2 Heat the remaining butter in the casserole and cook the onion and garlic for 2–3 minutes. Add the capsicum and mushrooms, and cook, stirring, for 3 minutes. Stir in the flour and cook for 1 minute. Add the wine, vinegar, tomato and tomato paste, and cook, stirring, for 2 minutes, or until slightly thickened.

3 Return the chicken to the casserole and make sure it is covered by the tomato and onion mixture. Place in the oven and cook, covered, for 1 hour, or until the chicken is tender. Stir in the olives and parsley. Season with salt and cracked black pepper, and serve with pasta.

NUTRITION PER SERVE
Protein 55 g; Fat 15 g; Carbohydrate 9.5 g; Dietary Fibre 5 g; Cholesterol 125 mg; 1675 kJ (401 cal)

Pour in the apricot nectar and stir to combine with the soup mix.

Add the apricot halves to the chicken and bake for 5 minutes more.

APRICOT CHICKEN

Preparation time: 10 minutes
Total cooking time: 1 hour
Serves 6

6 chicken thigh cutlets, skin removed
425 ml (14 fl oz) can apricot nectar
40 g (1 1/4 oz) packet French onion
    soup mix
425 g (14 oz) can apricot halves in natural
    juice, drained
1/4 cup (60 g/2 oz) sour cream

1 Preheat the oven to moderate 180°C (350°F/Gas 4). Put the chicken thigh cutlets in a casserole dish. Mix the apricot nectar with the French onion soup mix until well combined, and pour over the chicken.

2 Bake, covered, for 50 minutes, then add the apricot halves and bake for a further 5 minutes. Stir in the sour cream just before serving. Delicious served with creamy mashed potato or rice to soak up the juices.

NUTRITION PER SERVE
Protein 23 g; Fat 6 g; Carbohydrate 10 g;
Dietary Fibre 0 g; Cholesterol 63 mg;
780 kJ (187 cal)

NOTE: You can use low-fat sour cream in this recipe if you prefer.

Use your fingers to press the spice mixture over the silverside.

Pour the combined vinegar and water over the beef, orange and onion.

SPICED BEEF

Preparation time: 20 minutes
Total cooking time: 1 hour 40 minutes
Serves 4–6

¹/₃ cup (60 g/2 oz) soft brown sugar
1 teaspoon ground cinnamon
1 teaspoon ground nutmeg
1 teaspoon ground cardamom
1 teaspoon ground black pepper
1.5 kg (3 lb) piece fresh silverside, trimmed
1 orange, quartered
1 large onion, quartered
¹/₄ cup (60 ml/2 fl oz) red wine vinegar

1 Preheat the oven to warm 160°C (315°F/ Gas 2–3). Combine the sugar, cinnamon, nutmeg, cardamom and pepper in a small bowl. Rub the mixture all over the meat, pressing it on firmly with your fingers. Place the meat in a deep casserole dish.

2 Place the orange and onion around the meat, and pour in the vinegar combined with 1 cup (250 ml/8 fl oz) water. Bake, covered, for 1–1¹/₂ hours, or until the meat is tender.

3 Remove the meat from the dish, cover and set aside. Remove the orange pieces from the cooking liquid. Strain the remaining cooking liquid into a shallow saucepan and cook, uncovered, for 10 minutes, or until reduced by half. Serve the meat warm or cold, accompanied by the sauce.

NUTRITION PER SERVE (6)
Protein 56 g; Fat 5.5 g; Carbohydrate 10 g; Dietary Fibre 0.5 g; Cholesterol 168 mg; 1325 kJ (315 cal)

NOTES: To serve the silverside cold, refrigerate it overnight in the cooking liquid before draining.

A whole piece of rump or topside steak may be used in place of the fresh silverside.

Add the tomato, capsicum, vinegar, sugar and chilli powder to the onion mixture.

Arrange layers of corn chips, sauce and cheese in a casserole dish.

MEXICAN TOMATO CASSEROLE

Preparation time: 25 minutes
Total cooking time: 30 minutes
Serves 4–6

2 tablespoons oil
2 red onions, chopped
2 cloves garlic, crushed
6 ripe tomatoes, peeled, seeded
    and chopped
1 green capsicum, chopped
1 tablespoon red wine vinegar
1 teaspoon sugar
1/2 teaspoon chilli powder
375 g (12 oz) can corn kernels, drained
125 g (4 oz) plain corn chips
1 1/4 cups (155 g/5 oz) grated Cheddar
1 cup (250 g/8 oz) sour cream
1/2 cup (25 g/3/4 oz) chopped fresh chives

1 Preheat the oven to warm 160°C (315°F/Gas 2–3). Heat the oil in a medium saucepan over medium heat. Cook the onion and garlic for 3 minutes. Add the tomato, capsicum, vinegar, sugar and chilli powder. Cook for 6–7 minutes, or until the tomato has softened and most of the liquid has evaporated. Add the corn and stir over low heat for 3 minutes.
2 Arrange layers of corn chips, sauce and cheese in a casserole dish, finishing with cheese.
3 Spread the sour cream evenly over the casserole. Bake for 15 minutes. Sprinkle with chives before serving.

NUTRITION PER SERVE (6)
Protein 13 g; Fat 37 g; Carbohydrate 26 g; Dietary Fibre 5.5 g; Cholesterol 79 mg; 2030 kJ (485 cal)

NOTE: You can use low-fat sour cream if you prefer.

Using tongs, gently add the fish cubes to the hotpot mixture.

FISH, GINGER AND TOMATO HOTPOT

**Preparation time: 20 minutes +
    20 minutes soaking**
Total cooking time: 1 hour
Serves 4

1 tablespoon peanut oil
1 onion, cut into thin wedges
1 small fresh red chilli, sliced
3 cloves garlic, finely chopped
2 cm x 2 cm (³/₄ inch x ³/₄ inch) piece
    fresh ginger, julienned
¹/₂ teaspoon ground turmeric
425 g (14 oz) can diced tomatoes
1 litre chicken stock
1 tablespoon tamarind purée
80 g (2³/₄ oz) dried rice stick noodles
600 g (1 ¹/₄ lb) snapper fillets, skin removed,
    cut into 3 cm (1 ¹/₄ inch) cubes
fresh coriander leaves, to garnish

1 Preheat the oven to hot 220°C (425°F/Gas 7). Heat the oil in a frying pan over medium–high heat, and cook the onion for 1–2 minutes, or until softened. Add the chilli, garlic and ginger, and cook for a further 30 seconds. Add the ground turmeric, tomato, chicken stock and tamarind purée, and bring to the boil over high heat. Transfer to a 2.5 litre heatproof hotpot or casserole dish and bake, covered, for 40 minutes.

2 Place the rice stick noodles in a large heatproof bowl and cover with warm water. Soak the noodles for 15–20 minutes, or until al dente. Drain, rinse and drain again.

3 Remove the hotpot from the oven and stir in the drained noodles. Add the fish cubes, then cover and return to the oven for a further 10 minutes, or until the fish is cooked through. Serve sprinkled with some fresh coriander leaves.

NUTRITION PER SERVE
Protein 36 g; Fat 8 g; Carbohydrate 24 g; Dietary Fibre 3 g; Cholesterol 92 mg; 1310 kJ (315 cal)

Cook the pasta in a saucepan of salted boiling water until al dente.

Combine the cream of mushroom soup, sour cream and curry powder.

INDIVIDUAL CHICKEN AND PASTA CASSEROLES

Preparation time: 15 minutes
Total cooking time: 45 minutes
Serves 4

200 g (6½ oz) spiral pasta
425 g (14 oz) can cream of mushroom or broccoli soup
1 cup (250 g/8 oz) sour cream
1 teaspoon curry powder
1 barbecued chicken
250 g (8 oz) broccoli, cut into small pieces
1 cup (80 g/2¾ oz) fresh breadcrumbs
1½ cups (185 g/6 oz) grated Cheddar

1 Preheat the oven to moderate 180°C (350°F/Gas 4). Bring a saucepan of salted water to the boil, add the pasta and cook for 10–12 minutes, or until al dente. Drain.
2 Combine the soup, sour cream and curry powder, and season with freshly ground black pepper.
3 Remove the meat from the chicken. Discard the carcass and roughly chop the chicken. Combine the chicken with the cooked pasta, broccoli and soup mixture. Spoon the mixture into four lightly greased 2 cup (500 ml/ 16 fl oz) ovenproof dishes, and sprinkle with the combined breadcrumbs and grated cheese. Bake for 25–30 minutes, or until the cheese melts.

NUTRITION PER SERVE
Protein 67 g; Fat 47 g; Carbohydrate 55 g; Dietary Fibre 7.5 g; Cholesterol 254 mg; 3812 kJ (911 cal)

Remove the backbone and any excess fat from the inside of the duck.

Add the duck portions to the cabbage mixture, pressing them into the liquid.

DUCK WITH JUNIPER BERRIES

Preparation time: 35 minutes
Total cooking time: 1 hour 50 minutes
Serves 4

1.8 kg (3 lb 10 oz) duck
1 Granny Smith apple, peeled and
    thinly sliced
1 leek, cut into large chunks
1/2 small red cabbage, shredded
2 bay leaves
2 sprigs fresh thyme
6 juniper berries, lightly crushed
1/4 teaspoon black peppercorns
1 1/2 cups (375 ml/12 fl oz) chicken stock
1 cup (250 ml/8 fl oz) orange juice
50 g (1 3/4 oz) butter, chopped
2 tablespoons soft brown sugar
1/3 cup (80 ml/2 3/4 fl oz) cider vinegar
1 1/2 teaspoons cornflour
sprigs fresh chervil, to serve

1 Preheat the oven to moderate 180°C (350°F/Gas 4). Cut the duck in half by cutting down both sides of the backbone and through the breastbone. Discard the backbone. Cut each duck half into 4 portions, removing any fat. Brown the duck portions in a lightly oiled, heavy-based frying pan over medium heat; remove and set aside.

2 Drain the frying pan of all but 1 tablespoon of oil, reserving the excess. Cook the apple until golden all over; remove and set aside. Add 1 tablespoon of the fat to the pan and lightly brown the leek.

3 Add the cabbage, bay leaves, thyme, juniper berries and peppercorns, and cook, stirring, for 10 minutes, or until the cabbage softens. Transfer to a large flameproof casserole dish. Add the stock and orange juice and bring to the boil. Add the duck, pressing gently into the liquid, then cover and bake for 1 1/2 hours.

4 Remove the duck and keep warm. Drain the liquid into a saucepan. Simmer for 5 minutes, or until reduced to 1 cup (250 ml/8 fl oz). Stir in the butter, sugar and vinegar. Blend the cornflour with 1 tablespoon water and stir into the mixture until it boils and thickens.

5 Stir the apple and half the sauce into the cabbage mixture, and season to taste. Spoon onto a serving plate, top with the duck, drizzle with sauce and garnish with chervil to serve.

NUTRITION PER SERVE
Protein 50 g; Fat 30 g; Carbohydrate 25 g;
Dietary Fibre 4 g; Cholesterol 335 mg;
2250 kJ (540 cal)

Cover the porcini mushrooms with boiling water and soak until rehydrated.

Lightly toss the chicken pieces in the flour and shake off any excess.

CHICKEN AND MUSHROOM CASEROLE

Preparation time: 20 minutes +
 5 minutes soaking
Total cooking time: 1 hour
Serves 4

20 g (³/₄ oz) dried porcini mushrooms
1.5 kg (3 lb) chicken pieces
¹/₄ cup (30 g/1 oz) seasoned plain flour
2 tablespoons oil
1 large onion, chopped
2 cloves garlic, crushed
¹/₄ cup (60 ml/2 fl oz) chicken stock
¹/₃ cup (80 ml/2³/₄ fl oz) white wine
425 g (14 oz) can peeled whole tomatoes
1 tablespoon balsamic vinegar
3 sprigs fresh thyme
1 bay leaf
300 g (10 oz) field mushrooms,
 thickly sliced

1 Preheat the oven to moderate 180°C (350°F/Gas 4). Put the porcini mushrooms in a bowl and cover with ¹/₄ cup (60 ml/2 fl oz) boiling water. Leave for 5 minutes, or until the mushrooms are rehydrated.

2 Lightly toss the chicken in the seasoned flour to coat, and shake off any excess.

3 Heat the oil in a flameproof casserole dish, and cook the chicken over medium heat in batches until well browned all over. Set aside. Add the onion and garlic to the casserole, and cook for 3–5 minutes, or until the onion softens. Stir in the chicken stock.

4 Return the chicken to the casserole with the porcini mushrooms (and any remaining liquid), wine, tomatoes, vinegar, thyme and bay leaf. Cover and bake for 30 minutes.

5 After 30 minutes, remove the lid and add the field mushrooms. Return to the oven and cook, uncovered, for 15–20 minutes, or until the sauce thickens slightly. Serve immediately.

NUTRITION PER SERVE
Protein 55 g; Fat 10 g; Carbohydrate 7 g; Dietary Fibre 4 g; Cholesterol 115 mg; 1515 kJ (360 cal)

LAMB SHANKS WITH PUY LENTILS

Preparation time: 25 minutes
Total cooking time: 1 hour 45 minutes
Serves 4

⅓ cup (80 ml/2¾ fl oz) olive oil
4 French-trimmed lamb shanks
   (280 g/9 oz each) (see NOTE)
6 cloves garlic, unpeeled
1 onion, thinly sliced
1 red capsicum, sliced
2 cloves garlic, crushed
400 g (13 oz) can peeled tomatoes, chopped
1 cup (250 ml/8 fl oz) white wine
1 bay leaf
1 cinnamon stick
2 strips orange rind
1½ cups (320 g/11 oz) Puy lentils
400 g (13 oz) can cannellini beans, rinsed
   and drained
2 spring onions, sliced
pinch saffron threads
1 teaspoon ground coriander
1 teaspoon ground cumin
¼ cup (7 g/ ¼ oz) chopped fresh
   flat-leaf parsley

1 Preheat the oven to moderately hot 200°C (400°F/Gas 6). Heat half the oil in a large, deep flameproof casserole dish, add the shanks in batches and cook over medium heat for 4

minutes, or until the shanks are brown on all sides. Remove from the dish.
2 Place the unpeeled garlic cloves on a baking tray and drizzle with half the remaining oil.
3 Add the onion, capsicum and crushed garlic to the casserole dish and cook until golden. Stir in the tomato, wine, bay leaf, cinnamon stick and orange rind, return all the shanks, then cover and transfer to the oven. Cook for 1 hour, then uncover and cook for a further 30 minutes, or until the shanks are tender and the meat is just falling off the bone. Keep warm. Add the tray with the garlic cloves to the oven 15 minutes before the shanks will be ready, and cook until they are soft. Cool slightly, then peel.
4 Meanwhile, place the lentils in a saucepan, cover with 1.5 litres water and bring to the boil. Cook over high heat for 20 minutes, or until tender. Drain, reserving the cooking liquid.
5 Place the garlic in a food processor with the cannellini beans and a little of the reserved lentil cooking liquid, and process until smooth and creamy, then season to taste with salt and cracked black pepper. Cover and keep warm. Add more of the cooking liquid if it starts to thicken and dry out.
6 Heat the remaining oil in a large frying pan, add the spring onion and spices, and cook over medium heat for 3 minutes, or until fragrant. Stir in the lentils and parsley, and cook until warmed through.
7 Place a mound of lentils on each plate, stand the shanks in the lentils and drizzle with some of the cooking liquid. Serve a spoonful of the bean purée on the side.

NUTRITION PER SERVE
Protein 70 g; Fat 35 g; Carbohydrate 45 g; Dietary Fibre 2 g; Cholesterol 130 mg; 3437 kJ (820 cal)

NOTE: French-trimmed lamb shanks are lamb shanks that have the meat scraped back to make a neat lamb 'drumstick'. You can use regular lamb shanks instead.

Cook the lamb shanks in batches until brown all over.

Drain the soaked and cooked soy beans well in a colander.

Cook the sausages in a frying pan, turning frequently, until brown all over.

PORK SAUSAGE AND SOY BEAN CASSEROLE

Preparation time: 25 minutes + soaking
Total cooking time: 4 hours
Serves 4

1¹/₂ cups (325 g/11 oz) dried soy beans
8 thin pork sausages
2 tablespoons soy bean oil, or oil
1 red onion, chopped
4 cloves garlic, chopped
1 large carrot, diced
1 celery stick, diced
2 x 415 g (13 oz) cans chopped tomatoes
1 tablespoon tomato paste
1 cup (250 ml/8 fl oz) white wine
2 sprigs fresh thyme
1 teaspoon dried oregano
1 tablespoon fresh oregano, chopped

1 Soak the soy beans in cold water for at least 8 hours. Drain well. Place in a large saucepan with enough fresh water to cover. Bring to the boil, then reduce the heat and slowly simmer for 1¹/₄–2 hours—keep the beans covered with water during cooking; drain.

2 Prick the sausages all over. Cook in a frying pan, turning, for 10 minutes, or until browned. Drain on paper towels.

3 Heat the oil in a 3.5 litre flameproof casserole dish over medium heat. Cook the onion and garlic for 3–5 minutes, or until softened. Add the carrot and celery. Cook, stirring, for 5 minutes. Stir in the tomato, tomato paste, wine, thyme and dried oregano, and bring to the boil. Reduce the heat and simmer, stirring often, for 10 minutes, or until reduced and thickened slightly.

4 Preheat the oven to warm 160°C (315°F/ Gas 2–3). Add the sausages, beans and 1 cup (250 ml/8 fl oz) water to the casserole dish. Bake, covered, for 2 hours. Stir occasionally, adding more water to keep the beans covered.

5 Return the casserole dish to the stove, skim off any fat, then reduce the liquid until thickened slightly. Remove the thyme and stir in the oregano.

NUTRITION PER SERVE
Protein 46 g; Fat 58 g; Carbohydrate 20 g; Dietary Fibre 23 g; Cholesterol 93 mg; 3479 kJ (830 cal)

Arrange the chicken thighs and sauce on top of the cheese in a star shape.

Bake the casserole until it is bubbling and the cheese is melted.

MEXICAN CHICKEN CASSEROLE

Preparation time: 15 minutes
Total cooking time: 1 hour
Serves 4

³/₄ cup (165 g/5¹/₂ oz) short-grain rice
300 g (10 oz) can red kidney beans, drained and thoroughly rinsed
3¹/₂ tablespoons chopped fresh coriander leaves
1 tablespoon oil
600 g (1 ¹/₄ lb) chicken thigh fillets
2 x 200 g (6¹/₂ oz) jars spicy taco sauce
2 cups (250 g/8 oz) grated Cheddar
¹/₂ cup (125 g/4 oz) sour cream

1 Preheat the oven to moderate 180°C (350°F/Gas 4). Lightly grease a 7 cm (2³/₄ inch) deep, 21 cm (8¹/₂ inch) round casserole dish. Bring a large saucepan of water to the boil, add the rice and cook for 10–12 minutes, stirring occasionally. Drain.
2 In the prepared dish, combine the beans and 1¹/₂ tablespoons of the coriander, then add the rice and toss together. Lightly press the mixture so the beans are mixed into the rice and the mixture is flat.
3 Heat the oil in a large frying pan over medium–high heat. Sauté the chicken thighs for 3 minutes, then turn over. Add the spicy taco sauce, and cook for a further 3 minutes.
4 To assemble, spread half the cheese over the rice. Arrange the chicken and sauce on top in a star shape, sprinkle with 1¹/₂ tablespoons of the coriander, then sprinkle with the remaining cheese. Cover with foil.

5 Bake for 35–40 minutes, or until the mixture is bubbling and the cheese is melted and slightly browned—remove the foil for the last 5 minutes of cooking. Cut into four servings with a knife and scoop out carefully, keeping the layers intact. Serve sprinkled with the remaining coriander and a dollop of sour cream.

NUTRITION PER SERVE
Protein 52 g; Fat 50 g; Carbohydrate 66 g;
Dietary Fibre 6 g; Cholesterol 235 mg;
3825 kJ (915 cal)

Trim the leaves and base from the celery sticks, then cut into thick slices.

Heat the oil and butter, then brown the meat in batches over high heat.

VEAL AND FENNEL CASSEROLE

Preparation time: 20 minutes
Total cooking time: 2 hours 15 minutes
Serves 4–6

1 tablespoon oil
30 g (1 oz) butter
4 veal shanks, cut into 4 cm (1½ inch)
    pieces (see NOTE)
1 large onion, sliced
1 clove garlic, crushed
2 celery sticks, thickly sliced
3 carrots, thickly sliced
2 small fennel bulbs, quartered
¼ cup (30 g/1 oz) plain flour
425 g (14 oz) can crushed tomatoes
⅓ cup (80 ml/2¾ fl oz) white wine
1 cup (250 ml/8 fl oz) chicken stock
1 tablespoon chopped fresh thyme
12 black olives

1 Preheat the oven to moderate 180°C (350°F/Gas 4). Heat the oil and butter in a large, heavy-based saucepan and brown the meat quickly in batches on both sides over high heat. Transfer to a large, shallow casserole dish.
2 Add the onion and garlic to the pan, and cook over medium heat until soft. Add the celery, carrot and fennel, and cook for 2 minutes. Add the flour, stir until golden, then add the tomato, wine, stock and thyme. Bring to the boil, reduce the heat and simmer for 5 minutes, or until thickened. Season with salt and freshly ground pepper.
3 Add the sauce to the veal; cover and bake for 1½–2 hours, or until tender. Scatter with olives to serve.

NUTRITION PER SERVE (6)
Protein 20 g; Fat 8 g; Carbohydrate 10 g; Dietary Fibre 3 g; Cholesterol 80 mg; 840 kJ (200 cal)

NOTE: Many butchers sell veal shanks already cut into pieces. You will need 12 medium pieces for this recipe.

Cook the shanks quickly in batches in the oil in a frying pan.

Cook the leek in the frying pan, stirring, until the leek is tender.

LAMB SHANKS WITH GARLIC

Preparation time: 20 minutes
Total cooking time: 1 hour 25 minutes
Serves 6

6 large lamb shanks
1 tablespoon oil
2 leeks, sliced
1 sprig fresh rosemary
1 cup (250 ml/8 fl oz) dry white wine
1 bulb garlic
oil, for brushing

1 Preheat the oven to moderate 180°C (350°F/Gas 4). Season the lamb shanks. Heat the oil in a frying pan over medium–high heat. Cook the lamb shanks quickly in batches until well browned. Drain on paper towels, then place in a casserole dish.

2 Cook the leek in the frying pan until tender. Add to the lamb shanks with the rosemary and wine.

3 Cut the garlic horizontally through the centre. Brush the cut surfaces with a little oil. Place cut-side up in the casserole, but not covered by liquid. Bake, covered, for 1 hour. Remove the lid and bake for a further 15 minutes. Discard the rosemary. Serve with steamed vegetables and crusty bread on which to spread the roasted garlic.

NUTRITION PER SERVE
Protein 33 g; Fat 18 g; Carbohydrate 2 g; Dietary Fibre 2 g; Cholesterol 101 mg; 1350 kJ (320 cal)

Brown the chicken pieces in batches in a frying pan over medium heat.

Rub the butter into the flour until the mixture is fine and crumbly.

CHICKEN PAPRIKA WITH DUMPLINGS

Preparation time: 20 minutes
Total cooking time: 1 hour 10 minutes
Serves 4–6

2 tablespoons oil
1.6 kg (3 ¼ lb) chicken, cut into
    10 pieces
1 large onion, chopped
1 clove garlic, crushed
1 teaspoon sweet paprika
1 teaspoon dried thyme
2 tablespoons plain flour
½ cup (125 ml/4 fl oz) chicken stock
410 g (13 oz) can peeled tomatoes, crushed
2 carrots, sliced

DUMPLINGS
1 cup (125 g/4 oz) self-raising flour
20 g (¾ oz) butter, chopped
2 teaspoons finely chopped fresh parsley
2 teaspoons finely chopped fresh chives
½ teaspoon dried mixed herbs
⅓ cup (80 ml/2¾ fl oz) buttermilk

1 Heat the oil in a frying pan. Brown the chicken in batches over medium–high heat, then place in a deep 3 litre casserole dish.
2 Add the onion and garlic to the pan, stirring until soft. Reduce the heat to low. Add the paprika, thyme and flour, and cook, stirring, for 2 minutes. Gradually stir in the stock. Add the tomato, and season. Pour the mixture over the chicken. Add the carrot. Cover and bake for 30 minutes.

3 To make the dumplings, sift the flour into a bowl. Rub in the butter until fine and crumbly. Stir in the herbs and almost all the buttermilk. Mix to a soft dough, adding more buttermilk if necessary. Turn the dough out onto a floured surface and gather into a ball. Divide into 8 portions and roll each into a ball. Arrange the dumplings on top of the casserole. Bake, uncovered, for 20 minutes. Serve immediately.

NUTRITION PER SERVE (6)
Protein 44 g; Fat 36 g; Carbohydrate 25 g; Dietary Fibre 3 g; Cholesterol 200 mg; 2480 kJ (595 cal)

Cook the oxtail pieces in small batches in the hot oil.

Cook the onion and carrot, stirring, for 5 minutes over medium heat.

BRAISED OXTAIL CASSEROLE

Preparation time: 15 minutes
Total cooking time: 2 hours
Serves 6

1/4 cup (60 ml/2 fl oz) oil
16 small pieces oxtail, about 1.5 kg (3 lb)
4 baby potatoes, halved
1 large onion, chopped
2 carrots, chopped
250 g (8 oz) button mushrooms
2 tablespoons plain flour
3 cups (750 ml/24 fl oz) beef stock
1 teaspoon dried marjoram leaves
2 tablespoons Worcestershire sauce

1 Preheat the oven to moderate 180°C (350°F/Gas 4). Heat 2 tablespoons of the oil in a saucepan over medium–high heat. Cook the oxtail quickly in small batches until well browned. Place in a deep casserole dish and add the potato.

2 Heat the remaining oil in the pan. Cook the onion and carrot, stirring, over medium heat for 5 minutes. Transfer to the casserole dish. Add the mushrooms to the pan, and cook, stirring, for 5 minutes. Stir in the flour. Reduce the heat to low, and stir for 2 minutes.

3 Add the stock gradually, stirring until the liquid boils and thickens. Add the marjoram and Worcestershire sauce. Pour into the casserole dish. Bake, covered, for 1 1/2 hours. Stir, then bake, uncovered, for a further 30 minutes.

NUTRITION PER SERVE
Protein 35 g; Fat 53 g; Carbohydrate 16 g; Dietary Fibre 3.5 g; Cholesterol 102 mg; 2825 kJ (675 cal)

Curries

SPICY PRAWNS

Preparation time: 30 minutes +
15 minutes standing
Total cooking time: 1 hour
Serves 4–6

1 kg (2 lb) raw medium prawns, peeled
    and deveined, tails intact (reserve shells
    and heads)
1 teaspoon ground turmeric
¼ cup (60 ml/2 fl oz) oil
2 onions, finely chopped
4–6 cloves garlic, finely chopped
1–2 small fresh green chillies, seeded
    and chopped
2 teaspoons ground cumin
2 teaspoons ground coriander
1 teaspoon paprika
⅓ cup (90 g/3 oz) plain yoghurt
⅓ cup (80 ml/2¾ fl oz) thick cream
⅓ cup (20 g/¾ oz) chopped fresh coriander
    leaves

1 Bring 1 litre water to the boil in a large
saucepan. Add the reserved prawn shells
and heads, reduce the heat and simmer for
2 minutes. Skim any scum that forms on the
surface during cooking with a skimmer or slotted
spoon. Drain, discard the shells and heads, and
return the liquid to the pan. You will need 3 cups
(750 ml/24 fl oz) liquid. Make up with water,
if necessary. Add the turmeric and peeled
prawns, and cook for 1 minute, or until the
prawns just turn pink. Remove the prawns and
set the stock aside.

2 Heat the oil in a large saucepan. Cook the
onion, stirring, for 8 minutes, or until light
golden brown. Take care not to burn the onion.
Add the garlic and chilli, cook for 2 minutes,
then add the cumin, coriander and paprika, and
cook, stirring, for 2–3 minutes, or until fragrant.
3 Gradually add the reserved prawn stock, bring
to the boil and cook, stirring occasionally, for
35 minutes, or until the mixture has reduced by
half and thickened.
4 Remove from the heat and stir in the yoghurt.
Add the prawns and stir over low heat for
2–3 minutes, or until the prawns are warmed
through, but do now allow the mixture to boil.
Stir in the cream and coriander leaves. Cover
and leave to stand for 15 minutes to allow the
flavors to infuse. Reheat gently and serve
with rice.

NUTRITION PER SERVE (6)
Protein 35 g; Fat 17 g; Carbohydrate 3 g;
Dietary Fibre 1 g; Cholesterol 270 mg;
1293 kJ (310 cal)

NOTE: You can remove the prawn tails, if you
prefer.

Skim any scum on the surface with a skimmer or a
slotted spoon.

Cut the meat across the grain and at an angle into thin slices.

Add the meat to the wok and cook in batches until browned.

THAI BEEF AND PUMPKIN CURRY

Preparation time: 20 minutes
Total cooking time: 1 hour 30 minutes
Serves 6

2 tablespoons oil
750 g (1½ lb) blade steak, thinly sliced
4 tablespoons Musaman curry paste (see page 251)
2 cloves garlic, finely chopped
1 onion, sliced lengthways
6 curry leaves, torn
3 cups (750 ml/24 fl oz) coconut milk
450 g (14 oz) butternut pumpkin, roughly diced
2 tablespoons chopped unsalted peanuts
1 tablespoon palm sugar or soft brown sugar
2 tablespoons tamarind purée
2 tablespoons fish sauce
curry leaves, extra, to garnish

1 Heat a wok or frying pan over high heat. Add the oil and swirl to coat the side. Add the meat in batches and cook for 5 minutes, or until browned. Remove the meat from the wok.

2 Add the curry paste, garlic, onion and curry leaves to the wok, and stir to coat. Return the meat to the wok and cook, stirring, over medium heat for 2 minutes.

3 Add the coconut milk to the wok, then reduce the heat and simmer for 45 minutes. Add the diced pumpkin and simmer for 25–30 minutes, or until the meat and the vegetables are tender and the sauce has thickened.

4 Stir in the peanuts, palm sugar, tamarind purée and fish sauce, and simmer for 1 minute. Garnish with curry leaves. Serve with steamed rice.

NUTRITION PER SERVE
Protein 33 g; Fat 43 g; Carbohydrate 16 g; Dietary Fibre 4.5 g; Cholesterol 66 mg; 2403 kJ (574 cal)

Place the curry paste ingredients in a food processor and process until smooth.

Cook the onion slices for 5 minutes, or until the onion is soft.

GREEN TOFU CURRY

Preparation time: 20 minutes
Total cooking time: 20 minutes
Serves 6

CURRY PASTE
10 small fresh green chillies
50 g (1¾ oz) red Asian shallots, peeled
2 cloves garlic
1 cup (50 g/1¾ oz) finely chopped coriander
    stems and roots
1 stem lemon grass (white part only),
    chopped
2 tablespoons grated fresh galangal
1 tablespoon ground coriander
1 teaspoon ground cumin
1 teaspoon black peppercorns
½ teaspoon ground turmeric
1 tablespoon lime juice

2 tablespoons oil
1 onion, sliced
400 ml (13 fl oz) can coconut cream
4–5 kaffir lime leaves, torn
500 g (1 lb) firm tofu, cut into 2 cm
    (¾ inch) cubes
1 tablespoon lime juice
1 tablespoon shredded fresh Thai basil

1 To make the curry paste, place all the ingredients in a food processor and process until smooth.
2 Heat the oil in a frying pan, add the onion and cook for 5 minutes, or until soft. Add 4 tablespoons curry paste (or more for a stronger flavor) and cook, stirring, for 2 minutes. Stir in the coconut cream and 1 cup (250 ml/ 8 fl oz) water, and season with salt. Bring to the boil and add the lime leaves and tofu. Reduce the heat and simmer for 8 minutes, stirring often. Stir in the lime juice and Thai basil, and serve.

NUTRITION PER SERVE
Protein 3.5 g; Fat 25 g; Carbohydrate 3 g;
Dietary Fibre 1.5 g; Cholesterol 0 mg;
1020 kJ (242 cal)

NOTE: The recipe for the curry paste makes cup, but you will only need ⅓ cup. Freeze the remaining paste in two portions to use at a later date.

Trim the pork of any excess fat or sinew and cut into cubes.

Cook the pork in small batches over medium heat until browned.

PORK VINDALOO

Preparation time: 20 minutes
Total cooking time: 2 hours
Serves 4

¼ cup (60 ml/2 fl oz) oil
1 kg (2 lb) pork fillets, cut into bite-size
   pieces
2 onions, finely chopped
4 cloves garlic, finely chopped
1 tablespoon finely chopped fresh ginger
1 tablespoon garam masala
2 teaspoons brown mustard seeds
4 tablespoons vindaloo paste

1 Heat the oil in a saucepan, add the pork in small batches and cook over medium heat for 5–7 minutes, or until browned. Remove from the pan.
2 Add the onion, garlic, ginger, garam masala and mustard seeds to the pan, and cook, stirring, for 5 minutes, or until the onion is soft.
3 Return all the meat to the pan, add the vindaloo paste and cook, stirring, for 2 minutes. Add 2½ cups (625 ml/21 fl oz) water and bring to the boil. Reduce the heat and simmer, covered, for 1½ hours, or until the meat is tender. Serve with boiled rice and pappadums.

NUTRITION PER SERVE
Protein 58 g; Fat 20 g; Carbohydrate 4 g; Dietary Fibre 2 g; Cholesterol 125 mg; 1806 kJ (430 cal)

Dry-fry the shrimp over low heat until they turn dark orange.

Place the shrimp in a mortar and pestle, and pound until finely ground.

CHICKEN KAPITAN

Preparation time: 35 minutes
Total cooking time: 1 hour 20 minutes
Serves 4–6

1 teaspoon small dried shrimp
⅓ cup (80 ml/2¾ fl oz) oil
6–8 fresh red chillies, seeded and finely chopped
4 cloves garlic, finely chopped
3 stems lemon grass (white part only), finely chopped
2 teaspoons ground turmeric
10 candlenuts
2 large onions, chopped
1 cup (250 ml/8 fl oz) coconut milk
1.5 kg (3 lb) chicken, cut into 8 pieces
½ cup (125 ml/4 fl oz) coconut cream
2 tablespoons lime juice

1 Put the shrimp in a frying pan and dry-fry over low heat, shaking the pan regularly, for 3 minutes, or until the shrimp are dark orange and are giving off a strong aroma. Transfer to a mortar and pestle, and pound until finely ground. Alternatively, process in a food processor.

2 Place half the oil, the chilli, garlic, lemon grass, turmeric and candlenuts in a food processor, and process in short bursts until very finely chopped, regularly scraping down the side of the bowl.

3 Heat the remaining oil in a wok or frying pan, add the onion and ¼ teaspoon salt, and cook, stirring regularly, over low heat for 8 minutes, or until golden.

4 Add the spice mixture and shrimp, and stir for 5 minutes. If the mixture begins to stick, add 2 tablespoons of the coconut milk. It is important to cook the mixture thoroughly to develop the flavors.

5 Add the chicken to the wok and cook, stirring, for 5 minutes, or until beginning to brown. Stir in the remaining coconut milk and 1 cup (250 ml/8 fl oz) water, and bring to the boil. Reduce the heat and simmer for 50 minutes, or until the chicken is cooked and the sauce has thickened slightly. Add the coconut cream and bring the mixture back to the boil, stirring constantly. Add the lime juice and serve immediately with rice.

NUTRITION PER SERVE (6)

Protein 58 g; Fat 30 g; Carbohydrate 4 g; Dietary Fibre 2 g; Cholesterol 125 mg; 2211 kJ (528 cal)

Peel the prawns, remove the veins and keep the tails intact.

Cook the coconut milk and the curry paste until the oil separates.

COCONUT SEAFOOD AND TOFU CURRY

Preparation time: 30 minutes
Total cooking time: 30 minutes
Serves 4

2 tablespoons soy bean oil, or oil
500 g (1 lb) firm white fish (ling, perch), cut into 2 cm (³/₄ inch) cubes
250 g (8 oz) raw prawns, peeled and deveined, tails intact
2 x 400 ml (13 fl oz) cans coconut milk
1 tablespoon red curry paste (page 250)
4 fresh or 8 dried kaffir lime leaves
2 tablespoons fish sauce
2 tablespoons finely chopped fresh lemon grass (white part only)
2 cloves garlic, crushed
1 tablespoon finely chopped fresh galangal
1 tablespoon shaved palm sugar or soft brown sugar

300 g (10 oz) silken firm tofu, cut into 1.5 cm (⁵/₈ inch) cubes
¹/₂ cup (125 g/4 oz) bamboo shoots, julienned
1 large fresh red chilli, thinly sliced
2 teaspoons lime juice
spring onions, chopped, to garnish
fresh coriander leaves, chopped, to garnish

1 Heat the oil in a large frying pan or wok over medium heat. Sear the fish and prawns for 1 minute on each side. Remove the fish and prawns from the pan.

2 Place ¹/₄ cup (60 ml/2 fl oz) of the coconut milk and the curry paste in the pan, and cook over medium heat for 2 minutes, or until fragrant and the oil separates. Add the remaining coconut milk, kaffir lime leaves, fish sauce, lemon grass, garlic, galangal, palm sugar and 1 teaspoon salt. Cook over low heat for 15 minutes.

3 Add the tofu cubes, bamboo shoots and sliced chilli. Simmer for a further 3–5 minutes. Return to medium heat, add the seafood and lime juice, and cook for a further 3 minutes, or until the seafood is just cooked. Remove from the heat.

4 Serve the curry with steamed rice and garnish with the spring onion and coriander leaves.

NUTRITION PER SERVE

Protein 50 g; Fat 58 g; Carbohydrate 15 g; Dietary Fibre 4 g; Cholesterol 180 mg; 3201 kJ (765 cal)

Cook the onion in the ghee for 5 minutes, or until the onion is soft.

Remove the lid and simmer the curry until the liquid thickens.

LAMB ROGAN JOSH

Preparation time: 25 minutes
Total cooking time: 1 hour 40 minutes
Serves 4–6

1 tablespoon ghee or oil
2 onions, chopped
¹/₂ cup (125 g/4 oz) plain yoghurt
1 teaspoon chilli powder
1 tablespoon ground coriander
2 teaspoons ground cumin
1 teaspoon ground cardamom
¹/₂ teaspoon ground cloves
1 teaspoon ground turmeric
3 cloves garlic, crushed
1 tablespoon grated fresh ginger
400 g (13 oz) can chopped tomatoes
1 kg (2 lb) boned leg of lamb, cut into
   2.5 cm (1 inch) cubes
¹/₄ cup (30 g/1 oz) slivered almonds
1 teaspoon garam masala
chopped fresh coriander leaves, to garnish

1 Heat the ghee in a large saucepan, add the onion and cook, stirring, for 5 minutes, or until soft. Stir in the yoghurt, chilli powder, coriander, cumin, cardamom, cloves, turmeric, garlic and ginger. Add the tomato and 1 teaspoon salt, and simmer for 5 minutes.

2 Add the lamb and stir until coated. Cover and cook over low heat, stirring occasionally, for 1–1¹/₂ hours, or until the lamb is tender. Uncover and simmer until the liquid thickens.

3 Meanwhile, toast the almonds in a dry frying pan over medium heat for 3–4 minutes, shaking the pan gently, until the nuts are golden brown. Remove from the pan at once to prevent them burning.

4 Add the garam masala to the curry and mix through well. Sprinkle the slivered almonds and coriander leaves over the top, and serve.

NUTRITION PER SERVE (6)
Protein 40 g; Fat 13 g; Carbohydrate 5.5 g;
Dietary Fibre 2 g; Cholesterol 122 mg;
1236 kJ (295 cal)

Heat a wok until very hot, add the peanut oil and swirl to coat.

Stir-fry the spring onion, garlic and red curry paste until fragrant.

THAI DUCK AND PINEAPPLE CURRY

Preparation time: 10 minutes
Total cooking time: 15 minutes
Serves 4–6

1 tablespoon peanut oil
8 spring onions, sliced on the diagonal into
   3 cm (1 1/4 inch) lengths
2 cloves garlic, crushed
2–4 tablespoons red curry paste
   (see page 250)
750 g (1 1/4 lb) Chinese roast duck, chopped
400 ml (13 fl oz) can coconut milk
450 g (14 oz) can pineapple pieces in
   syrup, drained
3 kaffir lime leaves
1/4 cup (15 g/1/2 oz) chopped fresh coriander
2 tablespoons chopped fresh mint

1 Heat a wok until very hot, add the peanut oil and swirl to coat the side. Add the spring onion, garlic and red curry paste, and stir-fry for 1 minute, or until fragrant.
2 Add the roast duck pieces, coconut milk, drained pineapple pieces, kaffir lime leaves, and half the fresh coriander and mint. Bring to the boil, then reduce the heat and simmer for 10 minutes, or until the duck is heated through and the sauce has thickened slightly. Stir in the remaining fresh coriander and mint, and serve with steamed jasmine rice.

NUTRITION PER SERVE (6)
Protein 24 g; Fat 25 g; Carbohydrate 4 g; Dietary Fibre 2 g; Cholesterol 140 mg; 1415 kJ (340 cal)

Boil the milk and lemon juice, and stir for a few seconds as the milk curdles.

Cover the paneer curds with a plate, weigh it down and leave it to set.

MATTAR PANEER (CHEESE AND PEA CURRY)

Preparation time: 30 minutes +
   30 minutes draining + 4 hours setting
Total cooking time: 40 minutes
Serves 6

PANEER
2 litres full-cream milk
$^1/_3$ cup (80 ml/2$^3/_4$ fl oz) lemon juice
oil, for deep-frying

CURRY PASTE
2 large onions
3 cloves garlic
1 teaspoon grated fresh ginger
1 teaspoon cumin seeds
3 dried red chillies
1 teaspoon cardamom seeds
4 cloves
1 teaspoon fennel seeds
2 pieces cassia bark

500 g (1 lb) frozen peas
2 tablespoons oil
400 g (13 oz) tomato purée
1 tablespoon garam masala
1 teaspoon ground coriander
$^1/_4$ teaspoon ground turmeric
1 tablespoon cream
fresh coriander leaves, to garnish

1 Place the milk in a large saucepan, bring to the boil, stir in the lemon juice and turn off the heat. Stir the mixture for 1–2 seconds as it curdles. Place in a colander and leave for 30 minutes for the whey to drain off. Place the paneer curds on a clean, flat surface, cover with a plate, weigh down and leave for at least 4 hours.
2 To make the curry paste, place the ingredients in a spice grinder or mortar and pestle, and grind to a smooth paste.
3 Cut the solid paneer into 2 cm ($^3/_4$ inch) cubes. Fill a deep heavy-based saucepan one-third full of oil and heat to 180°C (350°F), or until a cube of bread browns in 15 seconds.

Cook the paneer in batches for 2–3 minutes, or until golden. Drain on paper towels.
4 Cook the peas in a saucepan of boiling water for 3 minutes, or until tender. Drain.
5 Heat the oil in a large saucepan, add the curry paste and cook over medium heat for 4 minutes, or until fragrant. Add the tomato purée, spices, cream and $^1/_2$ cup (125 ml/ 4 fl oz) water. Season with salt, and simmer over medium heat for 5 minutes. Add the paneer and peas, and cook for 3 minutes. Garnish with fresh coriander leaves, and serve hot.

NUTRITION PER SERVE
Protein 18 g; Fat 28 g; Carbohydrate 27 g; Dietary Fibre 7 g; Cholesterol 50 mg; 1788 kJ (427 cal)

Place all the curry paste ingredients in a food processor and process until smooth.

Cook the coconut cream and curry paste until it splits and becomes oily.

PANANG BEEF (THAI BEEF AND PEANUT CURRY)

Preparation time: 30 minutes +
5 minutes soaking
Total cooking time: 1 hour 30 minutes
Serves 4–6

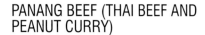

CURRY PASTE
8–10 large dried red chillies
6 red Asian shallots, chopped
6 cloves garlic, chopped
1 teaspoon ground coriander
1 tablespoon ground cumin
1 teaspoon white pepper
2 stems lemon grass (white part only),
    bruised and sliced
1 tablespoon chopped fresh galangal
6 coriander roots
2 teaspoons shrimp paste
2 tablespoons roasted peanuts
peanut oil, if needed

1 tablespoon peanut oil
400 ml (13 fl oz) can coconut cream (do not
    shake the can)
1 kg (2 lb) round or blade steak, thinly sliced
400 ml (13 fl oz) can coconut milk
4 kaffir lime leaves, whole
1/3 cup (90 g/3 oz) crunchy peanut butter
1/4 cup (60 ml/2 fl oz) lime juice
2 1/2 tablespoons fish sauce
3–4 tablespoons palm sugar or soft
    brown sugar
fresh Thai basil leaves, to garnish
1 tablespoon chopped peanuts, extra, to
    garnish (optional)

1 To make the curry paste, soak the chillies in boiling water for 5 minutes, or until soft. Remove the stem and seeds, then chop. Place all the curry paste ingredients in a food processor and process to a smooth paste. Add a little peanut oil if it is too thick.

2 Place the oil and the thick cream from the top of the coconut cream (reserving the rest) in a large saucepan over high heat. Add

6–8 tablespoons of the curry paste and cook, stirring, for 5 minutes, or until fragrant. Cook for 5–10 minutes, or until the coconut cream splits and becomes oily.

3 Add the beef, the reserved coconut cream, coconut milk, lime leaves and peanut butter, and cook for 8 minutes, or until the beef just starts to change color. Reduce the heat and simmer for 1 hour, or until the beef is tender.

4 Stir in the lime juice, fish sauce and palm sugar, and transfer to a serving dish. Garnish with the Thai basil leaves, and extra peanuts, if desired, and serve immediately.

NUTRITION PER SERVE (6)
Protein 8 g; Fat 30 g; Carbohydrate 5.5 g;
Dietary Fibre 4 g; Cholesterol 0 mg;
1293 kJ (310 cal)

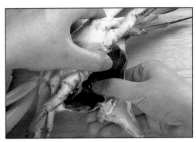

Pull back the apron and remove the top shell from the crabs.

Remove the intestines and grey feathery gills from the crabs.

CRAB CURRY

Preparation time: 25 minutes
Total cooking time: 20 minutes
Serves 6

4 raw large blue swimmer or mud crabs
1 tablespoon oil
1 large onion, finely chopped
2 cloves garlic, crushed
1 stem lemon grass (white part only),
    finely chopped
1 teaspoon sambal oelek
1 teaspoon ground cumin
1 teaspoon ground turmeric
1 teaspoon ground coriander
270 ml (9 fl oz) coconut cream
2 cups (500 ml/16 fl oz) chicken stock
$^1/_3$ cup (20 g/$^3/_4$ oz) firmly packed fresh basil
    leaves

1 Pull back the apron and remove the top shell from the crabs. Remove the intestines and grey feathery gills. Cut each crab into four pieces. Use a cracker to crack the claws open; this will make it easier to eat later and will also allow the flavors to get into the crab meat.
2 Heat the oil in a large saucepan or wok. Add the onion, garlic, lemon grass and sambal oelek, and cook for 2–3 minutes, or until softened.
3 Add the cumin, turmeric, coriander and $^1/_2$ teaspoon salt, and cook for a further 2 minutes, or until fragrant.
4 Stir in the coconut cream and stock. Bring to the boil, then reduce the heat, add the crab pieces and cook, stirring occasionally, for 10 minutes, or until the liquid has reduced and thickened slightly and the crabs are cooked. Stir in the basil and serve with rice.

NUTRITION PER SERVE
Protein 0.5 g; Fat 7 g; Carbohydrate 1.5 g; Dietary Fibre 0.5 g; Cholesterol 20 mg; 290 kJ (70 cal)

Process the curry paste ingredients in a food processor until smooth.

Stir in the coconut cream and cook until thickened slightly.

MUSAMAN VEGETABLE CURRY

Preparation time: 25 minutes
Total cooking time: 45 minutes
Serves 4–6

CURRY PASTE
1 tablespoon oil
1 teaspoon coriander seeds
1 teaspoon cumin seeds
8 cloves
1/2 teaspoon fennel seeds
seeds from 4 cardamom pods
6 red Asian shallots, chopped
3 cloves garlic, chopped
1 teaspoon finely chopped lemon grass
   (white part only)
1 teaspoon finely chopped fresh galangal
4 large dried red chillies
1 teaspoon ground nutmeg
1 teaspoon white pepper

1 tablespoon oil
250 g (8 oz) baby onions
500 g (1 lb) small new potatoes
300 g (10 oz) carrots, cut into 3 cm
   (1 1/4 inch) pieces
225 g (7 oz) can whole champignons,
   drained
1 cinnamon stick
1 kaffir lime leaf
1 bay leaf
1 cup (250 ml/8 fl oz) coconut cream
1 tablespoon lime juice
3 teaspoons grated palm sugar or soft brown
   sugar
1 tablespoon shredded fresh Thai basil
   leaves
1 tablespoon crushed roasted peanuts
fresh Thai basil leaves, extra, to garnish

1 To make the curry paste, heat the oil in a frying pan over low heat, add the coriander, cumin, cloves, fennel seeds and cardamom seeds, and cook for 1–2 minutes, or until fragrant. Place in a food processor and add the shallots, garlic, lemon grass, galangal, chillies, nutmeg and white pepper. Process until smooth, adding a little water as necessary.

2 Heat the oil in a large saucepan, add the curry paste and cook, stirring, over medium heat for 2 minutes, or until fragrant. Add the vegetables, cinnamon stick, kaffir lime leaf and bay leaf, and season with salt. Add enough water to cover—about 2 cups (500 ml/ 16 fl oz)—and bring to the boil. Reduce the heat and simmer, covered, stirring frequently, for 30–35 minutes, or until the vegetables are cooked. Stir in the coconut cream and cook, uncovered, for 4 minutes, stirring frequently, until thickened slightly. Stir in the lime juice, palm sugar and shredded Thai basil. Add a little water if the sauce is too dry. Garnish with the peanuts and Thai basil leaves.

NUTRITION PER SERVE (6)
Protein 4.5 g; Fat 17 g; Carbohydrate 21 g; Dietary Fibre 4.5 g; Cholesterol 0 mg; 6368 kJ (254 cal)

Lift off the thick cream from the top of the can of coconut cream.

Simmer the coconut cream and curry paste until the oil separates.

GREEN CHICKEN CURRY

Preparation time: 40 minutes
Total cooking time: 30 minutes
Serves 4–6

2 cups (500 ml/16 fl oz) coconut cream
(do not shake the can—see NOTE)
4 tablespoons green curry paste
(see page 250)
2 tablespoons grated palm sugar or soft
brown sugar
2 tablespoons fish sauce
4 kaffir lime leaves, finely shredded
1 kg (2 lb) chicken thigh or breast fillets,
cut into thick strips
200 g (6^1/$_2$ oz) bamboo shoots, cut into thick
strips
100 g (3^1/$_2$ oz) snake beans, cut into
5 cm (2 inch) lengths
^{1}/$_2$ cup (15 g/^{1}/$_2$ oz) fresh Thai basil leaves

1 Place ^{1}/$_2$ cup (125 ml/4 fl oz) of the thick coconut cream from the top of the can in a wok, and bring to the boil. Add the curry paste, then reduce the heat and simmer for 15 minutes, or until fragrant and the oil starts to separate from the cream. Add the palm sugar, fish sauce and kaffir lime leaves to the pan.
2 Stir in the remaining coconut cream and the chicken, bamboo shoots and beans, and simmer for 15 minutes, or until the chicken is tender. Stir in the Thai basil and serve with rice.

NUTRITION PER SERVE (6)
Protein 40 g; Fat 22 g; Carbohydrate 11 g;
Dietary Fibre 2 g; Cholesterol 85 mg;
1698 kJ (405 cal)

NOTE: Do not shake the can of coconut cream because good-quality coconut cream has a layer of very thick cream at the top that has separated from the rest of the cream. This has a higher fat content, which causes it to split or separate more readily than the rest of the coconut cream or milk.

Trim the meat of excess fat or sinew and cut it into cubes.

Cook the onion in a large frying pan over medium heat until browned.

MADRAS BEEF CURRY

Preparation time: 20 minutes
Total cooking time: 1 hour 45 minutes
Serves 4

1 tablespoon oil or ghee
1 onion, chopped
3–4 tablespoons Madras curry paste
    (see page 248)
1 kg (2 lb) skirt or chuck steak, cut into
    2.5 cm (1 inch) cubes
¼ cup (60 g/2 oz) tomato paste
1 cup (250 ml/8 fl oz) beef stock

1 Heat the oil in a large frying pan, add the onion and cook over medium heat for 10 minutes, or until browned. Add the curry paste and stir for 1 minute, or until fragrant. Then add the meat and cook, stirring, until coated with the curry paste.
2 Stir in the tomato paste and stock. Reduce the heat and simmer, covered, for 1¼ hours, and then uncovered for 15 minutes, or until the meat is tender.

NUTRITION PER SERVE
Protein 53 g; Fat 15 g; Carbohydrate 4.5 g; Dietary Fibre 1.5 g; Cholesterol 170 mg; 1514 kJ (362 cal)

Grind all the ingredients for the curry paste in a food processor or spice grinder until smooth.

Cook the onion over medium heat until it is just starting to brown.

CHU CHEE TOFU

Preparation time: 20 minutes
Total cooking time: 20 minutes
Serves 6

CURRY PASTE
10 small fresh red chillies
50 g (1³/₄ oz) red Asian shallots, peeled
1 tablespoon finely chopped coriander stem
   and root
1 stem lemon grass (white part only),
   chopped
2 tablespoons grated fresh galangal
2 cloves garlic
1 tablespoon ground coriander
1 teaspoon ground cumin
1 teaspoon black peppercorns
¹/₂ teaspoon ground turmeric
1 tablespoon lime juice

1 tablespoon oil
1 onion, finely chopped
2 cups (500 ml/16 fl oz) coconut milk
200 g (6¹/₂ oz) fried tofu puffs, halved
   on the diagonal
fresh coriander sprigs, to garnish

1 To make the curry paste, place all the ingredients in a food processor or spice grinder and process until smooth.
2 Heat the oil in a large saucepan, add the onion and cook over medium heat for 4–5 minutes, or until starting to brown. Add 3 tablespoons of the curry paste and cook, stirring, for 2 minutes.
3 Stir in the coconut milk and ¹/₂ cup (125 ml/ 4 fl oz) water, and season with salt. Bring slowly to the boil, stirring constantly. Add the tofu puffs, then reduce the heat and simmer, stirring frequently, for 5 minutes, or until the sauce thickens slightly. Garnish with the fresh coriander sprigs.

NUTRITION PER SERVE
Protein 2.5 g; Fat 23 g; Carbohydrate 5.5 g; Dietary Fibre 2.5 g; Cholesterol 1.5 mg; 980 kJ (234 cal)

LAMB KORMA

Preparation time: 30 minutes +
**   1 hour marinating**
Total cooking time: 1 hour 10 minutes
Serves 4–6

2 kg (4 lb) leg of lamb, boned
1 onion, chopped
2 teaspoons grated fresh ginger
3 cloves garlic
2 teaspoons ground coriander
2 teaspoons ground cumin
1 teaspoon cardamom seeds
large pinch cayenne pepper
2 tablespoons ghee or oil
1 onion, extra, sliced
2½ tablespoons tomato paste
½ cup (125 g/4 oz) plain yoghurt
½ cup (125 ml/4 fl oz) coconut cream
½ cup (50 g/1¾ oz) ground almonds
toasted slivered almonds, to serve

1 Trim any excess fat or sinew from the lamb, cut it into 3 cm (1¼ inch) cubes and place in a large bowl.
2 Place the chopped onion, grated ginger, garlic, ground coriander, ground cumin, cardamom seeds, cayenne pepper and ½ teaspoon salt in a food processor. Process the ingredients until they form a smooth paste. Add the spice mixture to a large bowl with the cubed lamb and mix well to coat the lamb in the spice mixture. Leave to marinate for 1 hour.
3 Heat the ghee in a large saucepan, add the sliced onion and cook, stirring, over low heat for 7 minutes, or until the onion is soft. Add the lamb and spice mixture, and cook, stirring constantly, for 8–10 minutes, or until the lamb changes color. Stir in the tomato paste, yoghurt, coconut cream and ground almonds.
4 Reduce the heat and simmer the curry, covered, stirring occasionally, for 50 minutes, or until the meat is tender. Add a little water if the mixture becomes too dry. Season the curry with salt and pepper, and garnish with the toasted slivered almonds. Serve with steamed rice.

NUTRITION PER SERVE (6)

Protein 80 g; Fat 23 g; Carbohydrate 5 g; Dietary Fibre 2 g; Cholesterol 240 mg; 2280 kJ (545 cal)

NOTE: Korma curries can also be made using beef or chicken. Korma refers to the style of curry—rich and smooth, and including almonds.

Trim any excess fat or sinew from the lamb and cut it into cubes.

Process the spice mixture in a food processor until it forms a smooth paste.

Halve the cucumber, remove the seeds and finely chop the flesh.

Cook the onion, garlic and spices in a heavy-based pan.

PORK AND TAMARIND CURRY

Preparation time: 20 minutes
Total cooking time: 1 hour 50 minutes
Serves 6

¹/₃ cup (80 ml/2³/₄ fl oz) oil
2 onions, thickly sliced
4 large cloves garlic, crushed
3 tablespoons Sri Lankan curry powder
  (see page 248)
1 tablespoon grated fresh ginger
10 dried curry leaves or 5 fresh curry leaves
2 teaspoons chilli powder
¹/₄ teaspoon fenugreek seeds
1.25 kg (2 lb 8 oz) lean shoulder pork,
  cubed
1 stem lemon grass (white part only),
  finely chopped
2 tablespoons tamarind purée
4 cardamom pods, crushed
400 ml (13 fl oz) can coconut cream

CUCUMBER SAMBAL
1–2 large cucumbers, halved, seeded and
  finely chopped
2 cups (500 g/16 oz) plain yoghurt
2 tablespoons fresh coriander leaves,
  finely chopped
1 tablespoon lemon juice
2 cloves garlic, crushed

1 Heat the oil in a heavy-based Dutch oven or deep, lidded frying pan. Add the onion, garlic, curry powder, ginger, curry leaves, chilli powder, fenugreek and 1 teaspoon salt, and cook, stirring, over medium heat for 5 minutes.

2 Add the pork, lemon grass, tamarind purée, cardamom and 1¹/₂ cups (375 ml/12 fl oz) hot water, then reduce the heat and simmer, covered, for 1 hour.

3 Stir in the coconut cream and simmer, uncovered, for 40–45 minutes, or until the sauce has reduced and become thick and creamy.

4 To make the cucumber sambal, place the cucumber in a bowl and stir in the yoghurt, coriander, lemon juice and garlic. Season to taste.

5 Serve the curry with the cucumber sambal and steamed basmati rice.

NUTRITION PER SERVE
Protein 55 g; Fat 30 g; Carbohydrate 9.5 g;
Dietary Fibre 3 g; Cholesterol 110 mg;
2260 kJ (540 cal)

Cook the onion over medium heat until it is just starting to brown.

Add the beans and cook until the vegetables are just tender.

VEGETABLE CURRY

Preparation time: 20 minutes
Total cooking time: 30 minutes
Serves 6

250 g (8 oz) potatoes, cut into 2 cm
   (³/₄ inch) cubes
250 g (8 oz) pumpkin, cut into 2 cm
   (³/₄ inch) cubes
200 g (6¹/₂ oz) cauliflower, broken into
   florets
150 g (5 oz) yellow squash, quartered
2 tablespoons oil
2 onions, chopped
3 tablespoons Indian curry powder
   (see page 248)
400 g (13 oz) can crushed tomatoes
1 cup (250 ml/8 fl oz) vegetable stock
150 g (5 oz) green beans, cut into 4 cm
   (1¹/₂ inch) lengths
¹/₃ cup (90 g/3 oz) plain yoghurt
¹/₄ cup (40 g/1 ¹/₄ oz) sultanas

1 Cook the potato and pumpkin in a saucepan of boiling water for 6 minutes, then remove. Add the cauliflower and squash, cook for 4 minutes, then remove.
2 Heat the oil in a large saucepan, add the onion and cook, stirring, over medium heat for 8 minutes, or until starting to brown.
3 Add the Indian curry powder and stir for 1 minute, or until fragrant. Stir in the crushed tomato and vegetable stock, and combine well.
4 Add the chopped potato, pumpkin, cauliflower and squash, and cook for 5 minutes, then add the green beans and cook for a further 2–3 minutes, or until the vegetables are just tender.
5 Add the yoghurt and sultanas, and stir to combine. Simmer for 3 minutes, or until thickened slightly. Season to taste with salt and black pepper, and serve with lemon wedges.

NUTRITION PER SERVE
Protein 7 g; Fat 8.5 g; Carbohydrate 20 g; Dietary Fibre 7 g; Cholesterol 2.5 mg; 805 kJ (192 cal)

Using wetted hands, form tablespoons of the mixture into balls.

Cook the onion, garlic and ginger over medium heat until lightly golden.

FISH KOFTAS IN TOMATO CURRY SAUCE

Preparation time: 40 minutes
Total cooking time: 30 minutes
Serves 6

750 g (1½ lb) firm fish fillets, such as snapper or ling, roughly chopped
1 onion, chopped
2–3 cloves garlic, chopped
1 tablespoon grated fresh ginger
⅓ cup (20 g/¾ oz) chopped fresh coriander leaves
1 teaspoon garam masala
¼ teaspoon chilli powder
1 egg, lightly beaten
oil, for shallow-frying

TOMATO CURRY SAUCE
2 tablespoons oil
1 large onion, finely chopped
3–4 cloves garlic, finely chopped
1 tablespoon grated fresh ginger
1 teaspoon ground turmeric
1 teaspoon ground cumin
1 teaspoon ground coriander
½ teaspoon garam masala
¼ teaspoon chilli powder
2 x 400 g (13 oz) cans crushed tomatoes
¼ cup (25 g/¾ oz) chopped fresh coriander

1 Place the fish in a food processor and process until smooth. Add the onion, garlic, ginger, coriander leaves, garam masala, chilli powder and egg, and process using the pulse button until well combined. Using wetted hands, form 1 tablespoon of the mixture into a ball. Repeat with the remaining mixture.

2 To make the tomato curry sauce, heat the oil in a large saucepan, add the onion, garlic and ginger, and cook, stirring frequently, over medium heat for 8 minutes, or until lightly golden.

3 Add the spices and cook, stirring, for 2 minutes, or until aromatic. Add the crushed tomato and 1 cup (250 ml/8 fl oz) water, then reduce the heat and simmer, stirring frequently, for 15 minutes, or until the sauce has reduced and thickened.

4 Meanwhile, heat 2 cm (¾ inch) of the oil in a large frying pan. Add the fish koftas in three to four batches and cook for 3 minutes, or until browned all over. Drain on paper towels.

5 Add the koftas to the sauce and simmer over low heat for 5 minutes, or until heated through. Gently fold in the coriander, season with salt and serve with steamed rice and chapatis.

NUTRITION PER SERVE
Protein 30 g; Fat 15 g; Carbohydrate 7 g;
Dietary Fibre 3 g; Cholesterol 118 mg;
1145 kJ (273 cal)

NOTE: The fish mixture is quite moist. Wetting your hands will stop the mixture from sticking to them.

Remove any excess fat or sinew from the chicken, then cut it into even-size pieces.

Add the spices, salt and water to the wok, and cook until thickened.

BALTI CHICKEN

Preparation time: 25 minutes
Total cooking time: 1 hour
Serves 6

1 kg (2 lb) chicken thigh fillets
1/3 cup (80 ml/2¾ fl oz) oil
1 large red onion, finely chopped
4–5 cloves garlic, finely chopped
1 tablespoon grated fresh ginger
2 teaspoons ground cumin
2 teaspoons ground coriander
1 teaspoon ground turmeric
½ teaspoon chilli powder
425 g (14 oz) can chopped tomatoes
1 green capsicum, cut into 3 cm
   (1 ¼ inch) cubes
1–2 small fresh green chillies, seeded and
   finely chopped
1/3 cup (20 g/¾ oz) chopped fresh coriander
2 chopped spring onions, to garnish

1 Remove any excess fat or sinew from the chicken thigh fillets and cut into 4–5 pieces.
2 Heat a large wok over high heat, add the oil and swirl to coat the side. Add the onion and stir-fry over medium heat for 5 minutes, or until softened but not browned. Add the garlic and ginger, and stir-fry for 3 minutes.
3 Add the spices, 1 teaspoon salt and ¼ cup (60 ml/2 fl oz) water. Increase the heat to high and stir-fry for 2 minutes, or until the mixture has thickened. Take care not to burn.
4 Add the tomato and 1 cup (250 ml/8 fl oz) water and cook, stirring often, for a further 10 minutes, or until the mixture is thick and pulpy and the oil comes to the surface.
5 Add the chicken to the wok, reduce the heat and simmer, stirring often, for 15 minutes. Add the capsicum and chilli, and simmer for 25 minutes, or until the chicken is tender. Add a little water if the mixture is too thick. Stir in the coriander and garnish with the spring onion. Serve with rice.

NUTRITION PER SERVE
Protein 40 g; Fat 17 g; Carbohydrate 5 g;
Dietary Fibre 2 g; Cholesterol 83 mg;
1370 kJ (327 cal)

NOTE: This curry is traditionally cooked in a Karahi or Balti pan, which is a round-bottomed, cast-iron, two-handled dish. A wok makes a good substitute.

BALINESE SEAFOOD CURRY

Preparation time: 20 minutes +
20 minutes marinating
Total cooking time: 20 minutes
Serves 6

CURRY PASTE
2 tomatoes, peeled, seeded and roughly
  chopped
5 small fresh red chillies, seeded and chopped
5 cloves garlic, chopped
2 stems lemon grass (white part only), sliced
1 tablespoon coriander seeds, dry-roasted
  and ground
1 teaspoon shrimp powder, dry-roasted
  (see NOTE)
1 tablespoon ground almonds
$1/4$ teaspoon ground nutmeg
1 teaspoon ground turmeric
3 tablespoons tamarind purée

1 tablespoon lime juice
250 g (8 oz) swordfish, cut into 3 cm
  (1 $1/4$ inch) cubes
$1/4$ cup (60 ml/2 fl oz) oil
2 red onions, chopped
2 small fresh red chillies, seeded and sliced
400 g (13 oz) raw medium prawns, peeled
  and deveined, tails intact
250 g (8 oz) calamari tubes, cut into
  1 cm ($1/2$ inch) rings
$1/2$ cup (125 ml/4 fl oz) fish stock
fresh Thai basil leaves, shredded, to garnish

1 To make the curry paste, place all the
ingredients in a blender or food processor,
and blend to a thick paste.
2 Place the lime juice in a bowl and season
with salt and freshly ground black pepper. Add
the swordfish, toss to coat well and leave to
marinate for 20 minutes.
3 Heat the oil in a saucepan or wok, add the
onion, sliced red chilli and curry paste, and
cook, stirring occasionally, over low heat for
10 minutes, or until fragrant.
4 Add the swordfish and prawns, and stir
to coat in the curry paste mixture. Cook for
3 minutes, or until the prawns just turn pink,
then add the calamari and cook for 1 minute.
5 Add the stock and bring to the boil, then
reduce the heat and simmer for 2 minutes, or
until the seafood is cooked and tender. Season
to taste with salt and freshly ground black
pepper. Garnish with the shredded fresh
basil leaves.

NUTRITION PER SERVE
Protein 30 g; Fat 14 g; Carbohydrate 3.5 g;
Dietary Fibre 2 g; Cholesterol 210 mg;
1100 kJ (263 cal)

NOTE: If you cannot purchase shrimp powder,
place some dried baby shrimp in a mortar and
pestle and grind to a fine powder. Alternatively,
you can place them in the small bowl of a food
processor and process to a fine powder.

Remove the seeds from the chillies, and roughly
chop the flesh.

Peel and devein the raw prawns, leaving the
tails intact.

Cook the lamb neck chops in batches in a large frying pan until browned.

Stir the spices to prevent them from sticking to the base of the pan.

LAMB NECK CURRY

Preparation time: 30 minutes
Total cooking time: 1 hour 35 minutes
Serves 4–6

1 tablespoon oil
8 best lamb neck chops (see NOTE)
2 onions, sliced
3 cloves garlic, finely chopped
2 teaspoons finely chopped fresh ginger
1 small fresh green chilli, seeded and finely chopped
1/2 teaspoon ground cumin
1 teaspoon ground fennel
1 1/2 teaspoons ground turmeric
1 1/2 teaspoons chilli powder
2 teaspoons garam masala
1 star anise
1 cinnamon stick
5 curry leaves
2 bay leaves
2 cups (500 ml/16 fl oz) beef stock
8 tomatoes, peeled and quartered

1 Heat the oil in a large frying pan and cook the lamb in batches for 5–8 minutes, or until browned. Place the chops in a large saucepan.
2 Add the onion to the frying pan and cook, stirring frequently, for 5 minutes, or until soft and browned. Stir in the garlic, ginger and chilli, and cook for 1 minute. Then stir in the cumin, fennel, turmeric, chilli powder, garam masala, star anise, cinnamon stick, curry leaves and bay leaves, and cook, stirring to prevent sticking, for a further 1 minute.
3 Add 2 tablespoons cold water to the frying pan, mix well, and then add the beef stock. Bring to the boil, then pour over the lamb. Stir in the tomato, reduce the heat and simmer, covered, for 1 1/4 hours. Serve with jasmine rice tossed with coriander.

NUTRITION PER SERVE (6)
Protein 17 g; Fat 7 g; Carbohydrate; 5 g; Dietary Fibre 5 g; Cholesterol 48 mg; 658 kJ (157 cal)

NOTE: Best lamb neck chops come from the meat just under the shoulder and are sweeter, leaner and meatier than lamb neck.

Trim the chicken of any excess fat or sinew and cut into bite-size pieces.

Place the curry paste ingredients in a food processor and process to a thick paste.

NONYA CHICKEN CURRY

Preparation time: 20 minutes
Total cooking time: 35 minutes
Serves 4

CURRY PASTE
2 red onions, chopped
4 small fresh red chillies, seeded and sliced
4 cloves garlic, sliced
2 stems lemon grass (white part only), sliced
3 cm x 2 cm (1¹/₄ inch x ³/₄ inch) piece fresh galangal, sliced
8 kaffir lime leaves, roughly chopped
1 teaspoon ground turmeric
¹/₂ teaspoon shrimp paste, dry-roasted

2 tablespoons oil
750 g (1¹/₂ lb) chicken thigh fillets, cut into bite-size pieces
400 ml (13 fl oz) can coconut milk
3 tablespoons tamarind purée
1 tablespoon fish sauce
3 kaffir lime leaves, shredded

1 To make the curry paste, place all the ingredients in a food processor or blender and process to a thick paste.
2 Heat a wok or large saucepan over high heat, add the oil and swirl to coat the side. Add the curry paste and cook, stirring occasionally, over low heat for 8–10 minutes, or until fragrant. Add the chicken and stir-fry with the paste for 2–3 minutes.
3 Add the coconut milk, tamarind purée and fish sauce to the wok, and simmer, stirring occasionally, for 15–20 minutes, or until the chicken is tender. Garnish with the lime leaves. Serve with rice and steamed bok choy.

NUTRITION PER SERVE
Protein 45 g; Fat 35 g; Carbohydrate 7.5 g; Dietary Fibre 3.5 g; Cholesterol 94 mg; 2175 kJ (520 cal)

Remove the thick coconut cream from the top of the can.

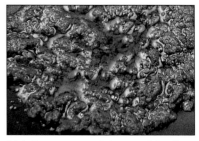

Stir in the curry paste and simmer until the oil begins to separate.

CHU CHEE SEAFOOD

Preparation time: 30 minutes
Total cooking time: 20 minutes
Serves 4

2 x 270 ml (9 fl oz) cans coconut cream
   (do not shake the cans)
3 tablespoons chu chee curry paste
   (see page 251)
500 g (1 lb) scallops, with roe removed
500 g (1 lb) raw medium king prawns,
   peeled and deveined, tails intact
2–3 tablespoons fish sauce
2–3 tablespoons palm sugar or soft
   brown sugar
8 kaffir lime leaves, finely shredded
2 fresh red chillies, thinly sliced
1 cup (30 g/1 oz) fresh Thai basil leaves

1 Place 1 cup (250 ml/8 fl oz) of the thick coconut cream from the top of the can in a wok. Heat until just boiling, then stir in the curry paste, reduce the heat and simmer for 10 minutes, or until fragrant and the oil begins to separate.
2 Stir in the remaining coconut cream, scallops and prawns, and cook for 5 minutes, or until tender. Add the fish sauce, palm sugar, kaffir lime leaves and chilli, and cook for 1 minute. Stir in half the basil and garnish with the remaining leaves.

NUTRITION PER SERVE
Protein 44 g; Fat 30 g; Carbohydrate 23 g; Dietary Fibre 3 g; Cholesterol 230 mg; 2253 kJ (538 cal)

Using a sharp knife, cut the meat across the grain into thin strips.

Boil the thick coconut cream until the oil separates from the cream.

RED BEEF AND EGGPLANT CURRY

Preparation time: 40 minutes
Total cooking time: 1 hour 30 minutes
Serves 4

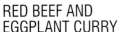

1 cup (250 ml/8 fl oz) coconut cream
  (do not shake the can)
2 tablespoons red curry paste (see page 250)
500 g (1 lb) round or topside steak, cut into
  strips (see NOTE)
2 tablespoons fish sauce
1 tablespoon palm sugar or soft brown sugar
5 kaffir lime leaves, halved
2 cups (500 ml/16 fl oz) coconut milk
8 Thai eggplants, halved
2 tablespoons finely shredded fresh Thai
  basil leaves

1 Place the thick coconut cream from the top of the can in a wok and bring to the boil. Boil for 10 minutes, or until the oil starts to separate. Add the curry paste and simmer, stirring to prevent it sticking to the bottom, for 5 minutes, or until fragrant.
2 Add the meat and cook, stirring, for 3–5 minutes, or until it changes color. Add the fish sauce, palm sugar, lime leaves, coconut milk and remaining coconut cream, and simmer for 1 hour, or until the meat is tender and the sauce has slightly thickened.
3 Add the eggplant and cook for 10 minutes, or until tender. If the sauce is too thick, add a little water. Stir in half the shredded basil leaves. Garnish with the remaining basil leaves and serve with rice.

NUTRITION PER SERVE
Protein 30 g; Fat 43 g; Carbohydrate 10 g;
Dietary Fibre 5 g; Cholesterol 85 mg;
2276 kJ (544 cal)

NOTE: Cut the meat into 5 x 5 x 2 cm (2 x 2 x
¾ inch) pieces, then cut across the grain at a
45° angle into 5 mm (¼ inch) thick slices.

Cook the onion in a large saucepan until it is golden brown.

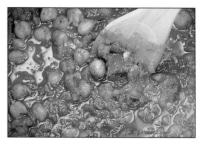

Add the drained chickpeas and cook until the sauce has thickened.

CHANNA MASALA (CHICKPEA CURRY)

Preparation time: 10 minutes +
overnight soaking
Total cooking time: 1 hour 15 minutes
Serves 6

1 cup (220 g/7 oz) dried chickpeas
2 tablespoons oil
2 onions, finely chopped
2 large ripe tomatoes, chopped
$^1/_2$ teaspoon ground coriander
1 teaspoon ground cumin
1 teaspoon chilli powder
$^1/_4$ teaspoon ground turmeric
1 tablespoon channa (chole) masala
  (see NOTE)
20 g ($^3/_4$ oz) ghee or butter
1 small white onion, sliced
fresh mint and coriander leaves, to garnish

1 Place the chickpeas in a bowl, cover with water and leave to soak overnight. Drain, rinse and place in a large saucepan. Cover with plenty of water and bring to the boil, then reduce the heat and simmer for 40 minutes, or until soft. Drain.

2 Heat the oil in a large saucepan, add the onion and cook over medium heat for 15 minutes, or until golden brown. Add the tomato, ground coriander and cumin, chilli powder, turmeric, channa (chole) masala and 2 cups (500 ml/16 fl oz) cold water, and cook for 10 minutes, or until the tomato is soft. Add the chickpeas, season well with salt and cook for 7–10 minutes, or until the sauce thickens. Transfer to a serving dish. Place the ghee or butter on top and allow to melt before serving. Garnish with sliced onion and fresh mint and coriander leaves.

NUTRITION PER SERVE
Protein 8 g; Fat 11 g; Carbohydrate 17 g; Dietary Fibre 6 g; Cholesterol 8.5 mg; 835 kJ (200 cal)

NOTE: Channa (chole) masala is a spice blend specifically used in this dish. It is available at Indian grocery stores. Garam masala (see page 249 for a recipe) can be used as a substitute, but this will alter the final flavor.

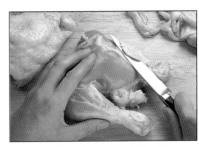

Remove the skin and any excess fat from the chicken pieces.

Using a large knife, cut each chicken Maryland into three even pieces.

VIETNAMESE CHICKEN CURRY

Preparation time: 30 minutes + overnight refrigeration
Total cooking time: 1 hour 10 minutes
Serves 6

4 large chicken Marylands (leg and
    thigh pieces)
1 tablespoon good-quality Indian
    curry powder
1 teaspoon caster sugar
1/3 cup (80 ml/2¾ fl oz) oil
500 g (1 lb) orange sweet potato, cut into
    3 cm (1¼ inch) cubes
1 large onion, cut into thin wedges
4 cloves garlic, chopped
1 stem lemon grass (white part only),
    finely chopped
2 bay leaves
1 large carrot, cut into 1 cm (½ inch) pieces
    on the diagonal
400 ml (13 fl oz) can coconut milk

1 Remove the skin and any excess fat from the chicken. Pat dry with paper towels and cut each piece into 3 even pieces, making 12 pieces. Place the curry powder, sugar, ½ teaspoon black pepper and 2 teaspoons salt in a bowl, and mix well. Rub the curry mixture into the chicken pieces. Place the chicken on a plate, cover with plastic wrap and refrigerate overnight.
2 Heat the oil in a large saucepan. Add the sweet potato cubes and cook over medium heat for 3 minutes, or until lightly golden. Remove with a slotted spoon.
3 Remove all but 2 tablespoons of the oil from the pan. Add the onion and cook, stirring, for 5 minutes. Then add the garlic, lemon grass and bay leaves, and cook for 2 minutes.
4 Add the chicken and cook, stirring, over medium heat for 5 minutes, or until the chicken is well coated in the mixture and starting to change color. Add 1 cup (250 ml/8 fl oz) water and simmer, covered, for 20 minutes. Stir once or twice.

5 Stir in the carrot, sweet potato and coconut milk, and simmer, uncovered, stirring occasionally, for 30 minutes, or until the chicken is cooked and tender. Be careful not to break up the sweet potato cubes. Serve with steamed rice or rice stick noodles.

NUTRITION PER SERVE
Protein 26 g; Fat 30 g; Carbohydrate 17 g; Dietary Fibre 3.5 g; Cholesterol 50 mg; 1787 kJ (427 cal)

Process the onion and garlic in a food processor until smooth.

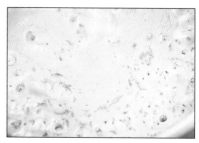

Cook the coconut milk over medium heat until reduced and the oil has separated.

BEEF RENDANG

Preparation time: 20 minutes
Total cooking time: 2 hours 30 minutes
Serves 6

2 onions, roughly chopped
2 cloves garlic, crushed
400 ml (13 fl oz) can coconut milk
2 teaspoons ground coriander seeds
1/2 teaspoon ground fennel seeds
2 teaspoons ground cumin seeds
1/4 teaspoon ground cloves
1.5 kg (3 lb) chuck steak, cut into
    3 cm (1¼ inch) cubes
4–6 small fresh red chillies, chopped
1 tablespoon lemon juice
1 stem lemon grass (white part only),
    bruised, cut lengthways
2 teaspoons grated palm sugar or soft
    brown sugar

1 Place the onion and garlic in a food processor, and process until smooth, adding water, if necessary.

2 Place the coconut milk in a large saucepan and bring to the boil, then reduce the heat to medium and cook, stirring occasionally, for 15 minutes, or until the milk has reduced by half and the oil has separated. Do not allow the milk to brown.

3 Add the coriander, fennel, cumin and cloves to the pan, and stir for 1 minute. Add the meat and cook for 2 minutes, or until it changes color. Add the onion mixture, chilli, lemon juice, lemon grass and sugar. Cook, covered, over medium heat for 2 hours, or until the liquid has reduced and the mixture has thickened. Stir frequently to prevent it sticking to the bottom of the pan.

4 Uncover and continue cooking until the oil from the coconut milk begins to emerge again, letting the curry develop color and flavor. Be careful that it does not burn. The curry is cooked when it is brown and dry.

NUTRITION PER SERVE
Protein 53 g; Fat 20 g; Carbohydrate 5.5 g; Dietary Fibre 1.5 g; Cholesterol 168 mg; 1775 kJ (424 cal)

Place all the curry paste ingredients in a food processor and process to a smooth paste.

Cook the curry paste and crushed garlic in a wok until fragrant.

JUNGLE CURRY PRAWNS

**Preparation time: 30 minutes +
  10 minutes soaking**
Total cooking time: 15 minutes
Serves 6

CURRY PASTE
10–12 dried red chillies
4 red Asian shallots, chopped
4 cloves garlic, sliced
1 stem lemon grass (white part only), sliced
1 tablespoon finely chopped fresh galangal
2 small coriander roots, chopped
1 tablespoon finely chopped fresh ginger
1 tablespoon shrimp paste, dry-roasted
1/4 cup (60 ml/2 fl oz) oil

1 tablespoon oil
1 clove garlic, crushed
1/4 cup (40 g/1 1/4 oz) ground candlenuts
1 tablespoon fish sauce
300 ml (10 fl oz) fish stock
1 tablespoon whisky
600 g (1 1/4 lb) raw prawns, peeled and
  deveined, tails intact
1 small carrot, slivered
200 g (6 1/2 oz) snake beans, cut into
  2 cm (3/4 inch) lengths
50 g (1 3/4 oz) bamboo shoots
3 kaffir lime leaves, crushed
fresh Thai basil leaves, to garnish

1 To make the curry paste, soak the chillies in 1 cup (250 ml/8 fl oz) boiling water for 10 minutes, then drain and place in a food processor with the remaining curry paste ingredients. Season with salt and white pepper, and process to a smooth paste.

2 Heat a wok over medium heat, add the oil and stir to coat the side. Add 3 tablespoons of the curry paste and the garlic, and cook, stirring constantly, for 5 minutes, or until fragrant. Stir in the candlenuts, fish sauce, stock, whisky, prawns, vegetables and lime leaves, and bring to the boil. Reduce the heat and simmer for 5 minutes, or until the prawns and vegetables are cooked through. Garnish with the Thai basil leaves and black pepper.

NUTRITION PER SERVE
Protein 23 g; Fat 15 g; Carbohydrate 3 g;
Dietary Fibre 2.5 g; Cholesterol 150 mg;
990 kJ (235 cal)

DUM ALU
(SMOTHERED POTATOES)

Preparation time: 20 minutes
Total cooking time: 30 minutes
Serves 6

CURRY PASTE
4 cardamom pods
1 teaspoon grated fresh ginger
2 cloves garlic
6 small fresh red chillies
1 teaspoon cumin seeds
¼ cup (40 g/1¼ oz) raw cashew
   nut pieces
1 tablespoon white poppy seeds (khus)
   (see NOTE)
1 cinnamon stick
6 cloves

1 kg (2 lb) potatoes, cubed
2 onions, roughly chopped
2 tablespoons oil
½ teaspoon ground turmeric
1 teaspoon besan (chickpea flour)
1 cup (250 g/8 oz) plain yoghurt
fresh coriander leaves, to garnish

1 To make the curry paste, lightly crush the cardamom pods with the flat side of a heavy knife. Remove the seeds, discarding the pods. Place the seeds and the remaining curry paste ingredients in a food processor, and process to a smooth paste.

2 Bring a large saucepan of lightly salted water to the boil. Add the potato and cook for 5–6 minutes, or until just tender. Drain.

3 Place the onion in a food processor and process in short bursts until it is finely ground but not puréed. Heat the oil in a large saucepan, add the ground onion and cook over low heat for 5 minutes. Add the curry paste and cook, stirring, for a further 5 minutes, or until fragrant. Stir in the potato, turmeric, salt to taste and 1 cup (250 ml/8 fl oz) water.

4 Reduce the heat and simmer, tightly covered, for 10 minutes, or until the potato is cooked but not breaking up and the sauce has thickened slightly.

5 Combine the besan with the yoghurt, add to the potato mixture and cook, stirring, over low heat for 5 minutes, or until thickened again. Garnish with the coriander leaves.

NUTRITION PER SERVE
Protein 7.5 g; Fat 11 g; Carbohydrate 27 g; Dietary Fibre 3.5 g; Cholesterol 6.5 mg; 1010 kJ (240 cal)

NOTE: White poppy seeds (khus) should not be mistaken for black and do not yield opium. They are off-white, odourless and flavorless until roasted when they have a slight sesame aroma and flavor. If they are not available, replace the poppy seeds with sesame seeds.

Add the curry paste to the onion and cook until the mixture is fragrant.

Simmer until the potato is cooked but not breaking up.

Place the curry paste ingredients in a food processor and process to a thick paste.

Use a sharp knife to trim any excess fat from the duck breast fillets.

DUCK AND COCONUT CURRY

Preparation time: 20 minutes
Total cooking time: 1 hour 15 minutes
Serves 6

CURRY PASTE
1 red onion, chopped
2 cloves garlic
2 coriander roots, chopped
2 teaspoons chopped fresh ginger
1¹/₂ teaspoons coriander seeds,
   dry-roasted and ground
1 teaspoon cardamom seeds,
   dry-roasted and ground
1 teaspoon fenugreek seeds,
   dry-roasted and ground
1 teaspoon brown mustard seeds,
   dry-roasted and ground
10 black peppercorns, ground
2 teaspoons garam masala
¹/₄ teaspoon ground turmeric
2 teaspoons tamarind purée

6–8 duck breast fillets
1 red onion, sliced
¹/₂ cup (125 ml/4 fl oz) white vinegar
2 cups (500 ml/16 fl oz) coconut milk
2 tablespoons fresh coriander leaves

1 To make the curry paste, place all the ingredients in a food processor and process to a thick paste.
2 Trim any excess fat from the duck fillets, then place, skin-side down, in a large saucepan and cook over medium heat for 10 minutes, or until the skin is brown and any remaining fat has melted. Turn the fillets over and cook for 5 minutes, or until tender. Remove and drain on paper towels.
3 Reserve 1 tablespoon duck fat, discarding the remaining fat. Add the onion and cook for 5 minutes, then add the curry paste and stir over low heat for 10 minutes, or until fragrant.

4 Return the duck to the pan and stir to coat with the paste. Stir in the vinegar, coconut milk, 1 teaspoon salt and ¹/₂ cup (125 ml/4 fl oz) water. Simmer, covered, for 45 minutes, or until the fillets are tender. Stir in the coriander leaves just prior to serving. Serve with rice and naan bread.

NUTRITION PER SERVE
Protein 55 g; Fat 33 g; Carbohydrate 5.5 g; Dietary Fibre 2.5 g; Cholesterol 323 mg; 2256 kJ (540 cal)

Process the curry paste ingredients together to a smooth paste.

Add the coconut cream and cook, stirring, until the sauce has thickened.

INDONESIAN VEGETABLE AND COCONUT CURRY

Preparation time: 20 minutes
Total cooking time: 35 minutes
Serves 6

CURRY PASTE
5 candlenuts
75 g (2½ oz) red Asian shallots
2 cloves garlic
2 teaspoons sambal oelek
¼ teaspoon ground turmeric
1 teaspoon grated fresh galangal
1 tablespoon peanut butter

2 tablespoons oil
1 onion, sliced
400 ml (13 fl oz) can coconut cream
200 g (6½ oz) carrots, julienned
200 g (6½ oz) snake beans, cut into
    7 cm (2¾ inch) lengths

300 g (10 oz) Chinese cabbage, roughly
    shredded
100 g (3½ oz) fresh shiitake mushrooms
¼ teaspoon sugar

1 To make the curry paste, place the candlenuts, red Asian shallots, garlic, sambal oelek, turmeric, galangal and peanut butter in a food processor, and process to a smooth paste.
2 Heat the oil in a large saucepan over low heat. Cook the curry paste, stirring, for 5 minutes, or until fragrant. Add the onion and cook for 5 minutes. Stir in ¼ cup (60 ml/2 fl oz) coconut cream and cook, stirring constantly, for 2 minutes, or until thickened. Add the carrot and snake beans, and cook over high heat for 3 minutes. Stir in the Chinese cabbage, mushrooms and 1 cup (250 ml/8 fl oz) water. Cook over high heat for 8–10 minutes, or until the vegetables are nearly cooked.

3 Stir in the remaining coconut cream and the sugar, and season to taste with salt. Bring to the boil, stirring constantly, then reduce the heat and simmer for 8–10 minutes to allow the flavors to develop. Serve hot.

NUTRITION PER SERVE
Protein 5 g; Fat 22 g; Carbohydrate 7.5 g;
Dietary Fibre 5 g; Cholesterol 0 mg;
1025 kJ (245 cal)

Heat the oil in a saucepan, add the onion and cook until turning golden.

Add the curry paste to the pan and cook until the mixture is fragrant.

YELLOW VEGETABLE CURRY

Preparation time: 20 minutes
Total cooking time: 45 minutes
Serves 6

¼ cup (60 ml/2 fl oz) oil
1 onion, finely chopped
2 tablespoons yellow curry paste
  (see page 250)
250 g (8 oz) potato, diced
200 g (6½ oz) zucchini, diced
150 g (5 oz) red capsicum, diced
100 g (3½ oz) beans, trimmed
50 g (1¾ oz) bamboo shoots, sliced
1 cup (250 ml/8 fl oz) vegetable stock
400 ml (13 fl oz) can coconut cream
fresh Thai basil leaves, to garnish

1 Heat the oil in a large saucepan, add the onion and cook over medium heat for 4–5 minutes, or until softened and just turning golden. Add the yellow curry paste and cook, stirring, for 2 minutes, or until fragrant.

2 Add all the vegetables and cook, stirring, over high heat for 2 minutes. Pour in the vegetable stock, reduce the heat to medium and cook, covered, for 15–20 minutes, or until the vegetables are tender. Cook, uncovered, over high heat for 5–10 minutes, or until the sauce has reduced slightly.

3 Stir in the coconut cream, and season with salt. Bring to the boil, stirring frequently, then reduce the heat and simmer for 5 minutes. Garnish with the Thai basil leaves.

NUTRITION PER SERVE
Protein 4 g; Fat 24 g; Carbohydrate 12 g; Dietary Fibre 3.5 g; Cholesterol 0.5 mg; 1157 kJ (276 cal)

Squeeze the blanched spinach to remove any excess moisture.

Process the cooked spinach in a food processor until smooth.

LAMB AND SPINACH CURRY

Preparation time: 30 minutes
Total cooking time: 2 hours 20 minutes
Serves 6

1 kg (2 lb) English spinach
¹/₂ cup (125 ml/4 fl oz) oil
1.5 kg (3 lb) lamb, cut into 3 cm
   (1¹/₄ inch) cubes (see NOTE)
2 red onions, finely chopped
6 cloves garlic, crushed
1¹/₂ tablespoons grated fresh ginger
2 bay leaves
2 tablespoons ground coriander
1 tablespoon ground cumin
1 teaspoon ground turmeric
2 large vine-ripened tomatoes, peeled,
   seeded and chopped
2–3 small fresh green chillies, seeded and
   finely chopped

100 g (3¹/₂ oz) plain thick yoghurt
1 cinnamon stick
2 teaspoons garam masala

1 Preheat the oven to warm 170°C (325°F/Gas 3). Trim the spinach and quickly blanch in simmering water. Drain, cool slightly and squeeze to remove any excess moisture, then place in a food processor and process until smooth.
2 Heat half the oil in a large saucepan. Add the lamb pieces in batches and cook over high heat for 4–5 minutes, or until browned. Remove the lamb from the pan.
3 Heat the remaining oil in the saucepan. Add the onion and cook, stirring frequently, for 10 minutes, or until golden brown but not burnt. Add the garlic, ginger and bay leaves, and cook, stirring, for 3 more minutes.
4 Add the spices and cook, stirring, for 2 minutes, or until fragrant. Add the tomato and chilli, and stir over low heat for 5 minutes, or

until the tomato is thick and pulpy. Remove from the heat and cool for 5 minutes. Transfer to a 4 litre casserole dish and stir in the yoghurt.
5 Return the meat to the dish and add the cinnamon stick and 1 teaspoon salt. Bake, covered, for 1 hour and then uncovered for a further 15 minutes. Stir in the spinach and garam masala, and cook, stirring occasionally, for 15 minutes, or until the meat is tender. Remove the bay leaves and cinnamon stick, and serve with rice or pilaf.

NUTRITION PER SERVE
Protein 60 g; Fat 30 g; Carbohydrate 5 g;
Dietary Fibre 6.5 g; Cholesterol 170 mg;
2240 kJ (533 cal)

NOTE: Ask your butcher to bone and cut the lamb for you. A 2.2 kg (4 lb 6¹/₂ oz) leg will yield about 1.5 kg (3 lb) meat.

Lightly crush the cardamom pods with the back of a heavy knife.

Add the beef to the pan and stir to coat with the spices.

BEEF AND LENTIL CURRY

Preparation time: 45 minutes +
10 minutes soaking
Total cooking time: 1 hour 50 minutes
Serves 6

3–4 small dried red chillies
¼ cup (60 ml/2 fl oz) oil
2 red onions, cut into thin wedges
4 cloves garlic, finely chopped
1 tablespoon grated fresh ginger
1 tablespoon garam masala
3 cardamom pods, lightly crushed
1 cinnamon stick
2 teaspoons ground turmeric
750 g (1½ lb) chuck or gravy beef, diced
400 g (13 oz) can chopped tomatoes
½ cup (95 g/3 oz) brown or green lentils
½ cup (125 g/4 oz) red lentils
200 g (6½ oz) pumpkin, diced
150 g (5 oz) baby eggplant, quartered
   lengthways, diced

125 g (4 oz) baby English spinach
1 tablespoon tamarind purée
2 tablespoons grated palm sugar or soft
   brown sugar

1 Soak the chillies in boiling water for 10 minutes, then drain and finely chop.
2 Heat the oil in a large saucepan. Add the onion and cook, stirring, over medium heat for 5 minutes, or until soft. Add the garlic and ginger, and cook for a further 2 minutes.
3 Add the chopped chilli, garam masala, cardamom pods, cinnamon stick, turmeric and ½ teaspoon coarsely ground black pepper. Cook, stirring, for 2 minutes, or until fragrant. Add the beef and stir constantly for 3–4 minutes, or until the meat changes color and is well coated in the spices.
4 Add the tomato, lentils, 1 teaspoon salt and 3 cups (750 ml/24 fl oz) water. Simmer, covered, for 1 hour, or until the lentils are tender. Stir frequently to prevent any of the mixture sticking to the base of the pan. Add a little extra water, if necessary.

5 Add the pumpkin and eggplant to the pan, and cook, covered, for 20 minutes, or until the beef and vegetables are tender and the sauce thickens. Stir in the spinach, tamarind purée and palm sugar, and cook, covered, for a further 10 minutes. Remove the cinnamon stick, and serve.

NUTRITION PER SERVE
Protein 34 g; Fat 14 g; Carbohydrate 22 g; Dietary Fibre 6.5 g; Cholesterol 84 mg; 1452 kJ (347 cal)

NOTE: This dish is traditionally served with rice that has been cooked pilaff-style with well-browned, slow-cooked onion slices.

Dry-fry the dried chillies, spices and desiccated coconut until fragrant.

Place the dry-fried spices in a food processor and finely grind.

GOAN FISH CURRY

Preparation time: 20 minutes
Total cooking time: 35 minutes
Serves 6

1/4 cup (60 ml/2 fl oz) oil
1 large onion, finely chopped
4–5 cloves garlic, chopped
2 teaspoons grated fresh ginger
4–6 small dried red chillies
1 tablespoon coriander seeds
2 teaspoons cumin seeds
1 teaspoon ground turmeric
1/4 teaspoon chilli powder
1/3 cup (30 g/1 oz) desiccated coconut
270 ml (9 fl oz) coconut milk
2 tomatoes, peeled and chopped
2 tablespoons tamarind purée
1 tablespoon white vinegar

6 curry leaves
1 kg (2 lb) boneless, skinless firm fish fillets, such as flake or ling, cut into 8 cm (3 inch) pieces

1 Heat the oil in a large saucepan. Add the onion and cook, stirring, over low heat for 10 minutes, or until softened and lightly golden. Add the garlic and ginger, and cook for a further 2 minutes.

2 Meanwhile, place the dried chillies, coriander seeds, cumin seeds, turmeric, chilli powder and coconut in a frying pan, and dry-fry, stirring constantly, over medium heat for 2 minutes, or until the mixture is aromatic. Place in a food processor or spice grinder and finely grind.

3 Add the spice mixture, coconut milk, chopped tomato, tamarind purée, vinegar and curry leaves to the onion mixture. Stir to mix thoroughly, add 1 cup (250 ml/8 fl oz) water and simmer for 10 minutes, or until the tomato has softened and the mixture has thickened slightly. Stir frequently to prevent sticking.

4 Add the fish and cook, covered, over low heat for 10 minutes, or until cooked through. Stir gently once or twice during cooking and add a little water if the mixture is too thick. Serve immediately with rice and pappadums.

NUTRITION PER SERVE
Protein 37 g; Fat 27 g; Carbohydrate 4 g; Dietary Fibre 3 g; Cholesterol 117 mg; 1685 kJ (400 cal)

Mash the tamarind pulp with a fork, then strain and reserve the liquid.

Cook the beef in batches over high heat until well browned.

MUSAMAN BEEF CURRY

Preparation time: 30 minutes
Total cooking time: 1 hour 45 minutes
Serves 4

1 tablespoon tamarind pulp
2 tablespoons oil
750 g (1½ lb) lean stewing beef, cubed
2 cups (500 ml/16 fl oz) coconut milk
4 cardamom pods, bruised
2 cups (500 ml/16 fl oz) coconut cream
2–3 tablespoons Musaman curry paste
   (see page 251)
8 baby onions, peeled (see NOTE)
8 baby potatoes, peeled (see NOTE)
2 tablespoons fish sauce
2 tablespoons palm sugar or soft brown
   sugar
½ cup (80 g/2¾ oz) unsalted peanuts,
   roasted and ground
fresh coriander leaves, to garnish

1 Place the tamarind pulp and ½ cup (125 ml/ 4 fl oz) boiling water in a bowl and set aside to cool. When cool, mash the pulp to dissolve in the water, then strain and reserve the liquid. Discard the pulp.
2 Heat the oil in a wok or a large saucepan and cook the beef in batches over high heat for 5 minutes, or until browned. Reduce the heat, add the coconut milk and cardamom, and simmer for 1 hour, or until the beef is tender. Remove the beef, strain and reserve the beef and cooking liquid.
3 Heat the coconut cream in the wok and stir in the curry paste. Cook for 5 minutes, or until the oil starts to separate from the cream.
4 Add the onions, potatoes, fish sauce, palm sugar, peanuts, beef mixture, reserved cooking liquid and tamarind water, and simmer for 25–30 minutes. Garnish with fresh coriander leaves. Serve with rice.

NUTRITION PER SERVE
Protein 52 g; Fat 77 g; Carbohydrate 35 g; Dietary Fibre 7.5 g; Cholesterol 115 mg; 4324 kJ (1033 cal)

NOTE: Use small onions and potatoes, about 25–30 g (¾–1 oz) each.

Cook the chicken pieces over high heat, in batches, until browned.

Cook the onion for 10 minutes, or until soft and golden brown.

CHICKEN CURRY WITH APRICOTS

Preparation time: 40 minutes +
** 1 hour soaking**
Total cooking time: 1 hour 10 minutes
Serves 6–8

18 dried apricots
1 tablespoon ghee or oil
2 x 1.5 kg (3 lb) chickens, jointed
3 onions, thinly sliced
1 teaspoon grated fresh ginger
3 cloves garlic, crushed
3 large fresh green chillies, seeded and
  finely chopped
1 teaspoon cumin seeds
1 teaspoon chilli powder
½ teaspoon ground turmeric
4 cardamom pods, bruised
4 large tomatoes, peeled and cut
  into eighths

1 Soak the dried apricots in 1 cup (250 ml/ 8 fl oz) hot water for 1 hour.
2 Melt the ghee in a large saucepan, add the chicken in batches and cook over high heat for 5–6 minutes, or until browned. Remove from the pan. Add the onion and cook, stirring often, for 10 minutes, or until the onion has softened and turned golden brown.
3 Add the ginger, garlic and chopped green chilli, and cook, stirring, for 2 minutes. Stir in the cumin seeds, chilli powder and ground turmeric, and cook for a further 1 minute.
4 Return the chicken to the pan, add the cardamom, tomato and apricots, with any remaining liquid, and mix well. Simmer, covered, for 35 minutes, or until the chicken is tender.
5 Remove the chicken, cover and keep warm. Bring the liquid to the boil and boil rapidly, uncovered, for 5 minutes, or until it has thickened slightly. To serve, spoon the liquid over the chicken. Serve with steamed rice mixed with raisins, grated carrot and toasted flaked almonds.

NUTRITION PER SERVE (8)
Protein 44 g; Fat 6.5 g; Carbohydrate 6.5 g; Dietary Fibre 2.5 g; Cholesterol 100 mg; 1105 kJ (264 cal)

Stews

SPICED BEEF AND POTATOES

Preparation time: 15 minutes
Total cooking time: 1 hour 40 minutes
Serves 4

SPICE PASTE
2 onions, chopped
2 cloves garlic, chopped
2 teaspoons grated lemon rind
2 small fresh red chillies, chopped
2 teaspoons ground coriander
2 teaspoons ground cumin
1 teaspoon ground turmeric
$^{1}/_{2}$ teaspoon ground cardamom
1 teaspoon garam masala

2 tablespoons oil
1 kg (2 lb) lean chuck steak, cut into
    3 cm (1$^{1}/_{4}$ inch) cubes
$^{3}/_{4}$ cup (185 ml/6 fl oz) coconut cream
1 tablespoon tamarind sauce
500 g (1 lb) baby potatoes, halved

1 To make the spice paste, combine all the ingredients in a food processor or blender, and process for 1 minute, or until very finely chopped.

2 Heat the oil in a heavy-based saucepan. Cook the meat quickly in small batches over medium–high heat until well browned. Drain on paper towels.

3 Add the spice paste to the pan and stir over medium heat for 2 minutes. Return the meat to the pan with the coconut cream, tamarind sauce and $^{1}/_{2}$ cup (125 ml/4 fl oz) water, and bring to the boil. Reduce the heat to a simmer and cook, covered, for 30 minutes, stirring occasionally.

4 Add the potato and cook, covered, for 30 minutes. Remove the lid and cook for 30 minutes, or until the meat is tender and almost all of the liquid has evaporated.

NUTRITION PER SERVE
Protein 57 g; Fat 25 g; Carbohydrate 25 g; Dietary Fibre 5 g; Cholesterol 168 mg; 2315 kJ (555 cal)

Trim the meat of excess fat and sinew and cut it into large cubes.

Return the meat to the pan with the coconut cream, tamarind sauce and water.

Coat the pork fillet pieces with the ground coriander and cracked pepper.

Heat some oil in a saucepan and cook the pork in batches until brown.

PORK AND CORIANDER STEW

Preparation time: 15 minutes +
  overnight marinating
Total cooking time: 1 hour 20 minutes
Serves 4–6

1½ tablespoons coriander seeds
800 g (1 lb 10 oz) pork fillet, cut into
  2 cm (¾ inch) cubes
1 tablespoon plain flour
¼ cup (60 ml/2 fl oz) olive oil
1 large onion, thinly sliced
1½ cups (375 ml/12 fl oz) red wine
1 cup (250 ml/8 fl oz) chicken stock
1 teaspoon sugar
sprigs fresh coriander, to garnish

1 Crush the coriander seeds in a mortar and pestle. Combine the pork, crushed seeds and ½ teaspoon cracked pepper in a bowl. Cover and marinate overnight in the refrigerator.
2 Combine the flour and pork, and toss to coat. Heat 2 tablespoons of the oil in a saucepan and cook the pork in batches over high heat for 1–2 minutes, or until brown. Remove.
3 Heat the remaining oil, add the onion and cook over medium heat for 2–3 minutes, or until just golden. Return the meat to the pan, add the red wine, stock and sugar, and season. Bring to the boil, then reduce the heat and simmer, covered, for 1 hour.
4 Remove the meat. Return the pan to the heat and boil over high heat for 3–5 minutes, or until the liquid is reduced and slightly thickened. Pour over the meat and top with coriander.

NUTRITION PER SERVE (6)
Protein 30 g; Fat 12 g; Carbohydrate 2.5 g;
Dietary Fibre 0 g; Cholesterol 65 mg;
1180 kJ (282 cal)

Roll tablespoons of the lamb and spice mixture into balls.

Add the garlic and spices to the onion, and cook until fragrant.

LAMB KEFTA

Preparation time: 30 minutes
Total cooking time: 40 minutes
Serves 4

1 kg (2 lb) lamb mince
1 onion, finely chopped
2 cloves garlic, finely chopped
2 tablespoons finely chopped fresh
   flat-leaf parsley
2 tablespoons finely chopped fresh
   coriander leaves
$^1/_2$ teaspoon cayenne pepper
$^1/_2$ teaspoon ground allspice
$^1/_2$ teaspoon ground ginger
$^1/_2$ teaspoon ground cardamom
1 teaspoon ground cumin
1 teaspoon paprika

SAUCE
2 tablespoons olive oil
1 onion, finely chopped
2 cloves garlic, finely chopped
2 teaspoons ground cumin
$^1/_2$ teaspoon ground cinnamon
1 teaspoon paprika
2 x 425 g (14 oz) cans chopped tomatoes
2 teaspoons harissa
$^1/_3$ cup (20 g/$^3/_4$ oz) chopped fresh coriander
   leaves

1 Preheat the oven to moderate 180°C (350°F/Gas 4). Lightly grease two baking trays. Place the lamb, onion, garlic, herbs and spices in a bowl, and mix together well. Season with salt and pepper. Roll tablespoons of the mixture into balls and place on the trays. Bake for 18–20 minutes, or until browned.
2 Meanwhile, to make the sauce, heat the oil in a large saucepan, add the onion and cook over medium heat for 5 minutes, or until soft. Add the garlic, cumin, cinnamon and paprika, and cook for 1 minute, or until fragrant.

3 Stir in the tomato and harissa, and bring to the boil. Reduce the heat and simmer for 20 minutes, then add the meatballs and simmer for 10 minutes, or until cooked through. Stir in the coriander, season well, and serve.

NUTRITION PER SERVE
Protein 53 g; Fat 37 g; Carbohydrate 10 g; Dietary Fibre 4 g; Cholesterol 158 mg; 2434 kJ (580 cal)

Trim the ends of the fennel, and slice the bulb thinly with a sharp knife.

Add the Pernod and wine to the softened fennel, leek and garlic mixture.

SEAFOOD AND FENNEL STEW

Preparation time: 10 minutes
Total cooking time: 30 minutes
Serves 6

2 tablespoons olive oil
1 large fennel bulb, thinly sliced
2 leeks, thinly sliced
2 cloves garlic, crushed
$^1/_2$ teaspoon paprika
2 tablespoons Pernod or Ricard
200 ml (6$^1/_2$ fl oz) dry white wine
18 mussels, scrubbed and beards removed
$^1/_4$ teaspoon saffron threads
$^1/_4$ teaspoon thyme leaves
6 baby octopus
16 raw prawns, peeled and deveined
500 g (1 lb) swordfish steaks, cut into
    large chunks
400 g (13 oz) baby new potatoes
fennel greens, to garnish

1 Heat the oil in a large saucepan over medium heat. Add the fennel, leek and garlic. Stir in the paprika, season lightly and cook for 8 minutes, or until softened. Add the Pernod and wine, and stir for 1 minute, or until reduced by a third.
2 Add the mussels, discarding any open ones. Cover and cook for 1 minute, or until opened, discarding any that do not open. Remove from the pan to cool; remove from the shells and set aside.
3 Add the saffron and thyme to the pan, and cook for 1–2 minutes, stirring. Adjust the seasoning and transfer to a large, flameproof casserole dish.
4 Use a small sharp knife to remove the octopus heads. Grasp the bodies and push the beaks out with your index finger; remove and discard. Slit the heads and remove the gut. Mix the octopus, prawns, fish and potatoes into the stew. Cover and cook gently for 10 minutes, or until tender. Add the mussels, cover and heat through. Garnish with fennel greens and serve.

NUTRITION PER SERVE
Protein 65 g; Fat 10 g; Carbohydrate 15 g; Dietary Fibre 5 g; Cholesterol 390 mg; 1840 kJ (440 cal)

Shape the lentil mixture into walnut-sized balls, and place on a foil-lined tray.

Fry the lentil balls in oil in batches over high heat, until golden brown.

LENTIL BHUJIA STEW

Preparation time: 30 minutes + overnight soaking + 30 minutes refrigeration
Total cooking time: 1 hour 10 minutes
Serves 4–6

2 cups (370 g/12 oz) green or brown lentils
1 large onion, grated
1 large potato, grated
1 teaspoon ground cumin
1 teaspoon ground coriander
1 teaspoon ground turmeric
3/4 cup (90 g/3 oz) plain flour
oil, for shallow-frying
2 cloves garlic, crushed
1 tablespoon grated fresh ginger
1 cup (250 ml/8 fl oz) tomato purée
2 cups (500 ml/16 fl oz) vegetable stock
1 cup (250 ml/8 fl oz) cream
200 g (6¹/₂ oz) green beans, topped, tailed
    and cut in half

2 carrots, sliced
2 hard-boiled eggs, chopped
sprigs fresh rosemary, to garnish

1 Soak the lentils overnight in cold water. Drain well. Squeeze the excess moisture from the lentils, onion and potato using a tea towel. Place them in a bowl with the ground spices and flour; mix well and leave for 10 minutes. With floured hands, shape the mixture into walnut-sized balls and place on a foil-lined tray. Cover and refrigerate for 30 minutes.

2 Heat 2 cm (³/₄ inch) of oil in a heavy-based frying pan. Cook the balls in batches over high heat until golden brown. Drain on paper towels.

3 Heat 2 tablespoons of oil in a saucepan and gently fry the garlic and ginger for 2 minutes. Stir in the purée, stock and cream. Bring to the boil, then reduce the heat and simmer for 10 minutes. Add the beans, lentil balls and carrot. Cook, covered, for 30 minutes, stirring twice. Add the egg and cook for 10 minutes. Garnish with rosemary to serve.

NUTRITION PER SERVE (6)
Protein 23 g; Fat 30 g; Carbohydrate 45 g;
Dietary Fibre 13 g; Cholesterol 125 mg;
2290 kJ (550 cal)

VARIATION: Split peas can be used in this recipe in place of the lentils. Soak them in cold water overnight, then drain well before using.

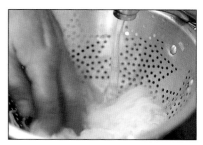

Rinse the noodles well in a colander, under cold running water.

Add the sauce and watercress, and cook briefly until the watercress has just wilted.

SUKIYAKI

Preparation time: 10 minutes
Total cooking time: 10 minutes
Serves 4

SAUCE
1/2–1 teaspoon dashi granules
1/3 cup (80 ml/2³/₄ fl oz) soy sauce
2 tablespoons sake
2 tablespoons mirin
1 tablespoon caster sugar

300 g (10 oz) shirataki noodles (see NOTE)
50 g (1³/₄ oz) lard
5 large spring onions, cut into 1 cm
    (1/2 inch) slices on the diagonal
16 fresh shiitake mushrooms, cut into
    smaller pieces if large
800 g (1 lb 10 oz) rump steak, thinly sliced
    across the grain
100 g (3¹/₂ oz) watercress, trimmed
4 eggs (optional)

1 To make the sauce, dissolve the dashi granules in 1/2 cup (125 ml/4 fl oz) water. Add the soy sauce, sake, mirin and sugar, and stir until combined.

2 Drain the noodles, then soak them in boiling water for 2 minutes. Rinse in cold water and drain well.

3 Melt the lard in a large frying pan over medium heat. Cook the spring onion, mushrooms and beef in batches, stirring, for 1–2 minutes each batch, or until just brown. Return the meat, spring onion and mushrooms to the pan, then add the sauce and watercress. Cook for 1 minute, or until heated through and the watercress has wilted—the sauce needs to just cover the ingredients but not drown them.

4 To serve, divide the noodles among four serving bowls and spoon the sauce evenly over the top. If desired, crack an egg into each bowl and break up through the sauce using chopsticks until it partially cooks.

NUTRITION PER SERVE
Protein 54 g; Fat 28 g; Carbohydrate 46 g;
Dietary Fibre 5 g; Cholesterol 342 mg;
2755 kJ (660 cal)

NOTE: Shirataki noodles are sold in Japanese supermarkets.

PONZU CHICKEN AND NOODLE HOTPOT

**Preparation time: 15 minutes +
  overnight refrigeration**
Total cooking time: 45 minutes
Serves 4

PONZU SAUCE
1 tablespoon lemon juice
1 tablespoon lime juice
1 tablespoon rice vinegar
1 tablespoon tamari
1½ tablespoons mirin
2½ tablespoons Japanese soy sauce
5 cm (2 inch) piece kombu (kelp), wiped
  with a damp cloth
1 tablespoon bonito flakes

900 g (1 lb 13 oz) chicken thigh cutlets, cut
  in half across the bone
10 cm (4 inch) piece kombu (kelp)
200 g (6½ oz) dried somen noodles

250 g (8 oz) fresh shiitake mushrooms,
  halved if large
1 carrot, thinly sliced
300 g (10 oz) baby English spinach leaves

1 To make the ponzu sauce, combine all the ingredients in a non-metallic bowl. Cover with plastic wrap and refrigerate overnight, then strain through a fine sieve.
2 Place the chicken and kombu in a large saucepan with 3½ cups (875 ml/28 fl oz) water. Bring to a simmer over medium heat. Cook for 20 minutes, or until the chicken is cooked, skimming the scum off the surface. Remove the chicken pieces and strain the broth. Transfer the broth and chicken pieces to a 2.5 litre flameproof casserole dish or Japanese nabe. Cover and continue to cook over low heat for 15 minutes.
3 Meanwhile, cook the noodles in a large saucepan of boiling water for 2 minutes, or until tender. Drain and rinse under cold running water.

4 Add the mushrooms and carrot to the chicken, and cook for 5 minutes. Place the noodles on top of the chicken, then top with the spinach. Cook, covered, for 2 minutes, or until the spinach has just wilted. Stir in 4–6 tablespoons of the ponzu sauce, or to taste. Serve immediately.

NUTRITION PER SERVE
Protein 32 g; Fat 9 g; Carbohydrate 37 g;
Dietary Fibre 6.5 g; Cholesterol 98 mg;
1515 kJ (360 cal)

NOTE: Traditionally, this dish would be served in a ceramic nabe dish, for your guests to help themselves.

Cook the veal shank pieces in batches until they are well browned.

Cook the onion, carrot, celery and bay leaf in oil until softened.

OSSO BUCO

Preparation time: 30 minutes
Total cooking time: 2 hours 20 minutes
Serves 4–6

12 meaty pieces veal shank, osso buco style
$^1/_3$ cup (40 g/1$^1/_4$ oz) seasoned plain flour
20 g ($^3/_4$ oz) butter
$^1/_3$ cup (80 ml/2$^3/_4$ fl oz) olive oil
1 onion, diced
1 carrot, diced
1 celery stick, diced
1 bay leaf
1 clove garlic, crushed
2 cups (500 ml/16 fl oz) veal or
   chicken stock
1 cup (250 ml/8 fl oz) white wine
$^1/_3$ cup (80 ml/2$^3/_4$ fl oz) lemon juice

GREMOLATA
$^2/_3$ cup (12 g/$^1/_4$ oz) fresh flat-leaf parsley
2 cloves garlic, finely chopped
1 tablespoon grated lemon rind

1 Lightly dust the veal shanks in the seasoned flour. Heat the butter and $^1/_4$ cup (60 ml/2 fl oz) of the oil in a large deep-sided frying pan over high heat until sizzling. Add the veal and cook in batches for 5 minutes, or until brown all over. Remove from the pan.
2 Heat the remaining oil in a large saucepan, add the onion, carrot, celery and bay leaf, and cook for 10 minutes, or until softened and starting to brown. Add the garlic, stock, wine and lemon juice, and stir to combine, scraping the bottom of the pan to remove any sediment. Add the veal to the pan, bring to the boil, then reduce the heat to low, cover and simmer for 1$^1/_2$–2 hours, or until the veal is very tender and falling off the bone and the sauce has reduced. Season to taste.

3 To make the gremolata, finely chop the parsley and mix together with the garlic and rind. Sprinkle over the osso buco just before serving. Serve with soft polenta.

NUTRITION PER SERVE (6)
Protein 53 g; Fat 17 g; Carbohydrate 7.5 g; Dietary Fibre 1.5 g; Cholesterol 205 mg; 1759 kJ (420 cal)

Process the almonds, bread, garlic, parsley and some of the stock to a smooth paste.

Quickly cook the fish and calamari in the oil in a frying pan.

CATALAN FISH STEW

Preparation time: 30 minutes
Total cooking time: 40 minutes
Serves 6–8

300 g (10 oz) red mullet fillets
400 g (13 oz) firm white fish fillets
300 g (10 oz) cleaned calamari
1.5 litres fish stock
1/3 cup (80 ml/2¾ fl oz) olive oil
1 onion, chopped
6 cloves garlic, chopped
1 small fresh red chilli, chopped
1 teaspoon paprika
pinch saffron threads
150 ml (5 fl oz) white wine
425 g (14 oz) can crushed tomatoes
16 raw medium prawns, peeled and
    deveined, tails intact
2 tablespoons brandy
24 black mussels, cleaned
1 tablespoon chopped fresh parsley

PICADA
2 tablespoons olive oil
2 slices day-old bread, cubed
2 cloves garlic
5 blanched almonds, toasted
2 tablespoons fresh flat-leaf
    parsley

1 Cut the fish and calamari into 4 cm (1½ inch) pieces. Place the stock in a large saucepan, bring to the boil and boil for 15 minutes, or until reduced by half.
2 To make the picada, heat the oil in a frying pan, add the bread and cook, stirring, for 2–3 minutes, or until golden, adding the garlic for the last minute. Place the almonds, bread, garlic and parsley in a food processor and process, adding enough of the stock to make a smooth paste.
3 Heat 2 tablespoons of the oil in a large saucepan, add the onion, garlic, chilli and paprika, and cook, stirring, for 1 minute. Add the saffron, wine, tomato and stock. Bring to the boil, then reduce the heat and simmer.

4 Heat the remaining oil in a frying pan and quickly fry the fish and calamari for 3–5 minutes. Remove from the pan. Add the prawns, cook for 1 minute and then pour in the brandy. Carefully ignite the brandy with a match and let the flames burn down. Remove from the pan.
5 Add the mussels to the stock and simmer, covered, for 2–3 minutes, or until opened. Discard any that do not open. Add all the seafood and the picada to the pan, stirring until the sauce has thickened and the seafood has cooked through. Season to taste, sprinkle with the parsley, and serve.

NUTRITION PER SERVE (8)
Protein 26 g; Fat 18 g; Carbohydrate 5 g;
Dietary Fibre 1.5 g; Cholesterol 136 mg;
1275 kJ (305 cal)

Cook the vegetables until they are coated in the spices and start to soften.

Once all the water has been absorbed, fluff the couscous with a fork.

VEGETABLE TAGINE

Preparation time: 20 minutes
Total cooking time: 1 hour
Serves 4–6

2 tablespoons oil
2 onions, chopped
1 teaspoon ground ginger
2 teaspoons ground paprika
2 teaspoons ground cumin
1 cinnamon stick
pinch saffron threads
1.5 kg (3 lb) vegetables, peeled and cut into large chunks (carrot, eggplant, orange sweet potato, parsnip, potato, pumpkin)
$^1/_2$ preserved lemon, rinsed, pith and flesh removed, thinly sliced
400 g (13 oz) can peeled tomatoes
1 cup (250 ml/8 fl oz) vegetable stock
100 g ($3^1/_2$ oz) dried pears, halved
50 g ($1^3/_4$ oz) pitted prunes
2 zucchini, cut into large chunks

300 g (10 oz) couscous
1 tablespoon olive oil
$^1/_4$ cup (7 g/$^1/_4$ oz) chopped fresh flat-leaf parsley
$^1/_3$ cup (50 g/$1^3/_4$ oz) almonds

1 Preheat the oven to moderate 180°C (350°F/Gas 4). Heat the oil in a large saucepan or ovenproof dish, add the onion and cook over medium heat for 5 minutes, or until soft. Add the spices and cook for 3 minutes.
2 Add the vegetables and cook, stirring, until coated with the spices and the vegetables begin to soften. Add the lemon, tomatoes, stock, pears and prunes. Cover, transfer to the oven and cook for 30 minutes. Add the zucchini and cook for 15–20 minutes, or until the vegetables are tender.
3 Cover the couscous with the olive oil and 2 cups (500 ml/16 fl oz) boiling water, and stand until all the water has been absorbed. Fluff with a fork.

4 Remove the cinnamon stick from the vegetables, then stir in the parsley. Serve on a large platter with the couscous formed into a ring and the vegetable tagine in the centre, sprinkled with the almonds.

NUTRITION PER SERVE (6)
Protein 8 g; Fat 15 g; Carbohydrate 33 g; Dietary Fibre 9 g; Cholesterol 0 mg; 1240 kJ (296 cal)

Cook the garlic, onion wedges and capsicum in a large saucepan.

Simmer the mixture for 40 minutes, or until the beans are cooked through.

BEAN AND CAPSICUM STEW

Preparation time: 20 minutes + soaking
Total cooking time: 1 hour 35 minutes
Serves 4–6

1 cup (200 g/6½ oz) dried haricot beans
   (see NOTE)
2 tablespoons olive oil
2 large cloves garlic, crushed
1 red onion, halved and cut into thin wedges
1 red capsicum, cut into 1.5 cm
   (⅝ inch) squares
1 green capsicum, cut into 1.5 cm
   (⅝ inch) squares
2 x 400 g (13 oz) cans chopped tomatoes
2 tablespoons tomato paste
2 cups (500 ml/16 fl oz) vegetable stock
2 tablespoons chopped fresh basil
⅔ cup (125 g/4 oz) Kalamata olives, pitted
1–2 teaspoons soft brown sugar

1 Put the beans in a large bowl, cover with cold water and soak overnight. Rinse well, then transfer to a saucepan, cover with cold water and cook for 45 minutes, or until just tender. Drain.
2 Heat the oil in a large saucepan. Cook the garlic and onion wedges over medium heat for 2–3 minutes, or until the onion is soft. Add the red and green capsicums, and cook for a further 5 minutes.
3 Stir in the tomato, tomato paste, stock and beans. Simmer, covered, for 40 minutes, or until the beans are cooked through. Stir in the basil, olives and sugar. Season with salt and pepper. Serve hot with crusty bread.

NUTRITION PER SERVE (6)
Protein 10 g; Fat 8 g; Carbohydrate 20 g;
Dietary Fibre 9.5 g; Cholesterol 0 mg;
825 kJ (197 cal)

NOTE: 1 cup of dried haricot beans yields about 2½ cups cooked beans. You can use 2½ cups canned haricot or borlotti beans instead if you prefer.

LAMB HOTPOT WITH RICE NOODLES

Preparation time: 20 minutes +
**   2 hours marinating**
Total cooking time: 2 hours
Serves 4

2 cloves garlic, crushed
2 teaspoons grated fresh ginger
1 teaspoon five-spice powder
¼ teaspoon ground white pepper
2 tablespoons Chinese rice wine
1 teaspoon sugar
1 kg (2 lb) boneless lamb shoulder, trimmed
    and cut into 3 cm (1¼ inch) pieces
30 g (1 oz) whole dried Chinese mushrooms
1 tablespoon peanut oil
1 large onion, cut into wedges
2 cm (¾ inch) piece fresh ginger, julienned
1 teaspoon Sichuan peppercorns, crushed
    or ground
2 tablespoons sweet bean paste
1 teaspoon black peppercorns, ground
    and toasted
2 cups (500 ml/16 fl oz) chicken stock
¼ cup (60 ml/2 fl oz) oyster sauce
2 star anise
¼ cup (60 ml/2 fl oz) Chinese rice
    wine, extra
80 g (2¾ oz) can sliced bamboo shoots
100 g (3½ oz) can water chestnuts, drained
    and sliced
400 g (13 oz) fresh rice noodles, cut into
    2 cm (¾ inch) wide strips
1 spring onion, sliced on the diagonal

1 Combine the garlic, grated ginger, five-spice powder, white pepper, rice wine, sugar and 1 teaspoon salt in a large bowl. Add the lamb and toss to coat. Cover and marinate for 2 hours.

2 Meanwhile, soak the mushrooms in boiling water for 20 minutes. Drain. Discard the stems and slice the caps.

3 Heat a wok over high heat, add the oil and swirl to coat. Stir-fry the onion, julienned ginger and Sichuan pepper for 2 minutes. Cook the lamb in three batches, stir-frying for 2–3 minutes each batch, or until starting to brown. Return all the lamb to the wok. Stir in the bean paste and black peppercorns, and cook for 3 minutes, or until the lamb is brown.

4 Add the stock and transfer to a 2 litre flameproof clay pot or casserole dish. Stir in the oyster sauce, star anise and extra rice wine and simmer, covered, over low heat for 1½ hours, or until the lamb is tender. Stir in the drained bamboo shoots and water chestnuts, and cook for 20 minutes. Add the mushrooms.

5 Cover the noodles with boiling water and gently separate. Drain and rinse the noodles, then add to the hotpot, stirring for 1–2 minutes, or until heated through. Serve sprinkled with spring onion.

NUTRITION PER SERVE

Protein 58 g; Fat 21 g; Carbohydrate 57 g; Dietary Fibre 4 g; Cholesterol 168 mg; 2805 kJ (670 cal)

Stir the bean paste and peppercorns into the lamb and onion mixture.

Toss the liver slices in the seasoned cornflour, shaking off the excess.

Cook the bacon in a heavy-based saucepan until crisp, then drain on paper towels.

LAMB'S LIVER AND BACON STEW

Preparation time: 10 minutes
Total cooking time: 30 minutes
Serves 6

1 lamb's liver, about 750 g (1½ lb)
  (see NOTE)
¼ cup (30 g/1 oz) cornflour
¼ teaspoon ground black pepper
6 rashers bacon, cut into large pieces
2 tablespoons oil
2 onions, thinly sliced
1 beef stock cube, crumbled

1 Wash the liver and cut it into thin slices, discarding any veins or discolored spots. Pat the liver dry with paper towels. Combine the cornflour and pepper. Toss the liver slices in the seasoned cornflour, shaking off the excess.
2 Cook the bacon in a heavy-based saucepan until crisp, then drain on paper towels. Heat the oil in the pan and cook the onion gently until golden, then remove from the pan.
3 Cook the liver quickly in small batches over medium heat until well browned, then drain on paper towels. Return the liver, bacon and onion to the pan. Dissolve the stock cube in 1 cup (250 ml/8 fl oz) boiling water, then gradually add to the pan. Stir over medium heat for 10 minutes, or until the liquid boils and thickens. Serve the stew immediately.

NUTRITION PER SERVE
Protein 36 g; Fat 30 g; Carbohydrate 9 g;
Dietary Fibre 0.5 g; Cholesterol 573 mg;
1850 kJ (440 cal)

NOTE: Soaking the liver in milk for 30 minutes before cooking will result in a milder taste.

Shape the pork medallions into rounds by securing a length of string around each one.

Cook the medallions in the oil for 2 minutes on each side, turning once.

BRAISED PORK WITH PRUNES

Preparation time: 15 minutes
Total cooking time: 30 minutes
Serves 4

4 lean pork loin medallions, about 175 g (6 oz) each
2 cups (500 ml/16 fl oz) chicken stock
2 tablespoons oil
1 large onion, cut into wedges
2 cloves garlic, crushed
1 tablespoon fresh thyme leaves
1 large tomato, peeled, seeded and finely chopped
$^{1}/_{2}$ cup (125 ml/4 fl oz) cream
16 pitted prunes

1 Shape the meat into rounds by securing a length of string around the medallions. Tie with a bow for easy removal. Bring the stock to the boil in a medium saucepan. Reduce the heat to a simmer and cook for 5 minutes, or until reduced to $^{3}/_{4}$ cup (185 ml/6 fl oz).

2 Heat the oil over high heat in a heavy-based frying pan. Cook the meat for 2 minutes each side to seal, turning once. Drain on paper towels.

3 Add the onion and garlic to the saucepan, and stir for 2 minutes. Return the meat to the pan with the thyme, tomato and stock, then reduce the heat to low. Cover the pan and bring slowly to simmering point. Simmer for 10 minutes, or until the meat is tender, turning once. Add the cream and prunes, and simmer for a further 5 minutes.

NUTRITION PER SERVE
Protein 45 g; Fat 25 g; Carbohydrate 20 g; Dietary Fibre 4 g; Cholesterol 138 mg; 2015 kJ (480 cal)

Toss the diced beef in the seasoned flour until evenly coated.

Slowly pour the red wine into the pan, scraping up any sediment with a wooden spoon.

BEEF BOURGUIGNONNE

Preparation time: 10 minutes
Total cooking time: 2 hours
Serves 4

1 kg (2 lb) diced beef
¼ cup (30 g/1 oz) seasoned plain flour
1 tablespoon oil
150 g (5 oz) bacon, diced
8 bulb spring onions, greens trimmed to
    2 cm (¾ inch)
200 g (6½ oz) button mushrooms
2 cups (500 ml/16 fl oz) red wine
2 tablespoons tomato paste
2 cups (500 ml/16 fl oz) beef stock
1 bouquet garni (see NOTE)

1 Toss the beef in the seasoned flour until evenly coated, shaking off any excess. Heat the oil in a large saucepan over high heat. Cook the beef in three batches for about 3 minutes, or until well browned all over, adding a little extra oil as needed. Remove from the pan.

2 Add the bacon to the pan and cook for 2 minutes, or until browned. Remove with a slotted spoon and add to the beef. Add the spring onions and mushrooms, and cook for 5 minutes, or until the onions are browned. Remove.

3 Slowly pour the red wine into the pan, scraping up any sediment from the bottom with a wooden spoon. Stir in the tomato paste and stock. Add the bouquet garni and return the beef, bacon and any juices. Bring to the boil, then reduce the heat and simmer for 45 minutes. Return the spring onions and mushrooms to the pan. Cook for 1 hour, or until the meat is very tender and the sauce is glossy. Serve with steamed new potatoes or mash.

NUTRITION PER SERVE
Protein 65 g; Fat 20 g; Carbohydrate 9.5 g; Dietary Fibre 3 g; Cholesterol 169 mg; 2363 kJ (563 cal)

NOTE: To make a bouquet garni, wrap the green part of a leek around a bay leaf, a sprig of thyme, a sprig of parsley and celery leaves, and tie with string. The combination of herbs can be varied according to taste.

Remove the peel and pith from the orange, and cut the flesh into segments.

Brown the chicken breasts and chorizo slices in the hot oil.

MADRID CHICKEN

Preparation time: 10 minutes
Total cooking time: 1 hour
Serves 4

1 orange
1 tablespoon olive oil
4 chicken breasts (skin and excess
   fat removed)
2 chorizo sausages (about 200 g/
   6¹/₂ oz), cut into 1 cm (¹/₂ inch) slices
1 cup (250 ml/8 fl oz) chicken stock
1 cup (250 g/8 oz) bottled tomato
   pasta sauce
12 Kalamata olives
Kalamata olives, extra, to garnish
fresh flat-leaf parsley, to garnish

1 Using a vegetable peeler, carefully cut 4 thin strips of orange rind (about 1 x 4 cm/¹/₂ x 1¹/₂ inches). Remove the peel and pith from the orange, and segment the flesh.
2 Heat the oil in a saucepan and brown the chicken and chorizo slices, in batches if necessary. (Leave the meat side of the chicken browning for 5 minutes.) Add the stock, tomato sauce and orange rind. Bring to the boil, then reduce the heat and simmer, covered, for 25 minutes.
3 Remove the lid, turn the chicken over and continue to simmer, uncovered, for about 25 minutes, or until the chicken is tender and the sauce reduced. Season with salt and freshly ground black pepper, and stir through the olives and orange segments. Garnish with extra olives and flat-leaf parsley.

NUTRITION PER SERVE
Protein 75 g; Fat 30 g; Carbohydrate 12 g; Dietary Fibre 3.5 g; Cholesterol 250 mg; 2553 kJ (610 cal)

NOTE: Chorizo sausages can be replaced with any spicy sausages.

Use strong kitchen scissors to cut through the sides of each bug tail.

Pull back the shell and pull out the bug flesh in one piece.

CREAMY GARLIC SEAFOOD STEW

Preparation time: 20 minutes
Total cooking time: 20 minutes
Serves 6

12 scallops, with roe
500 g (1 lb) skinless firm white fish fillets
(see NOTE)
6 raw Balmain bugs or crabs
500 g (1 lb) raw medium prawns
50 g (1³⁄₄ oz) butter
1 onion, finely chopped
5–6 large cloves garlic, finely chopped
¹⁄₂ cup (125 ml/4 fl oz) white wine
2 cups (500 ml/16 fl oz) cream
1¹⁄₂ tablespoons Dijon mustard
2 teaspoons lemon juice
2 tablespoons chopped fresh flat-leaf parsley

1 Slice or pull off any membrane or hard muscle from the scallops. Cut the fish into 2 cm (³⁄₄ inch) cubes. Cut the heads off the bugs, then use kitchen scissors to cut down around the sides of the tail so you can flap open the shell. Remove the flesh in one piece, then slice each piece in half. Peel and devein the prawns. Refrigerate all the seafood, covered, until ready to use.

2 Melt the butter in a frying pan and cook the onion and garlic over medium heat for 2 minutes, or until the onion is softened (be careful not to burn the garlic—it may turn bitter).

3 Add the wine to the pan and cook for 4 minutes, or until reduced by half. Stir in the cream, mustard and lemon juice, and simmer for 5–6 minutes, or until reduced to almost half.

4 Add the prawns to the pan and cook for 1 minute, then add the bug meat and cook for another minute, or until white. Add the fish and cook for 2 minutes, or until cooked through (the flesh will flake easily when tested with a fork). Finally, add the scallops and cook for 1 minute. If any of the seafood is still not cooked, cook for another minute or so, but be careful not to overcook as this will result in tough flesh. Remove the frying pan from the heat and toss the parsley through. Season to taste. Serve with salad and bread.

NUTRITION PER SERVE

Protein 39 g; Fat 46 g; Carbohydrate 4 g; Dietary Fibre 1 g; Cholesterol 316 mg; 2460 kJ (585 cal)

NOTE: Try using perch, ling, bream, tuna or blue-eye.

Cut between the head and the tentacles of the octopus.

Slit the head section and remove any gut from the inside.

GREEK OCTOPUS STEW

Preparation time: 25 minutes
Total cooking time: 1 hour 10 minutes
Serves 4–6

1 kg (2 lb) baby octopus
2 tablespoons olive oil
1 large onion, chopped
3 cloves garlic, crushed
1 bay leaf
3 cups (750 ml/24 fl oz) red wine
1/4 cup (60 ml/2 fl oz) red wine vinegar
400 g (13 oz) can crushed tomatoes
1 tablespoon tomato paste
1 tablespoon chopped fresh oregano
1/4 teaspoon ground cinnamon
small pinch ground cloves
1 teaspoon sugar
2 tablespoons finely chopped fresh
    flat-leaf parsley

1 Cut between the head and tentacles of the octopus, just below the eyes. Grasp the body and push the beak out and up through the centre of the tentacles with your fingers. Cut the eyes from the head by slicing off a small round. Discard the eye section. Carefully slit through one side, avoiding the ink sac, and remove any gut from inside. Rinse the octopus well under running water.

2 Heat the oil in a large saucepan, add the onion and cook over medium heat for 5 minutes, or until starting to brown. Add the garlic and bay leaf, and cook for 1 minute further. Add the octopus and stir to coat in the onion mixture.

3 Stir in the wine, vinegar, tomato, tomato paste, oregano, cinnamon, cloves and sugar. Bring to the boil, then reduce the heat and simmer for 1 hour, or until the octopus is tender and the sauce has thickened slightly. Stir in the parsley and season with salt and ground black pepper. Serve with a Greek salad and crusty bread to mop up the delicious juices.

NUTRITION PER SERVE (6)
Protein 29 g; Fat 8.5 g; Carbohydrate 3.5 g; Dietary Fibre 1.5 g; Cholesterol 332 mg; 1234 kJ (295 cal)

Halve the kidneys and remove the cores and fat.
Slice in half again.

Add half the Muscat to the onion and mushrooms,
and simmer for 3–4 minutes.

STEAK AND KIDNEY STEW

Preparation time: 35 minutes
Total cooking time: 2 hours 30 minutes
Serves 4–6

1 kg (2 lb) chuck steak, trimmed
8 lamb's kidneys
¼ cup (60 ml/2 fl oz) oil
1 rasher bacon, rind removed, cut
  into long, thin strips
40 g (1¼ oz) butter
1 large onion, chopped
300 g (10 oz) button mushrooms, halved
1 cup (250 ml/8 fl oz) Muscat
2–3 cloves garlic, crushed
¼ teaspoon ground allspice
½ teaspoon paprika
2 teaspoons coriander seeds, lightly crushed
1 tablespoon wholegrain mustard
1 cup (250 ml/8 fl oz) beef stock

2–3 tablespoons soft brown sugar
1–2 teaspoons fresh thyme
1–2 teaspoons fresh rosemary

1 Cut the steak into 2–3 cm (1 inch) cubes.
Cut the kidneys in half, remove the core and any
fat, then slice them in half again.
2 Heat 1 teaspoon of the oil in a large, heavy-
based saucepan. Add the bacon and cook
over medium heat until just crisp. Remove and
set aside.
3 Heat 2 tablespoons of the oil and 30 g (1 oz)
of the butter in the pan. Brown the steak cubes
in batches, then set aside.
4 Add the onion to the pan and cook for
3 minutes, or until soft and golden. Add the
mushrooms and cook, stirring, for 3 minutes,
until starting to brown. Stir in half the Muscat
and simmer for 3–4 minutes. Remove and
set aside.

5 Add the remaining oil and butter to the pan.
Stir in the garlic, allspice, paprika and
coriander, and cook for 1 minute. Add the
kidney and cook until just starting to brown. Stir
in the mustard and remaining Muscat, and
simmer for 2 minutes.
6 Stir in the bacon, steak, onion and
mushrooms. Stir in the stock, bring to the boil,
then reduce the heat, cover and simmer for
1 hour. Add the sugar. Simmer, covered, for
40 minutes, then uncovered for 20 minutes,
stirring in the herbs during the last 10 minutes.

NUTRITION PER SERVE (6)
Protein 40 g; Fat 20 g; Carbohydrate 15 g;
Dietary Fibre 2 g; Cholesterol 155 mg;
1830 kJ (440 cal)

Fry the eggplant in batches over high heat until browned on both sides.

Add the cider to the frying pan, scraping the brown bits from the side and base.

PORK AND EGGPLANT HOTPOT

Preparation time: 20 minutes
Total cooking time: 1 hour 40 minutes
Serves 4

olive oil, for cooking
375 g (12 oz) slender eggplant, cut into
    3 cm (1¼ inch) slices
8 bulb spring onions
400 g (13 oz) can chopped tomatoes
2 cloves garlic, crushed
2 teaspoons ground cumin
500 g (1 lb) pork fillet, cut into 3 cm
    (1¼ inch) thick slices
seasoned plain flour
⅔ cup (170 ml/5½ fl oz) cider
1 sprig fresh rosemary
2 tablespoons finely chopped toasted
    almonds

1 Heat ¼ cup (60 ml/2 fl oz) of oil in a large, heavy-based frying pan. Brown the eggplant in batches over high heat, adding oil as needed. Remove and set aside.
2 Quarter the spring onions along their length. Add some oil to the pan and fry the spring onion over medium heat for 5 minutes. Add the tomato, garlic and cumin, and cook for 2 minutes. Remove and set aside.
3 Coat the pork in the seasoned flour, shaking off any excess. Brown in batches over medium–high heat until golden, adding oil as needed. Remove and set aside.
4 Add the cider to the pan and stir well, scraping down the side and base. Allow to boil for 1–2 minutes, then add ½ cup (125 ml/ 4 fl oz) water. Reduce the heat and stir in the spring onion and tomato. Add the pork, season, and poke the rosemary sprig into the stew. Partially cover and simmer gently for 20 minutes.
5 Layer the eggplant on top, partially cover and cook for 25 minutes, or until the pork is tender. Just before serving, gently toss the almonds through.

NUTRITION PER SERVE
Protein 30 g; Fat 7 g; Carbohydrate 10 g; Dietary Fibre 5 g; Cholesterol 60 mg; 980 kJ (235 cal)

Coat the lamb in the spice marinade, then leave for 1 hour.

Cook the lamb in batches over high heat for 2–3 minutes, or until browned.

LAMB TAGINE

**Preparation time: 15 minutes +
    1 hour marinating**
Total cooking time: 1 hour 45 minutes
Serves 6–8

1.5 kg (3 lb) leg or shoulder of lamb, cut into
    2.5 cm (1 inch) pieces
3 cloves garlic, chopped
1/3 cup (80 ml/2¾ fl oz) olive oil
2 teaspoons ground cumin
1 teaspoon ground ginger
1 teaspoon ground turmeric
1 teaspoon paprika
1/2 teaspoon ground cinnamon
2 onions, thinly sliced
600 ml (20 fl oz) beef stock
1/4 preserved lemon, pulp discarded, rind
    rinsed and cut into thin strips
425 g (14 oz) can chickpeas, drained

35 g (1¼ oz) cracked green olives
1/4 cup (15 g/1/2 oz) chopped fresh coriander
    leaves

1 Place the lamb pieces in a non-metallic bowl, add the chopped garlic, 2 tablespoons of the olive oil and the ground cumin, ginger, turmeric, paprika, cinnamon, and 1/2 teaspoon ground black pepper and 1 teaspoon salt. Mix well to coat, then leave to marinate for 1 hour.
2 Heat the remaining olive oil in a large saucepan, add the lamb in batches and cook over high heat for 2–3 minutes, or until browned. Remove from the pan. Add the onion and cook for 2 minutes, then return the meat to the pan and add the beef stock. Reduce the heat and simmer, covered, for 1 hour.
3 Add the preserved lemon strips, drained chickpeas and olives, and cook, uncovered, for a further 30 minutes, or until the lamb is tender and the sauce has reduced and thickened. Stir in the coriander. Serve in bowls with couscous.

NUTRITION PER SERVE (8)
Protein 50 g; Fat 20 g; Carbohydrate 11 g;
Dietary Fibre 5.5 g; Cholesterol 124 mg;
1765 kJ (422 cal)

Roll up the cabbage leaf, tucking in the sides to enclose the filling.

CABBAGE ROLLS

Preparation time: 30 minutes
Total cooking time: 1 hour 35 minutes
Makes 12 large rolls

1 tablespoon olive oil
1 onion, finely chopped
large pinch allspice
1 teaspoon ground cumin
large pinch ground nutmeg
2 bay leaves
1 large head of cabbage
500 g (1 lb) lamb mince
1 cup (220 g/7 oz) short-grain rice
4 cloves garlic, crushed
⅓ cup (50 g/1¾ oz) toasted pine nuts
2 tablespoons finely chopped fresh mint
2 tablespoons finely chopped
    fresh flat-leaf parsley
1 tablespoon finely chopped raisins
1 cup (250 ml/8 fl oz) olive oil, extra

⅓ cup (80 ml/2¾ fl oz) lemon juice
extra virgin olive oil, to drizzle
lemon wedges, to serve

1 Heat the oil in a saucepan, add the onion and cook over medium heat for 10 minutes, or until golden. Add the allspice, cumin and nutmeg, and cook for 2 minutes, or until fragrant. Remove from the pan.
2 Bring a very large saucepan of water to the boil and add the bay leaves. Remove the tough outer leaves and about 5 cm (2 inches) of the core from the cabbage with a sharp knife, then place the cabbage into the boiling water. Cook for 5 minutes, then carefully loosen a whole leaf with tongs and remove. Continue to cook and remove the leaves until you reach the core. Drain, reserving the cooking liquid, and set aside to cool.

3 Take 12 equal-size leaves and cut a small 'v' from the core end of each leaf to remove the thickest part, then trim the firm central veins so that the leaf is as flat as possible. Place three-quarters of the remaining leaves into a very large saucepan to prevent the rolls catching on the base.
4 Combine the mince, onion mixture, rice, garlic, pine nuts, mint, parsley and raisins in a bowl, and season well. With the core end of the leaf closest to you, form 2 tablespoons of the mince mixture into an oval and place in the centre of the leaf. Roll up, tucking in the sides to enclose the filling. Repeat with the other 11 leaves and filling. Place the rolls tightly in a single layer in the lined saucepan, seam-side down.
5 Combine 2½ cups (625 ml/20 fl oz) of the cooking liquid with the extra olive oil, lemon juice and 1 teaspoon salt, and pour over the rolls (the liquid should just come to the top of the rolls). Lay the remaining leaves on top. Cover and bring to the boil, then reduce the heat and simmer for 1¼ hours, or until the filling is cooked. Remove with a slotted spoon and drizzle with extra virgin olive oil. Serve with lemon wedges.

NUTRITION PER ROLL
Protein 13 g; Fat 26 g; Carbohydrate 20 g;
Dietary Fibre 4 g; Cholesterol 28 mg;
1510 kJ (360 cal)

MOROCCAN SEAFOOD WITH CORIANDER

Preparation time: 50 minutes
Total cooking time: 50 minutes
Serves 6

2 tablespoons olive oil
2 red onions, roughly chopped
1 red capsicum, chopped
4 cloves garlic, crushed
2 teaspoons ground cumin
1 teaspoon ground coriander
2 teaspoons sweet paprika
$1/2$ teaspoon dried chilli flakes
1 cup (250 ml/8 fl oz) chicken or fish stock
425 g (14 oz) can chopped tomatoes
$1/3$ cup (80 ml/$2^3/4$ fl oz) orange juice
1 tablespoon sugar
$1/4$ cup (40 g/$1^1/4$ oz) seedless raisins
375 g (12 oz) baby new potatoes
500 g (1 lb) baby octopus, cleaned
12 raw king prawns, peeled and deveined,
   tails intact
1 kg (2 lb) thick white fish fillets, cut into
   chunks

CORIANDER PUREE
1 cup (30 g/1 oz) fresh coriander leaves
2 tablespoons ground almonds
$1/3$ cup (80 ml/$2^3/4$ fl oz) extra virgin olive oil
$1/2$ teaspoon ground cumin
1 teaspoon honey

1 Heat the olive oil in a large saucepan and cook the onion over medium heat for about 5 minutes, or until soft. Add the capsicum and garlic, and cook for another minute. Add the cumin, coriander, paprika and chilli flakes, and cook until fragrant.

2 Pour in the stock, tomato, orange juice, sugar and raisins, and bring to the boil. Add the potatoes, reduce the heat to low and gently simmer for 20–30 minutes, or until the potatoes are just tender. Season to taste.

3 Use a small sharp knife to remove the octopus heads; slit the heads open and remove the gut. Grasp the body firmly and push the beak out with your index finger; remove and discard. Add the octopus, prawns and fish to the pan and cook, covered, for 10 minutes, or until the fish flakes when tested with a fork.

4 To make the coriander purée, place the coriander leaves and ground almonds in a food processor. With the motor running, drizzle in the oil and process until smooth, then add the cumin, honey and salt to taste. Process until well combined.

5 To serve, dish the stew onto serving plates and drizzle a spoonful of purée on top. Serve with couscous and a green leaf salad.

NUTRITION PER SERVE
Protein 60 g; Fat 30 g; Carbohydrate 25 g;
Dietary Fibre 4 g; Cholesterol 175 mg;
2415 kJ (580 cal)

Peel and devein the prawns, and cut the cleaned octopus into bite-sized pieces.

Process the coriander leaves and ground almonds, gradually drizzling in the oil.

Grill the tomatoes until the skin is black and blistered and it will peel away easily.

Once the tortillas are crisp, break into pieces and put in the food processor.

MEXICAN BEEF STEW

Preparation time: 30 minutes
Total cooking time: 1 hour 30 minutes
Serves 6

500 g (1 lb) Roma tomatoes, halved
6 flour tortillas
1–2 fresh red chillies, finely chopped
1 tablespoon olive oil
1 kg (2 lb) stewing beef, cubed
$1/2$ teaspoon black pepper
2 onions, thinly sliced
$1^{1}/_{2}$ cups (375 ml/12 fl oz) beef stock
$1/4$ cup (60 g/2 oz) tomato paste
375 g (12 oz) can kidney beans, drained
1 teaspoon chilli powder
$1/2$ cup (125 g/4 oz) sour cream

1 Preheat the oven to moderate 180°C (350°F/Gas 4). Grill the tomatoes, skin-side up, under a hot grill for 6–8 minutes, or until the skin is black and blistered. Cool, remove the skin and roughly chop the flesh.

2 Bake 2 of the tortillas for 4 minutes, or until crisp. Break into pieces and put in a food processor with the tomato and chilli. Process for 30 seconds, or until almost smooth.

3 Heat the oil in a large heavy-based saucepan. Brown the beef in batches, season with pepper, then remove. Add the onion to the pan and cook for 5 minutes. Return the meat to the pan. Stir in the processed mixture, stock and tomato paste, and bring to the boil. Reduce the heat, cover and simmer for $1^{1}/_{4}$ hours. Add the beans and chilli powder, and heat through.

4 Grill the remaining tortillas for 2–3 minutes on each side, then cool and cut into wedges. Serve the stew with the sour cream, and toasted tortilla wedges on the side.

NUTRITION PER SERVE

Protein 50 g; Fat 20 g; Carbohydrate 40 g; Dietary Fibre 8 g; Cholesterol 125 mg; 2235 kJ (535 cal)

HINT: If this stew becomes thick during cooking, thin it with a little extra stock.

Stir the garlic and spices into the pan with the onion, and cook for 1 minute.

Add the crushed tomato, stock and burghul to the pan.

VEGETARIAN CHILLI

**Preparation time: 15 minutes +
    10 minutes soaking**
Total cooking time: 40 minutes
Serves 6–8

³/₄ cup (130 g/4¹/₂ oz) burghul (cracked
    wheat)
2 tablespoons olive oil
1 large onion, finely chopped
2 cloves garlic, crushed
1 teaspoon chilli powder
2 teaspoons ground cumin
1 teaspoon cayenne pepper
¹/₂ teaspoon ground cinnamon
2 x 400 g (13 oz) cans crushed tomatoes
3 cups (750 ml/24 fl oz) vegetable stock
440 g (14 oz) can red kidney beans, rinsed
    and drained
2 x 300 g (10 oz) cans chickpeas, rinsed
    and drained
310 g (10 oz) can corn kernels, drained
2 tablespoons tomato paste
corn chips and sour cream

1 Soak the burghul with 1 cup (250 ml/8 fl oz) hot water for 10 minutes. Heat the oil in a large heavy-based saucepan and cook the onion for 10 minutes, stirring often, until soft and golden.
2 Add the garlic, chilli powder, cumin, cayenne and cinnamon, and cook, stirring, for 1 minute.
3 Add the tomato, stock and burghul. Bring to the boil and simmer for 10 minutes. Stir in the beans, drained chickpeas, corn and tomato paste, and simmer for 20 minutes, stirring often. Serve with corn chips and sour cream.

NUTRITION PER SERVE (8)
Protein 7 g; Fat 10 g; Carbohydrate 18 g;
Dietary Fibre 7 g; Cholesterol 8 mg;
780 kJ (185 cal)

Add the chicken mince to the onion and cook until browned, breaking up any lumps.

Stir the tomato, tomato paste and water into the chicken mixture.

CHILLI CON POLLO

Preparation time: 10 minutes
Total cooking time: 45 minutes
Serves 4

1 tablespoon olive oil
1 onion, finely chopped
500 g (1 lb) chicken mince
1–2 teaspoons mild chilli powder
440 g (14 oz) can chopped tomatoes
2 tablespoons tomato paste
1–2 teaspoons soft brown sugar
425 g (14 oz) can red kidney beans, rinsed
    and drained

1 Heat the oil in a large saucepan. Add the chopped onion and cook over medium heat for 3 minutes, or until soft. Increase the heat to high and add the chicken mince. Cook until the chicken has browned, breaking up any lumps with a wooden spoon.

2 Add the chilli powder to the chicken and cook for 1 minute. Stir in the tomato, tomato paste and ½ cup (125 ml/4 fl oz) water.

3 Bring to the boil, then reduce the heat and simmer for 30 minutes. Stir through the sugar to taste and the kidney beans. Season. Serve with corn chips or in taco shells with sour cream.

NUTRITION PER SERVE
Protein 37 g; Fat 8.5 g; Carbohydrate 20 g;
Dietary Fibre 9 g; Cholesterol 60 mg;
1305 kJ (312 cal)

Add the tomato to the capsicum mixture, and simmer until it thickens.

Simmer until the liquid has been absorbed and the chicken is tender.

SPANISH CHICKEN AND RICE STEW

Preparation time: 10 minutes
Total cooking time: 1 hour
Serves 4

¼ cup (60 ml/2 fl oz) olive oil

4 chicken thighs and 6 drumsticks

1 large red onion, finely chopped

1 large green capsicum, two-thirds diced and one-third julienned

3 teaspoons sweet paprika

400 g (13 oz) can diced tomatoes

1¼ cups (275 g/9 oz) paella or arborio rice (see NOTE)

½ teaspoon ground saffron

1 Heat 2 tablespoons of the oil in a large deep frying pan over high heat. Season the chicken pieces well and brown in batches. Remove the chicken from the pan.

2 Reduce the heat to medium and add the remaining oil. Add the onion and the diced capsicum, and cook gently for 5 minutes. Stir in the sweet paprika and cook for 30 seconds. Add the tomato and simmer for 1–3 minutes, or until it thickens.

3 Stir in 3½ cups (875 ml/28 fl oz) boiling water, then add the rice and saffron. Return the chicken to the pan and stir to combine. Season to taste. Bring to the boil, then cover, reduce the heat to medium–low and simmer for 20–30 minutes, or until the liquid has been absorbed and the chicken is tender. Stir in the julienned capsicum, then allow to stand, covered, for 3–4 minutes before serving.

NUTRITION PER SERVE
Protein 92 g; Fat 45 g; Carbohydrate 57 g; Dietary Fibre 2.5 g; Cholesterol 433 mg; 4150 kJ (990 cal)

NOTE: Paella rice is a medium round grain from Spain. Calasparra is the most commonly available variety and can be purchased from fine food stores or Spanish delicatessens.

Peel the skin away from the crosses cut in the base of the tomatoes.

Cook the eggplant until softened but not browned, then remove.

RATATOUILLE

Preparation time: 30 minutes
Total cooking time: 40 minutes
Serves 4–6

100 ml (3¹/₂ fl oz) olive oil
500 g (1 lb) eggplant, cut into 2 cm (³/₄ inch)
   cubes
375 g (12 oz) zucchini, cut into 2 cm
   (³/₄ inch) slices
1 green capsicum, seeded, cut into
   2 cm (³/₄ inch) cubes
1 red onion, cut into 2 cm (³/₄ inch) wedges
3 cloves garlic, finely chopped
¹/₄ teaspoon cayenne pepper
2 teaspoons chopped fresh thyme
2 bay leaves
6 vine-ripened tomatoes, peeled and
   roughly chopped
1 tablespoon red wine vinegar
1 teaspoon caster sugar
¹/₄ cup (15 g/¹/₂ oz) shredded fresh basil

1 Heat 2 tablespoons of the oil in a large saucepan and cook the eggplant over medium heat for 4–5 minutes, or until soft but not browned. Remove all the eggplant from the pan.
2 Add 2 tablespoons oil to the pan and cook the zucchini slices for 3–4 minutes, or until softened. Remove the zucchini from the pan. Add the capsicum to the pan, cook for 2 minutes, then remove.
3 Heat the remaining oil in the pan, add the onion wedges and cook for 2–3 minutes, or until softened. Add the garlic, cayenne pepper, thyme and bay leaves, and cook, stirring, for 1 minute. Return the cooked eggplant, zucchini and capsicum to the pan, and add the tomato, vinegar and sugar. Simmer for 20 minutes, stirring occasionally. Stir in the basil and season with salt and black pepper. Serve hot or cold.

NUTRITION PER SERVE (6)
Protein 4 g; Fat 17 g; Carbohydrate 8.5 g;
Dietary Fibre 5.5 g; Cholesterol 0 mg;
826 kJ (197 cal)

NOTE: Ratatouille takes quite a long time to prepare and so is traditionally made in large quantities. It is then eaten over several days as an hors d'oeuvre, side dish or main meal.

Fill the squid hoods three-quarters full with the stuffing mixture.

Cook the stuffed squid hoods in a frying pan on all sides.

STUFFED SQUID STEW

Preparation time: 50 minutes
Total cooking time: 50 minutes
Serves 4

100 ml (3¹/₂ fl oz) olive oil
1 large onion, finely chopped
2 cloves garlic, crushed
1 cup (80 g/2³/₄ oz) fresh breadcrumbs
1 egg, lightly beaten
60 g (2 oz) kefalotyri cheese, grated
60 g (2 oz) haloumi cheese, grated
4 large or 8 small squid (1 kg/2 lb), cleaned
   (see NOTE)
1 small onion, finely chopped, extra
2 cloves garlic, crushed, extra
500 g (1 lb) firm ripe tomatoes, peeled
   and diced
150 ml (5 fl oz) red wine
1 tablespoon chopped fresh oregano
1 tablespoon chopped fresh flat-leaf parsley

1 Heat 2 tablespoons of the oil in a frying pan, add the onion and cook over medium heat for 3 minutes. Remove. Combine with the garlic, breadcrumbs, egg and cheese. Season.

2 Pat the squid hoods dry with paper towels and, using a teaspoon, fill them three-quarters full with the stuffing. Do not pack them too tightly or the stuffing mixture will swell and burst out during cooking. Secure the ends with wooden toothpicks.

3 Heat the remaining oil in a large frying pan, add the squid and cook for 1–2 minutes on all sides. Remove. Add the extra onion and cook over medium heat for 3 minutes, or until soft, then add the extra garlic and cook for a further 1 minute. Stir in the tomato and wine, and simmer for 10 minutes, or until thick and pulpy, then stir in the oregano and parsley. Return the squid to the pan and cook, covered, for 20–25 minutes, or until tender. Serve warm with the tomato sauce or cool with a salad.

NUTRITION PER SERVE
Protein 57 g; Fat 35 g; Carbohydrate 30 g;
Dietary Fibre 4 g; Cholesterol 558 mg;
2890 kJ (690 cal)

NOTE: Ask the fishmonger to clean the squid. Or, discard the tentacles and cartilage. Rinse the hoods under running water and pull off the skin.

Toss the veal strips in the flour, shaking off any excess flour.

Return the meat to the pan with the mustard, cream, wine, thyme and stock.

CREAMY VEAL AND MUSHROOM STEW

Preparation time: 20 minutes
Total cooking time: 2 hours
Serves 4

750 g (1½ lb) veal steaks, cut into
   1 cm (½ inch) strips
¼ cup (30 g/1 oz) plain flour
30 g (1 oz) butter
1 clove garlic, crushed
1 tablespoon Dijon mustard
1 cup (250 ml/8 fl oz) cream
½ cup (125 ml/4 fl oz) white wine
1 tablespoon chopped fresh thyme
1 cup (250 ml/8 fl oz) chicken stock
375 g (12 oz) button mushrooms, halved

1 Toss the meat in the flour, shaking off the excess. Heat the butter and garlic in a heavy-based saucepan. Add the meat and cook quickly in small batches over medium heat until well browned. Drain on paper towels.
2 Return the meat to the pan and add the mustard, cream, wine, thyme and stock. Bring to the boil, then reduce the heat and simmer, covered, for 1½ hours, stirring occasionally.
3 Add the mushrooms and cook for a further 15 minutes, or until the meat is tender. Delicious served with pasta and steamed vegetables.

NUTRITION PER SERVE
Protein 47 g; Fat 38 g; Carbohydrate 8.5 g; Dietary Fibre 3 g; Cholesterol 258 mg; 2425 kJ (580 cal)

Make two deep cuts in the thickest part of the chicken drumsticks.

Add the crushed garlic, lemon rind and rosemary to the drumsticks.

LEMON AND ROSEMARY CHICKEN STEW

Preparation time: 10 minutes
Total cooking time: 30 minutes
Serves 4

8 large chicken drumsticks
60 g (2 oz) butter
2 cloves garlic, crushed
2 teaspoons finely grated lemon rind
2 tablespoons chopped fresh rosemary
1 tablespoon plain flour
1¹/₂ cups (375 ml/12 fl oz) chicken stock
2 tablespoons lemon juice

1 Using a sharp knife, make two deep cuts in the thickest part of each chicken drumstick.
2 Melt the butter in a large frying pan. Add the drumsticks and cook over medium heat for 2 minutes on each side, or until brown. Add the garlic, lemon rind and rosemary.
3 Blend the flour, stock and lemon juice until smooth. Add to the pan and bring to the boil. Reduce the heat and simmer, covered, for 25 minutes, or until the drumsticks are tender, stirring occasionally. Season, and serve immediately.

NUTRITION PER SERVE
Protein 68 g; Fat 54 g; Carbohydrate 3.5 g; Dietary Fibre 0.5 g; Cholesterol 430 mg; 3205 kJ (765 cal)

HINT: To check whether chicken is cooked, insert a skewer into the thickest part. If the juice runs clear, the chicken is cooked.

Twist each sausage tightly in opposite directions so that it forms two short fat sausages.

Cook until all the water in the pan has evaporated and the sausages are lightly browned.

PORK SAUSAGE AND WHITE BEAN STEW

Preparation time: 25 minutes + overnight soaking
Total cooking time: 1 hour 40 minutes
Serves 4

350 g (11 oz) dried white haricot beans
150 g (5 oz) tocino, speck or pancetta, unsliced
1/2 leek, thinly sliced
2 cloves garlic
1 bay leaf
1 small fresh red chilli, halved and seeded
1 small onion
2 cloves
1 sprig fresh rosemary
3 sprigs fresh thyme
1 sprig fresh parsley
1/4 cup (60 ml/2 fl oz) olive oil
8 pork sausages
1/2 onion, finely chopped
1 green capsicum, finely chopped
1/2 teaspoon paprika
1/2 cup (125 ml/4 fl oz) tomato purée
1 teaspoon cider vinegar

1 Soak the beans overnight in cold water. Drain and rinse the beans under cold water. Put them in a large saucepan with the tocino, leek, garlic, bay leaf and chilli. Stud the onion with the cloves and add to the saucepan. Tie the rosemary, thyme and parsley together, and add to the saucepan. Pour in 3 cups (750 ml/ 24 fl oz) cold water and bring to the boil. Add 1 tablespoon of the oil, reduce the heat and simmer, covered, for about 1 hour, or until the beans are tender. When necessary, add a little more boiling water to keep the beans covered.

2 Prick each sausage 5 or 6 times and twist tightly in opposite directions in the middle to give 2 short fat sausages joined in the middle. Put in a single layer in a large frying pan and add enough cold water to reach halfway up their sides. Bring to the boil and simmer, turning two or three times, until all the water has evaporated and the sausages brown lightly in the little fat that is left in the pan. Remove from the pan and cut the short sausages apart. Add the remaining oil, the chopped onion and green capsicum to the pan, and fry over medium heat for 5–6 minutes. Stir in the paprika, cook for 30 seconds, then add the tomato purée. Season to taste. Cook, stirring, for 1 minute.

3 Remove the tocino, herb sprigs and any loose large pieces of onion from the bean mixture. Leave in any loose leaves from the herbs and any small pieces of onion. Add the sausages and sauce to the pan, and stir the vinegar through. Bring to the boil. Adjust the seasoning.

NUTRITION PER SERVE
Protein 39 g; Fat 51 g; Carbohydrate 43 g; Dietary Fibre 20 g; Cholesterol 99 mg; 3195 kJ (765 cal)

Return the duck to the pan with the processed sauce mixture.

Grind the almonds, garlic and brandy in a mortar and pestle or in a blender.

DUCK WITH PEARS

Preparation time: 20 minutes
Total cooking time: 1 hour 40 minutes
Serves 4

2 tablespoons olive oil
4 duck breasts
2 red onions, finely diced
1 carrot, finely diced
2 teaspoons fresh thyme
1 cup (250 ml/8 fl oz) chicken stock
2 ripe tomatoes, peeled, seeded and diced
4 green, firm pears, peeled, halved and
    cored (leaving the stems intact)
1 cinnamon stick
60 g (2 oz) blanched almonds,
    toasted, chopped
1 clove garlic
100 ml (3½ fl oz) brandy

1 Heat the oil in a heavy-based frying pan and cook the duck, skin-side down first, over medium heat until brown all over. Remove and set aside, reserving 4 tablespoons of the cooking fat.
2 Return 2 tablespoons of the fat to the pan. Add the onion, carrot and thyme, and cook over medium heat for 5 minutes, or until the onion has softened. Add the stock and tomato and bring to the boil. Reduce the heat and simmer for 30 minutes, with the lid slightly askew, or until the sauce has thickened and reduced. Cool slightly, then purée in a food processor until smooth. Return to the pan with the duck. Simmer gently over low heat for 30–40 minutes, or until the duck is tender.
3 While the duck is cooking, place the pears in a saucepan with the cinnamon and just cover with cold water. Bring to the boil, reduce the heat and simmer gently for 5 minutes, or until the pears are tender but still firm to the bite. Remove the pears, cover to keep warm and add ½ cup (125 ml/4 fl oz) of the pear poaching liquid to the tomato sauce.

4 Remove the duck from the sauce and keep warm. Grind the almonds, garlic and brandy together in a mortar and pestle or blender to make a smooth paste. Add to the tomato sauce, season, and cook for another 10 minutes.
5 Arrange the duck pieces on a serving plate and pour the sauce over the top. Arrange the warmed pears around the duck, and serve.

NUTRITION PER SERVE
Protein 45 g; Fat 54 g; Carbohydrate 27 g; Dietary Fibre 6.5 g; Cholesterol 250 mg; 3415 kJ (815 cal)

NOTE: The sauce adds an interesting finish to this Spanish dish, which is traditionally made with goose.

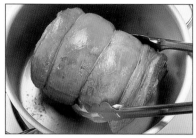

Cook the meat in the oil over medium–high heat until it is browned all over.

Add the stock to the pan with the wine, brandy, onion, garlic, tomato and herbs.

BEEF POT ROAST PROVENCALE

Preparation time: 15 minutes
Total cooking time: 2 hours 15 minutes
Serves 6

2 tablespoons oil
2 kg (4 lb) rolled beef brisket, trimmed
3 cups (750 ml/24 fl oz) beef stock
1 cup (250 ml/8 fl oz) red wine
1/4 cup (60 ml/2 fl oz) brandy
2 onions, quartered
3 cloves garlic, crushed
3 tomatoes, peeled, seeded and chopped
2 bay leaves
1/4 cup (15 g/1/2 oz) chopped fresh parsley
2 tablespoons fresh thyme leaves
12 pitted black olives
6 small carrots, thickly sliced
2 tablespoons plain flour

1 Heat the oil in a deep heavy-based saucepan. Cook the meat over medium–high heat until browned all over, then remove from the heat.
2 Add the stock to the pan with the wine, brandy, onion, garlic, tomato, bay leaves, parsley and thyme. Cover and bring to simmering point over low heat. Simmer for 1 1/2 hours.
3 Add the olives and carrot, and cook for 30 minutes. Remove the meat and leave it in a warm place, covered with foil, for 10 minutes before slicing.
4 Combine the flour and 1/4 cup (60 ml/2 fl oz) water to make a smooth paste. Add to the sauce, stir over medium heat until the sauce thickens, and cook for 3 minutes. Pour over the sliced meat to serve.

NUTRITION PER SERVE
Protein 70 g; Fat 11 g; Carbohydrate 11.5 g; Dietary Fibre 2.5 g; Cholesterol 150 mg; 2005 kJ (480 cal)

Toss the meat in the seasoned flour, shaking off the excess.

Cook the meat in batches until well browned, then drain on paper towels.

BRAISED BEEF IN RED WINE

Preparation time: 10 minutes
Total cooking time: 2 hours
Serves 6

¼ cup (30 g/1 oz) plain flour
¼ teaspoon ground black pepper
1 kg (2 lb) lean round or chuck steak, cut into 3 cm (1¼inch) cubes
1 tablespoon oil
15 g (½ oz) butter
12 baby onions
1 cup (250 ml/8 fl oz) beef stock
1 cup (250 ml/8 fl oz) red wine
2 tablespoons tomato paste
1 tablespoon French mustard
1 bay leaf
¼ teaspoon mixed dried herbs

1 Combine the flour and pepper. Toss the meat in the seasoned flour, shaking off the excess.
2 Heat the oil and butter in a heavy-based saucepan. Cook the meat quickly in batches over medium–high heat until well browned. Drain on paper towels.
3 Add the onions to the pan and cook over medium heat until golden brown. Return the meat to the pan and stir in the stock, wine, tomato paste, mustard and herbs. Bring to the boil, then reduce the heat and simmer, covered, for 1½ hours, or until the meat is tender, stirring occasionally.

NUTRITION PER SERVE
Protein 37 g; Fat 10 g; Carbohydrate 7.5 g; Dietary Fibre 1.5 g; Cholesterol 110 mg; 1235 kJ (295 cal)

Peel the skin from the tomatoes, then remove the seeds and chop.

Simmer the dhal mixture for 45 minutes, or until the split peas are soft.

SPICY VEGETABLE STEW WITH DHAL

**Preparation time: 25 minutes +
    2 hours soaking**
Total cooking time: 1 hour 35 minutes
Serves 4–6

DHAL
³/₄ cup (165 g/5¹/₂ oz) yellow split peas
5 cm (2 inch) piece fresh ginger, grated
2–3 cloves garlic, crushed
1 fresh red chilli, seeded and chopped

2 tablespoons oil
1 teaspoon yellow mustard seeds
1 teaspoon cumin seeds
1 teaspoon ground cumin
¹/₂ teaspoon garam masala
1 red onion, cut into thin wedges
3 tomatoes, peeled, seeded and chopped
3 slender eggplants, cut into 2 cm
    (³/₄ inch) slices

2 carrots, cut into 2 cm (³/₄ inch) slices
¹/₄ cauliflower, cut into florets
1¹/₂ cups (375 ml/12 fl oz) vegetable stock
2 small zucchini, cut into 3 cm
    (1¹/₄ inch) slices
¹/₂ cup (80 g/2³/₄ oz) frozen peas
¹/₂ cup (15 g/¹/₂ oz) fresh coriander leaves

1 To make the dhal, place the split peas in a bowl, cover with water and soak for 2 hours. Drain. Place in a large saucepan with the ginger, garlic, chilli and 3 cups (750 ml/24 fl oz) water. Bring to the boil, then reduce the heat and simmer for 45 minutes, or until soft.
2 Heat the oil in a large saucepan. Cook the spices over medium heat for 30 seconds, or until fragrant. Add the onion and cook for a further 2 minutes, or until the onion is soft. Stir in the tomato, eggplant, carrot and cauliflower.

3 Add the dhal purée and stock, mix together well and simmer, covered, for 45 minutes, or until the vegetables are tender. Stir occasionally. Add the zucchini and peas during the last 10 minutes of cooking. Stir in the coriander leaves and serve hot.

NUTRITION PER SERVE (6)
Protein 11 g; Fat 7 g; Carbohydrate 20 g;
Dietary Fibre 8.5 g; Cholesterol 17 mg;
780 kJ (186 cal)

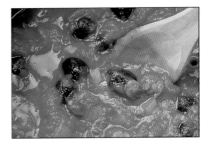

Simmer the chunky tomato sauce, stirring occasionally, until thick.

Cook the mussels until they open, and discard any that don't open.

MUSSEL AND TOMATO STEW

Preparation time: 15 minutes
Total cooking time: 30 minutes
Serves 4–6

1.5 kg (3 lb) black mussels
1/4 cup (60 ml/2 fl oz) olive oil
1 large onion, diced
4 cloves garlic, finely chopped
810 g (1 lb 10 oz) can diced tomatoes
1/4 cup (60 g/2 oz) tomato paste
1/4 cup (30 g/1 oz) pitted black olives
1 tablespoon capers
1/2 cup (125 ml/4 fl oz) fish stock
1/4 cup (7 g/1/4oz) chopped fresh
    flat-leaf parsley

1 Scrub the mussels with a stiff brush and pull out the hairy beards. Discard any damaged mussels, or those that don't close when tapped on the bench.

2 In a large saucepan, heat the olive oil and cook the onion and garlic over medium heat for 1–2 minutes, until softened. Add the tomato, tomato paste, olives, capers and fish stock. Bring to the boil, then reduce the heat and simmer, stirring occasionally, for 20 minutes, or until the sauce is thick.

3 Stir in the mussels and cover the saucepan. Shake or toss the mussels occasionally, and cook for 4–5 minutes, or until the mussels begin to open. Once they have all opened, remove the pan from the heat. Discard any unopened mussels.

4 Just before serving, toss the parsley through. Serve with crusty bread.

NUTRITION PER SERVE (6)
Protein 17 g; Fat 14 g; Carbohydrate 11 g;
Dietary Fibre 3 g; Cholesterol 35 mg;
973 kJ (233 cal)

MONGOLIAN LAMB HOTPOT

Preparation time: 15 minutes +
**   10 minutes soaking**
Total cooking time: 5 minutes
Serves 6

250 g (8 oz) dried rice vermicelli
600 g (1¼ lb) lamb backstraps, thinly sliced
    across the grain
4 spring onions, sliced
1.5 litres light chicken stock
3 cm x 6 cm (1¼ inch x 2½ inch) piece
    fresh ginger, cut into 6 slices
2 tablespoons Chinese rice wine
300 g (10 oz) silken firm tofu, cut into
    1.5 cm (⅝ inch) cubes
300 g (10 oz) Chinese broccoli, cut into
    4 cm (1½ inch) lengths
2 cups (90 g/3 oz) shredded Chinese
    cabbage

SAUCE
⅓ cup (80 ml/2¾ fl oz) light soy sauce
2 tablespoons Chinese sesame paste
1 tablespoon Chinese rice wine
1 teaspoon chilli and garlic paste

1 Place the vermicelli in a large heatproof
bowl, cover with boiling water and soak for
6–7 minutes. Drain well and divide among six
serving bowls. Top with the lamb slices and
spring onion.
2 To make the sauce, combine the soy sauce,
sesame paste, rice wine and the chilli and garlic
paste in a small bowl.
3 Place the stock, ginger and rice wine in a
2.5 litre flameproof hotpot or large saucepan.
Cover and bring to the boil over high heat. Add
the tofu, Chinese broccoli and Chinese cabbage
and simmer, uncovered, for 1 minute, or until
the broccoli has wilted. Divide the tofu, broccoli
and cabbage among the serving bowls, then
ladle on the hot stock. Drizzle a little of the
sauce on top and serve the rest on the side.

NUTRITION PER SERVE
Protein 36 g; Fat 16 g; Carbohydrate 32 g;
Dietary Fibre 4 g; Cholesterol 68 mg;
1770 kJ (425 cal)

NOTES: Make sure the stock is hot enough to
cook the thin slices of lamb.

This recipe traditionally uses a Chinese
steamboat—this is an aluminium pot with a
steam spout in the middle, placed on a propane
burner in the middle of the dining table. You
could use a fondue pot instead.

Cook the chicken pieces in batches until they are browned all over.

Simmer the chicken and stock, covered, until the chicken is cooked through.

CHICKEN WITH BALSAMIC VINEGAR

Preparation time: 5 minutes
Total cooking time: 50 minutes
Serves 4

2 tablespoons olive oil
8 (1.2 kg/2 lb 6½ oz) chicken pieces
½ cup (125 ml/4 fl oz) chicken stock
½ cup (125 ml/4 fl oz) dry white wine
½ cup (125 ml/4 fl oz) balsamic vinegar
40 g (1¼oz) chilled butter

1 Heat the oil in a large casserole dish over medium heat and cook the chicken, in batches, for 7–8 minutes, or until browned. Pour off any excess fat.

2 Add the stock, bring to the boil, then reduce the heat and simmer, covered, for 30 minutes, or until the chicken is cooked through.

3 Add the white wine and vinegar and increase the heat to high. Boil for 1 minute, or until the liquid has thickened. Remove from the heat, stir in the butter until melted, and season. Spoon the sauce over the chicken to serve, accompanied by roast potatoes and salad.

NUTRITION PER SERVE
Protein 40 g; Fat 25 g; Carbohydrate 0.5 g; Dietary Fibre 0 g; Cholesterol 165 mg; 1790 kJ (430 cal)

NOTE: Use a good-quality balsamic vinegar, as the cheaper varieties can be too acidic.

Grill the capsicums under a hot grill until the skin blackens and blisters.

Remove the skin from the cooked capsicums and slice them into thin strips.

ITALIAN SAUSAGE AND CHICKPEA STEW

Preparation time: 15 minutes
Total cooking time: 45 minutes
Serves 4

2 large red capsicums
1 tablespoon olive oil
2 large red onions, cut into thick wedges
2 cloves garlic, finely chopped
600 g (1¼lb) Italian-style thin pork sausages
300 g (10 oz) can chickpeas, drained
150 g (5 oz) flat mushrooms, thickly sliced
½ cup (125 ml/4 fl oz) dry white wine
2 bay leaves
2 teaspoons chopped fresh rosemary
400 g (13 oz) can diced tomatoes

1 Cut the capsicums into large pieces, removing the seeds and membrane. Place skin-side up, under a hot grill until the skin blackens and blisters. Allow to cool in a plastic bag. Peel away the skin, and slice diagonally into thick strips.

2 Meanwhile, heat the oil in a large non-stick frying pan. Add the onion and garlic, and stir over medium heat for 6 minutes, or until the onion is soft and browned. Remove the onion from the pan and set aside. Add the sausages to the same pan. Cook over medium heat, turning occasionally, for 8 minutes, or until the sausages are browned. Remove the sausages from the pan and slice diagonally into 3 cm (1¼ inch) pieces.

3 Combine the capsicum slices, onion, sausage pieces, chickpeas and mushrooms in the pan, and cook over medium–high heat.

4 Add the wine, bay leaves and rosemary to the pan. Bring to the boil, then reduce the heat to low and simmer for 3 minutes. Stir in the tomato and simmer for 20 minutes, or until the sauce has thickened slightly. Remove the bay leaves and season to taste with sugar, salt and cracked black pepper. Delicious served with fettuccine, noodles, grilled ciabatta bread, mashed potato, soft polenta or Parmesan shavings.

NUTRITION PER SERVE

Protein 20 g; Fat 25 g; Carbohydrate 25 g; Dietary Fibre 9.5 g; Cholesterol 50 mg; 1695 kJ (405 cal)

Put the baby brown onions in a bowl and cover with boiling water.

Add the butter and meat to the pan, and brown the meat well on all sides.

BEEF POT ROAST

Preparation time: 15 minutes
Total cooking time: 3 hours 15 minutes
Serves 6

300 g (10 oz) baby brown onions
2 carrots
3 parsnips, peeled
40 g (1¼ oz) butter
1–1.5 kg (2–3 lb) eye of silverside, trimmed
  of fat (see NOTE)
¼ cup (60 ml/2 fl oz) dry red wine
1 large tomato, finely chopped
1 cup (250 ml/8 fl oz) beef stock
mild or hot English mustard, to serve

1 Put the onions in a heatproof bowl and cover with boiling water. Leave for 1 minute, then drain well. Allow to cool, then peel off the skins.
2 Cut the carrots and parsnips in half lengthways, then into even-sized pieces. Heat half the butter in a large heavy-based saucepan that will tightly fit the meat (it will shrink during cooking), add the onions, carrot and parsnip, and cook, stirring, over medium–high heat until browned. Remove from the pan. Add the remaining butter to the pan and add the meat, browning well all over. Increase the heat to high and pour in the wine. Bring to the boil, then add the tomato and stock. Return to the boil, then reduce the heat to low, cover and simmer for 2 hours, turning once. Add the vegetables and simmer, covered, for 1 hour.
3 Remove the meat from the pan and put it on a board ready for carving. Cover with foil and leave it to stand while finishing the sauce.

4 Increase the heat to high and boil the pan juices with the vegetables for 10 minutes to reduce and thicken slightly. Skim off any excess fat, and taste before seasoning. Slice the meat and arrange on a serving platter or individual serving plates with the vegetables. Drizzle generously with the pan juices. Serve with mustard.

NUTRITION PER SERVE
Protein 60 g; Fat 10 g; Carbohydrate 95 g; Dietary Fibre 3.5 g; Cholesterol 185 mg; 1690 kJ (405 cal)

NOTE: Eye of silverside is a tender, long-shaped cut of silverside that carves easily into serving-sized pieces. A regular piece of silverside or topside may be substituted.

When the oil and butter are foaming, add the mushrooms and cook until soft.

Brown the chicken pieces in batches over high heat until the skin is golden and crisp.

CREAMY TOMATO AND CHICKEN STEW

Preparation time: 35 minutes
Total cooking time: 50 minutes
Serves 4–6

4 rashers bacon
2 tablespoons oil
50 g (1¾ oz) butter
300 g (10 oz) small button mushrooms, halved
1.5 kg (3 lb) chicken pieces
2 onions, chopped
2 cloves garlic, crushed
400 g (13 oz) can tomatoes
1 cup (250 ml/8 fl oz) chicken stock
1 cup (250 ml/8 fl oz) cream
2 tablespoons chopped fresh parsley
2 tablespoons fresh lemon thyme leaves

1 Chop the bacon into large pieces. Place a large, heavy-based saucepan over medium heat. Brown the bacon, stirring, then remove and set aside on paper towels.

2 Heat half the oil and one-third of the butter in the saucepan until foaming, then add the mushrooms and cook until they are softened and golden brown. Remove from the pan with a slotted spoon.

3 Add the remaining oil to the pan with a little more butter. When the oil is hot, brown the chicken pieces in batches over high heat until the skin is golden all over and a little crisp. Remove the chicken pieces from the pan and drain on paper towels.

4 Heat the remaining butter in the pan. Add the onion and garlic, and cook over medium–high heat for about 3 minutes, or until softened. Pour in the tomatoes, stock and cream. Return the bacon, mushrooms and chicken pieces to the pan, and simmer over medium–low heat for 25 minutes. Stir in the parsley and thyme, season with salt and freshly ground pepper, and simmer for another 5 minutes before serving.

NUTRITION PER SERVE (6)
Protein 70 g; Fat 40 g; Carbohydrate 7 g; Dietary Fibre 3 g; Cholesterol 215 mg; 2650 kJ (630 cal)

Toss the lamb cubes in the flour, shaking off any excess flour.

Brown the lamb in small batches, turning occasionally, then drain on paper towels.

LAMB AND MUSTARD STEW

Preparation time: 15 minutes
Total cooking time: 1 hour 40 minutes
Serves 4

750 g (1¹/₂ lb) lean lamb fillets, cut into
   2.5 cm (1 inch) cubes
¹/₂ cup (60 g/2 oz) plain flour
1 tablespoon oil
16 baby onions
1 cup (250 ml/8 fl oz) white wine
1 cup (250 ml/8 fl oz) chicken stock
¹/₂ cup (125 g/4 oz) Dijon mustard
2 tablespoons chopped fresh thyme

1 Toss the lamb cubes in the flour, shaking off any excess. Heat the oil in a heavy-based saucepan over high heat. Add the lamb in small batches and cook for 3 minutes, or until well browned, turning occasionally. Drain on paper towels.
2 Return the lamb to the pan. Add the onions, wine, stock, mustard and thyme. Bring to the boil, then reduce the heat to low and simmer, covered, for 1 hour, stirring occasionally. Remove the lid and simmer for another 30 minutes, or until the lamb is tender. Serve with pasta.

NUTRITION PER SERVE
Protein 46 g; Fat 11 g; Carbohydrate 18 g;
Dietary Fibre 2.5 g; Cholesterol 124 mg;
1655 kJ (395 cal)

NOTE: A small, boned leg of lamb is ideal for this dish.

Stir the onion, pork and paprika until the pork is browned on all sides.

Add the beef stock to the saucepan and bring to the boil.

PORK AND LENTIL STEW

Preparation time: 20 minutes
Total cooking time: 1 hour
Serves 4

1 tablespoon olive oil
2 onions, chopped
500 g (1 lb) lean diced pork
2 teaspoons sweet Hungarian paprika
1 teaspoon hot paprika
$1/2$ teaspoon dried thyme
2 tablespoons tomato paste
2 teaspoons soft brown sugar
$1/4$ cup (60 g/2 oz) red lentils
$1\frac{1}{2}$ cups (375 ml/12 fl oz) beef stock
1 tomato
2 tablespoons low-fat plain yoghurt

1 Heat the olive oil in a large, deep saucepan over high heat. Add the onion, pork and paprikas, and stir for 3–4 minutes, or until browned.

2 Add the thyme, tomato paste, sugar, lentils, stock, and salt and freshly ground black pepper. Bring to the boil, then reduce the heat to very low and cook, covered, for 20 minutes, stirring occasionally to prevent sticking. Uncover and cook for another 15–20 minutes, or until thickened.

3 Remove from the heat and set aside for 10 minutes. Cut the tomato in half and scoop out the seeds. Slice the flesh into thin strips.

4 Just before serving, stir the yoghurt into the stew. Scatter with the tomato strips and serve with rice, if desired.

NUTRITION PER SERVE
Protein 35 g; Fat 8 g; Carbohydrate 13 g; Dietary Fibre 4 g; Cholesterol 70 mg; 1110 kJ (265 cal)

Chop the carrots into small pieces, and thinly slice the celery sticks.

Dry-fry the spices over low heat, stirring the spices and shaking the pan.

PORK, BEER AND CHICKPEA STEW

Preparation time: 35 minutes
Total cooking time: 1 hour 30 minutes
Serves 4

2 teaspoons ground cumin
1 teaspoon ground coriander
1/2 teaspoon chilli powder
1/4 teaspoon ground cinnamon
400 g (13 oz) lean diced pork, trimmed
1 tablespoon plain flour
1 tablespoon olive oil
1 large onion, finely chopped
3 cloves garlic, finely chopped
2 large carrots, chopped
2 celery sticks, sliced
1/2 cup (125 ml/4 fl oz) chicken stock
1/2 cup (125 ml/4 fl oz) beer
2 ripe tomatoes, chopped

310 g (10 oz) can chickpeas, rinsed
   and drained
2 tablespoons chopped fresh parsley

1 Cook the cumin, coriander, chilli powder and cinnamon in a dry frying pan over low heat, shaking the pan, for 1 minute, or until aromatic.
2 Combine the pork with the spices and flour in a plastic bag, and toss well. Remove the pork and shake off any excess flour. Heat the oil in a large heavy-based saucepan over high heat and cook the pork, tossing regularly, for 8 minutes, or until lightly browned.
3 Add the onion, garlic, carrot, celery and half the stock to the pan, and toss well. Cover and cook for 10 minutes. Add the remaining stock, beer and tomato, and season with salt and pepper. Bring to the boil, then reduce the heat, cover with a tight-fitting lid and simmer over low heat for 1 hour. Gently shake the pan occasionally, but do not remove the lid during cooking. Stir in the chickpeas and parsley. Simmer, uncovered, for 5 minutes before serving.

NUTRITION PER SERVE
Protein 40 g; Fat 10 g; Carbohydrate 35 g; Dietary Fibre 15 g; Cholesterol 50 mg; 1720 kJ (410 cal)

AUTUMN VEGETABLE STEW

Preparation time: 25 minutes
Total cooking time: 30 minutes
Serves 4–6

185 g (6 oz) frozen broad beans, thawed
150 g (5 oz) baby onions
50 g (1¾ oz) butter
2 teaspoons olive oil
400 g (13 oz) small parsnips
150 g (5 oz) Jerusalem artichokes
2 tablespoons plain flour
2⅓ cups (580 ml/19 fl oz) chicken stock
300 ml (10 fl oz) cream
2 teaspoons grated lemon rind
1 teaspoon grated orange rind
400 g (13 oz) baby carrots, trimmed
500 g (1 lb) baby turnips, trimmed

1 Peel and discard the tough outer skin of the broad beans. Carefully peel the onions, leaving the flat root end attached, then cut a cross through the root end of each onion.
2 Heat the butter and oil in a large, heavy-based saucepan until foamy. Add the onions and cook for 7 minutes over low–medium heat, turning often to color evenly.

3 While the onions are browning, peel the parsnips and artichokes, and cut them into bite-size pieces. Add to the saucepan and toss well. Scatter the flour over the onion, parsnip and artichokes, toss to coat and cook for 2 minutes.
4 Stir in the chicken stock, cream, lemon rind and orange rind. Bring to the boil, stirring, then reduce the heat and simmer for 7 minutes, or until the vegetables are half-cooked.
5 Add the carrots and turnips, and toss well. Cover the pan and cook for 4–5 minutes, or until the vegetables are just tender. Season well with salt and freshly ground pepper, stir in the peeled broad beans to heat through, and serve.

NUTRITION PER SERVE (6)
Protein 7 g; Fat 30 g; Carbohydrate 25 g; Dietary Fibre 10 g; Cholesterol 90 mg; 1665 kJ (400 cal)

NOTES: Baby vegetables have a sweet, delicate flavor. If unavailable, choose the smallest vegetables and cook them for a few minutes longer.

Fresh broad beans can be used. Add them with the carrots and turnips.

Skin the broad beans and cut a cross through the root end of the peeled onions.

Peel the small parsnips and Jerusalem artichokes, and cut into bite-sized pieces.

Carefully cut between the head and the tentacles of the octopus, just below the eyes.

Carefully slit through one side of the head, avoiding the ink sac, and scrape out any gut.

PROVENCALE OCTOPUS

Preparation time: 25 minutes
Total cooking time: 1 hour 30 minutes
Serves 6

1 kg (2 lb) baby octopus
¹/₄ cup (60 ml/2 fl oz) olive oil
1 large brown onion, chopped
2 cloves garlic
500 g (1 lb) ripe tomatoes, peeled, seeded and chopped
1¹/₃ cups (330 ml/11 fl oz) dry white wine
¹/₄ teaspoon saffron threads
2 sprigs fresh thyme
2 tablespoons roughly chopped fresh flat-leaf parsley

1 To clean the octopus, use a small sharp knife and cut each head from the tentacles. Remove the eyes by cutting a round of flesh from the base of each head. To clean the heads, carefully slit them open and remove the gut. Rinse thoroughly. Cut the heads in half. Push out the beaks from the centre of the tentacles from the cut side. Cut the tentacles into sets of four or two, depending on the size of the octopus.
2 Blanch all the octopus in boiling water for 2 minutes, then drain and allow to cool slightly. Pat dry with paper towels.
3 Heat the olive oil in a heavy-based frying pan and cook the onion for 7–8 minutes over medium heat until lightly golden. Add the octopus and garlic to the pan, and cook for another 2–3 minutes. Add the tomato, wine, saffron and thyme. Add just enough water to cover the octopus.

4 Simmer, covered, for 1 hour. Uncover and cook for another 15 minutes, or until the octopus is tender and the sauce has thickened a little. The cooking time will vary depending upon the size of the octopus. Season to taste. Serve hot or at room temperature, sprinkled with chopped parsley.

NUTRITION PER SERVE
Protein 29 g; Fat 10.5 g; Carbohydrate 4.5 g; Dietary Fibre 1.5 g; Cholesterol 89 mg; 1120 kJ (270 cal)

Using a sharp knife, cut the green beans into long slices.

Add the chickpeas, pig's trotter and chorizo to the saucepan.

COCINO MADRILENO

Preparation time: 25 minutes + overnight soaking
Total cooking time: 2 hours 45 minutes
Serves 6–8

1 cup (220 g/7 oz) dried chickpeas
1 kg (2 lb) chicken, trussed
500 g (1 lb) piece lean beef brisket
250 g (8 oz) piece smoke-cured bacon
125 g (4 oz) tocino, streaky bacon or speck
1 pig's trotter
200 g (6¹/₂ oz) chorizo
1 onion, studded with 2 cloves
1 bay leaf
1 morcilla blood sausage (optional)
250 g (8 oz) green beans, sliced lengthways
250 g (8 oz) green cabbage, cut into sections through the heart
300 g (10 oz) silverbeet leaves, stalks removed
4 small potatoes
2 leeks, cut into 10 cm (4 inch) lengths
pinch saffron threads
75 g (2¹/₂ oz) dried rice vermicelli

1 Soak the chickpeas in cold water overnight. Drain and rinse. Tie loosely in a muslin bag.
2 Put 3 litres cold water in a very large, deep saucepan. Add the chicken, beef, bacon and tocino, and bring to the boil. Add the chickpeas, pig's trotter and chorizo, return to the boil, then add the onion, bay leaf and ¹/₂ teaspoon salt. Simmer, partially covered, for 2¹/₂ hours.
3 After 2 hours, bring a saucepan of water to the boil, add the morcilla and gently boil for 5 minutes. Drain and set aside. Tie the green beans loosely in a muslin bag. Pour 1 litre water into a large saucepan and bring to the boil. Add the beans, cabbage, silverbeet, potatoes, leek and saffron with 1 teaspoon of salt. Return to the boil and simmer for 30 minutes.

4 Strain the stock from both the meat and vegetable pans, and combine in a large saucepan. Bring to the boil, adjust the seasoning and add the vermicelli. Simmer for 6–7 minutes. Release the chickpeas and pile them in the centre of a large warm platter. Discard the tocino, then slice the meats and sausages. Arrange the meats and sausages in groups around the chickpeas at one end of the platter. Release the beans. Arrange the vegetables in groups around the other end. Spoon a little of the simmering broth (minus the vermicelli) over the meat, then pour the rest (with the vermicelli) into a soup tureen. Serve at once. It is traditional to serve the two dishes together, although the broth is eaten first.

NUTRITION PER SERVE (8)
Protein 51 g; Fat 27 g; Carbohydrate 26 g; Dietary Fibre 8 g; Cholesterol 158 mg; 2290 kJ (545 cal)

Use a sharp knife to score the thickest part of the chicken drumsticks.

Add the stock to the chicken and wine mixture, then cover and bring to the boil.

BRAISED CHICKEN AND LEEK IN WINE

Preparation time: 15 minutes
Total cooking time: 1 hour
Serves 4

2 tablespoons oil
1.2 kg (2 lb 6½ oz) chicken pieces
1 leek, thinly sliced
5 spring onions, thinly sliced on the diagonal
2 tablespoons fresh marjoram
150 ml (5 fl oz) white wine
400 ml (13 fl oz) chicken stock
100 ml (3½ fl oz) cream

1 Score the chicken drumsticks. Heat 1 tablespoon of the oil in a frying pan and cook the chicken pieces in batches for 3–4 minutes, or until browned.

2 Heat the remaining oil in a large casserole dish and cook the leek, spring onion and marjoram for 4 minutes, or until soft. Add the chicken and wine, and cook for 2 minutes. Add the stock, cover and bring to the boil. Reduce the heat and simmer for 30 minutes. Stir in the cream and simmer, uncovered, for 15 minutes, or until the chicken is tender. Season to taste. Serve with steamed rice.

NUTRITION PER SERVE
Protein 48 g; Fat 30 g; Carbohydrate 2.5 g; Dietary Fibre 1 g; Cholesterol 190 mg; 2065 kJ (493 cal)

Cook the chicken and spring onion until the chicken is golden.

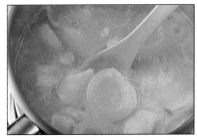

Add the apricot juice, apricots and stock to the pan, and bring to the boil.

SPICY APRICOT CHICKEN

Preparation time: 10 minutes
Total cooking time: 20 minutes
Serves 4

750 g (1½ lb) chicken thigh fillets,
    cut into 5 cm (2 inch) pieces
plain flour, for coating
2 tablespoons oil
2 teaspoons red curry paste (page 250)
2 spring onions, sliced
415 g (13 oz) can apricot halves in
    light syrup
½ cup (125 ml/4 fl oz) chicken stock
200 g (6½ oz) plain yoghurt
2 tablespoons chopped fresh
    coriander leaves
fresh coriander leaves, extra, to garnish

1 Lightly coat the chicken in the flour. Heat the oil in a saucepan, add the curry paste and stir over low heat for 1 minute. Add the spring onion and chicken, and cook, stirring, over medium heat for 2–3 minutes, or until the chicken is golden.

2 Drain the apricots and reserve ½ cup (125 ml/4 fl oz) apricot juice. Add the reserved juice, apricots and stock to the pan. Bring to the boil, then reduce the heat and simmer for 10 minutes, or until the chicken is tender.

3 Mix together the yoghurt and coriander, and place a spoonful of the mixture over each serving of chicken. Garnish with extra coriander leaves. Serve with couscous or rice.

NUTRITION PER SERVE
Protein 45 g; Fat 15 g; Carbohydrate 15 g; Dietary Fibre 2 g; Cholesterol 100 mg; 1622 kJ (388 cal)

Remove the lobster meat from the shell and cut it into small pieces.

When the onion is soft, add the chopped mushrooms, tomato, liquids and herbs.

CIOPPINO (SEAFOOD STEW)

**Preparation time: 30 minutes +
    30 minutes soaking**
Total cooking time: 1 hour
Serves 4

2 dried mushrooms
1 kg (2 lb) firm white fish fillets
375 g (12 oz) raw king prawns
1 raw lobster tail
12 mussels
¼ cup (60 ml/2 fl oz) olive oil
1 large onion, finely chopped
1 green capsicum, finely chopped
2–3 cloves garlic, crushed
425 g (14 oz) can crushed tomatoes
1 cup (250 ml/8 fl oz) white wine
1 cup (250 ml/8 fl oz) tomato juice
1 cup (250 ml/8 fl oz) fish stock
    (see NOTE)
1 bay leaf

2 sprigs fresh parsley
6 fresh basil leaves, chopped
1 tablespoon chopped fresh parsley

1 Soak the mushrooms in boiling water for 20 minutes. Cut the fish into bite-size pieces, removing any bones. Peel and devein the prawns, leaving the tails intact. Remove the meat from the lobster shell and cut into small pieces. Discard any open mussels; scrub the rest, remove the beards, then soak in cold water for 10 minutes. Drain the mushrooms, squeeze dry and chop finely.

2 Heat the oil in a heavy-based saucepan. Cook the onion, capsicum and garlic over medium heat, stirring, for about 5 minutes, or until the onion is soft. Add the mushrooms, tomato, wine, tomato juice, stock, bay leaf, parsley sprigs and chopped basil. Bring to the boil, reduce the heat, then cover and simmer for 30 minutes.

3 Layer the fish and prawns in a large pan. Add the sauce mixture, then cover and leave on low heat for 10 minutes, or until the prawns are pink and the fish is cooked. Add the lobster and mussels, and simmer for 2–3 minutes. Season to taste. Discard any unopened mussels, sprinkle with parsley, and serve with crusty bread.

NUTRITION PER SERVE
Protein 100 g; Fat 25 g; Carbohydrate 8 g; Dietary Fibre 3 g; Cholesterol 460 mg; 2905 kJ (695 cal)

NOTE: You can make your own fish stock for this recipe by simmering the trimmings from the fish, lobster and prawns in 1¼ cups (310 ml/10 fl oz) water for about 20 minutes, then straining the liquid.

Cut the steak into 3 cm (11/4 inch) cubes, using a sharp knife.

Add the brandy, stock, Worcestershire sauce and mustard to the onion mixture.

BEEF AND PEPPERCORN STEW

Preparation time: 15 minutes
Total cooking time: 2 hours
Serves 4

1 kg (2 lb) chuck steak, cut into 3 cm
   (1¼ inch) cubes
2 teaspoons cracked black peppercorns
40 g (1¼ oz) butter
2 tablespoons oil
1 large onion, thinly sliced
2 cloves garlic, sliced
1½ tablespoons plain flour
2 tablespoons brandy
3 cups (750 ml/24 fl oz) beef stock
1 tablespoon Worcestershire sauce
2 teaspoons Dijon mustard
500 g (1 lb) baby new potatoes
¼ cup (60 ml/2 fl oz) cream
2 tablespoons chopped fresh parsley

1 Toss the steak in the peppercorns. Heat half the butter and half the oil in a large heavy-based saucepan. Brown half the steak over high heat, then remove and set aside. Heat the remaining butter and oil, and brown the remaining steak. Remove from the pan and set aside.

2 Add the onion and garlic to the pan and cook, stirring, until the onion is golden. Add the flour and stir until browned. Remove from the heat.

3 Combine the brandy, beef stock, Worcestershire sauce and mustard, and gradually stir into the onion mixture. Return to the heat, add the steak and any juices, then simmer, covered, for 1¼ hours.

4 Add the potatoes and simmer, uncovered, for a further 30 minutes, or until the meat and potatoes are tender. Stir in the cream and parsley, and season to taste with salt and freshly ground pepper.

NUTRITION PER SERVE
Protein 60 g; Fat 30 g; Carbohydrate 20 g; Dietary Fibre 3 g; Cholesterol 215 mg; 2580 kJ (615 cal)

SICHUAN CHICKEN

Preparation time: 10 minutes
Total cooking time: 25 minutes
Serves 4

¹/₄ teaspoon five-spice powder
750 g (1¹/₂ lb) chicken thigh fillets, halved
2 tablespoons peanut oil
1 tablespoon julienned fresh ginger
1 teaspoon Sichuan peppercorns, crushed
1 teaspoon chilli bean paste (toban djan)
2 tablespoons light soy sauce
1 tablespoon Chinese rice wine
1¹/₄ cups (250 g/8 oz) jasmine rice
600 g (1¹/₄ lb) baby bok choy, leaves
    separated

1 Sprinkle the five-spice powder over the halved chicken fillets. Heat a wok until very hot, add half the oil and swirl to coat the side. Add the chicken pieces and cook for 2 minutes each side, or until browned. Remove from the wok.
2 Reduce the heat to medium. Add the julienned ginger to the wok and cook for 30 seconds. Add the crushed Sichuan peppercorns and chilli bean paste. Return the chicken pieces to the wok, add the soy sauce, wine and ¹/₂ cup (125 ml/4 fl oz) water, then simmer for 15–20 minutes, or until the chicken is cooked through.
3 Meanwhile, bring a large saucepan of water to the boil. Add the rice and cook for 12 minutes, stirring occasionally. Drain well.
4 Heat the remaining peanut oil in a saucepan. Add the baby bok choy and toss gently for 1 minute, or until the leaves wilt and the stems are tender. Serve with the chicken and boiled rice.

NUTRITION PER SERVE
Protein 42 g; Fat 24 g; Carbohydrate 52 g;
Dietary Fibre 2.5 g; Cholesterol 163 mg;
2465 kJ (590 cal)

MOROCCAN CHICKEN

Preparation time: 10 minutes +
5 minutes standing
Total cooking time: 35 minutes
Serves 4

1 tablespoon Moroccan spice blend
800 g (1 lb 10 oz) chicken thigh fillets,
 halved
1 tablespoon oil
60 g (2 oz) butter
1 large onion, cut into wedges
1 cinnamon stick
2 cloves garlic, crushed
2 tablespoons lemon juice
1 cup (250 ml/8 fl oz) chicken stock
¹/₃ cup (75 g/2¹/₂ oz) pitted prunes, halved
1¹/₂ cups (280 g/9 oz) couscous
lemon wedges, to serve

1 Sprinkle half the spice blend over the chicken. Heat the oil and 20 g (³/₄ oz) of the butter in a large deep-sided frying pan over medium heat. Cook the chicken in batches for 5 minutes, or until evenly browned. Remove from the pan, then add the onion and cinnamon stick, and cook for 2–3 minutes before adding the garlic. Return the chicken to the pan and add the lemon juice and the remaining spice blend. Season to taste, then cook, covered, for 5 minutes.

2 Add the stock and prunes to the pan, and bring to the boil. Reduce the heat to medium–low and cook, uncovered, for 15 minutes, or until the chicken is cooked and the liquid has reduced to a sauce. Before serving, stir 20 g (³/₄ oz) of the butter into the sauce.

3 About 10 minutes before the chicken is ready, place the couscous in a heatproof bowl, add 1¹/₂ cups (375 ml/12 fl oz) boiling water and stand for 3–5 minutes. Stir in the remaining butter and fluff with a fork until the butter has melted and the grains have separated. Serve with the chicken and lemon wedges.

Cook the chicken pieces in batches until they are evenly browned.

NUTRITION PER SERVE

Protein 47 g; Fat 32 g; Carbohydrate 56 g;
Dietary Fibre 3 g; Cholesterol 213 mg;
2905 kJ (695 cal)

NOTE: Depending on the quality and freshness of the Moroccan spice blend you buy, you may need to use a little more than specified in the recipe.

TURKEY OSSO BUCO

Preparation time: 25 minutes + thawing
Total cooking time: 1 hour 30 minutes
Serves 4–6

3 red capsicums
2.1 kg (4 lb 3 oz) frozen turkey hindquarters
  (legs with thighs), chopped (see NOTES)
seasoned plain flour
¼ cup (60 ml/2 fl oz) olive oil
60 g (2 oz) butter
¾ cup (185 ml/6 fl oz) chicken stock
¼ teaspoon dried chilli flakes
4 fresh sage leaves, chopped, or
  ½ teaspoon dried sage
2 cloves garlic, crushed
1 teaspoon finely grated lemon rind
150 g (5 oz) sliced pancetta, or thinly
  sliced bacon
1 sprig fresh rosemary
2 tablespoons chopped fresh flat-leaf parsley

1 Preheat the grill to high. Cut the capsicums in half, then remove the seeds and membranes. Place the capsicum halves skin-side up under the grill and cook for 5–8 minutes, or until the skin blackens and blisters. Transfer to a plastic bag, seal and allow to cool, then peel away the blackened skin. Cut the flesh into thick slices.
2 Thaw the turkey pieces in a single layer in the refrigerator. When they have thawed, pat the turkey pieces well with paper towels to remove all the excess moisture, then coat them well in the seasoned flour, dusting off any excess.
3 Heat the oil and butter in a large saucepan. Brown the turkey pieces in batches over medium–high heat, then drain the pan of excess oil.
4 Pour the chicken stock into the pan and stir well, scraping the base and side of the pan to mix in all the pan juices. Add the chilli flakes, sage, garlic and lemon rind, and cook, stirring, for 1 minute.
5 Return all the turkey pieces to the pan. Cover with the grilled capsicum slices, then layer the pancetta over the top to completely cover. Add the rosemary sprig, cover the pan and cook over low heat for 1 hour, or until the turkey is succulent, yet not falling off the bone.
6 Discard the rosemary sprig and transfer the pancetta, capsicum slices and turkey pieces to a serving plate. Cover and keep warm. If the sauce is a little thin, place it over high heat and simmer for 3–4 minutes to thicken. Stir in the chopped parsley, adjust the seasoning if necessary, then spoon the sauce around the turkey to serve.

NUTRITION PER SERVE (6)
Protein 65 g; Fat 55 g; Carbohydrate 5 g; Dietary Fibre 2 g; Cholesterol 345 mg; 4265 kJ (1020 cal)

NOTES: Ask your butcher or poulterer to saw the frozen turkey into 1.5–2 cm (¾ inch) pieces for you.

Pancetta is an Italian unsmoked bacon, rolled and cured with salt and spices, sold in many delicatessens. You could use prosciutto instead.

In batches, brown the turkey in the hot oil and butter over medium–high heat.

Cook the beef in the hot oil until it is well browned all over.

Add the stock, onion, garlic, tomato, cumin, turmeric, lemon rind and juice to the beef.

BEEF POT ROAST WITH EGGPLANT

Preparation time: 20 minutes
Total cooking time: 1 hour 25 minutes
Serves 4

2 tablespoons oil
1 kg (2 lb) piece lean topside beef
1 cup (250 ml/8 fl oz) beef stock
1 onion, sliced
1 clove garlic, crushed
4 large tomatoes, peeled, seeded and
  chopped
1 teaspoon ground cumin
1 teaspoon ground turmeric
1 teaspoon finely grated lemon rind
2 tablespoons lemon juice
1 medium eggplant, cut into 3 cm
  (1¼ inch) cubes

1 sweet potato, halved and cut into
  1 cm (½ inch slices)
2 tablespoons plain flour
1 tablespoon chopped fresh coriander

1 Heat the oil in a deep heavy-based saucepan. Add the meat and cook over medium–high heat until well browned on all sides.
2 Remove the pan from the heat and add the stock, onion, garlic, tomato, cumin, turmeric, lemon rind and lemon juice. Cover, bring slowly to simmering point over low heat and simmer for 45 minutes.
3 Add the eggplant and sweet potato, and cook, uncovered, for 30 minutes, or until the meat and vegetables are tender. Remove the meat and leave it in a warm place, covered with foil, for 10 minutes before slicing.
4 Combine the flour and ¼ cup (60 ml/2 fl oz) water to make a smooth paste. Add to the sauce with the coriander, stir over medium heat until the sauce boils and thickens, and cook for 3 minutes. Pour over the sliced meat to serve.

NUTRITION PER SERVE
Protein 60 g; Fat 18 g; Carbohydrate 18 g; Dietary Fibre 4.5 g; Cholesterol 123 mg; 1985 kJ (475 cal)

Using a large sharp knife, cut the topside steak into large cubes.

Cook the meat in small batches until browned, then drain on paper towels.

BEEF AND RED WINE STEW

Preparation time: 15 minutes
Total cooking time: 2 hours
Serves 6

30 g (1 oz) butter
2 tablespoons oil
1 kg (2 lb) topside steak, trimmed and cut
    into 3 cm (1¼ inch) cubes
100 g (3½ oz) bacon pieces, cut into 1.5 cm
    (⅝ inch) cubes
18 baby onions
2 cloves garlic, crushed
¼ cup (30 g/1 oz) plain flour
2 cups (500 ml/16 fl oz) red wine
3 cups (750 ml/24 fl oz) beef stock
300 g (10 oz) small mushrooms, halved

1 Heat the butter and oil in a heavy-based saucepan. Cook the meat quickly in small batches over medium–high heat until browned, then drain on paper towels.
2 Add the bacon, onions and garlic to the pan, and cook, stirring, for 2 minutes, or until browned. Add the flour and stir over low heat until lightly golden. Gradually pour in the wine and stock, and stir until smooth. Stir continuously over medium heat for 2 minutes, or until the mixture boils and thickens.
3 Return the meat to the pan and reduce the heat to a simmer. Cook, covered, for 1½ hours, or until the meat is tender, stirring occasionally. Add the mushrooms and cook for 15 minutes. Delicious served with mashed potato.

NUTRITION PER SERVE
Protein 45 g; Fat 17 g; Carbohydrate 10 g;
Dietary Fibre 2.5 g; Cholesterol 105 mg;
1800 kJ (430 cal)

Squeeze the broad beans to remove the tough outer skins.

Cook the onion for 3–4 minutes, or until it is soft but not brown.

CHICKEN, ARTICHOKE AND BROAD BEAN STEW

Preparation time: 15 minutes
Total cooking time: 1 hour 25 minutes
Serves 4

1 cup (155 g/5 oz) frozen broad beans
8 chicken thighs (skin removed, optional)
$^1/_2$ cup (60 g/2 oz) seasoned plain flour
2 tablespoons oil
1 large red onion, cut into small wedges
$^1/_2$ cup (125 ml/4 fl oz) dry white wine
$1^1/_4$ cups (310 ml/10 fl oz) chicken stock
2 teaspoons finely chopped fresh rosemary
340 g (11 oz) marinated artichokes, well
    drained and quartered
800 g (1 lb 10 oz) potatoes, cut into
    large cubes
60 g (2 oz) butter

1 Remove the skins from the broad beans. Coat the chicken in the flour, shaking off the excess. Heat the oil in a saucepan or flameproof casserole dish, then brown the chicken in two batches on all sides over medium heat. Remove and drain on paper towels.

2 Add the onion to the pan and cook for 3–4 minutes, or until soft but not brown. Increase the heat to high, pour in the wine and boil for 2 minutes, or until reduced to a syrup. Stir in 1 cup (250 ml/8 fl oz) of the stock and bring just to the boil, then return the chicken to the pan with the rosemary. Reduce the heat to low and simmer, covered, for 45 minutes.

3 Add the artichokes to the pan, increase the heat to high and return to the boil. Reduce to a simmer and cook, uncovered, for 10–15 minutes. Add the beans and cook for a further 5 minutes.

4 Meanwhile, cook the potato in a saucepan of boiling water for 15–20 minutes, or until tender. Drain, then return to the pan. Add the butter and the remaining stock, and mash with a potato masher. Serve on the side of the stew.

NUTRITION PER SERVE
Protein 76 g; Fat 47 g; Carbohydrate 43 g; Dietary Fibre 8.5 g; Cholesterol 334 mg; 3845 kJ (920 cal)

Brown the veal in batches over medium–high heat for 3 minutes.

Cover and simmer until the meat is tender and the sauce has thickened.

PAPRIKA VEAL WITH CARAWAY NOODLES

Preparation time: 10 minutes
Total cooking time: 1 hour 35 minutes
Serves 4

¹/₄ cup (60 ml/2 fl oz) oil
1 kg (2 lb) veal shoulder, diced
1 large onion, thinly sliced
3 cloves garlic, finely chopped
¹/₄ cup (60 g/2 oz) Hungarian paprika
¹/₂ teaspoon caraway seeds
2 x 400 g (13 oz) cans chopped tomatoes, one drained
350 g (11 oz) fresh fettuccine
40 g (1¹/₄ oz) butter, softened

1 Heat half the oil in a large saucepan over medium–high heat, then brown the veal in batches for 3 minutes per batch. Remove the veal from the pan and set aside with any pan juices.

2 Add the remaining oil to the pan and sauté the onion and garlic over medium heat for 5 minutes, or until softened. Add the paprika and ¹/₄ teaspoon of the caraway seeds, and stir for 30 seconds.

3 Add the chopped tomatoes and their liquid plus ¹/₂ cup (125 ml/4 fl oz) water. Return the veal to the pan with any juices, increase the heat to high and bring to the boil. Reduce the heat to low, then cover and simmer for 1¹/₄ hours, or until the meat is tender and the sauce has thickened.

4 About 15 minutes before the veal is ready, cook the pasta in a large saucepan of rapidly boiling salted water according to the packet instructions until al dente. Drain, then return to the pan. Stir in the butter and the remaining caraway seeds. Serve immediately with the paprika veal.

NUTRITION PER SERVE
Protein 68 g; Fat 25 g; Carbohydrate 73 g; Dietary Fibre 10 g; Cholesterol 231 mg; 3340 kJ (800 cal)

Add the vinegar, sugar, cloves, peppercorns, bay leaves, garlic and parsley to the meat.

Remove the sauce from the heat and stir in the cooked onion.

CORNED BEEF

Preparation time: 5 minutes
Total cooking time: 1 hour 40 minutes
Serves 6–8

1 tablespoon oil
1.5 kg (3 lb) piece corned silverside, trimmed
1 tablespoon white vinegar
1 tablespoon soft brown sugar
4 cloves
4 black peppercorns
2 bay leaves
1 clove garlic, crushed
1 large sprig fresh parsley
4 carrots
4 potatoes
6 small onions

ONION SAUCE
30 g (1 oz) butter
2 white onions, chopped
2 tablespoons plain flour
1⅓ cups (330 ml/11 fl oz) milk

HORSERADISH CREAM
¼ cup (60 ml/2 fl oz) horseradish relish
1 tablespoon white vinegar
½ cup (125 ml/4 fl oz) cream, whipped

1 Heat the oil in a deep, heavy-based saucepan. Cook the meat over medium–high heat, turning until well browned all over. Remove the pan from the heat and add the vinegar, sugar, cloves, peppercorns, bay leaves, garlic and parsley.

2 Pour over enough water to cover. Cover and return to the heat, reduce the heat and bring slowly to simmering point. Simmer for 30 minutes.

3 Cut the carrots and potatoes into large pieces and add to the pan with the onions. Simmer, covered, for 1 hour, or until tender. Remove the

vegetables and keep warm. Reserve ½ cup (125 ml/4 fl oz) of the cooking liquid.

4 To make the onion sauce, heat the butter in a small saucepan. Cook the onion gently for 10 minutes, or until soft but not browned. Transfer the onion to a bowl. Add the flour to the pan and stir over low heat for 2 minutes, or until the flour is lightly golden. Gradually add the milk and the reserved cooking liquid, and stir until the sauce boils and thickens. Boil for 1 minute, then remove from the heat and stir in the onion. Season to taste.

5 To make the horseradish cream, combine all of the ingredients in a bowl until smooth.

6 Drain the meat from the pan, discarding the remaining liquid and spices. Slice the meat, and serve it with the vegetables, onion sauce and horseradish cream.

NUTRITION PER SERVE (8)

Protein 37 g; Fat 13 g; Carbohydrate 19 g; Dietary Fibre 2.5 g; Cholesterol 111 mg; 1425 kJ (340 cal)

Cut the kidneys in half lengthways and remove the core and membrane.

Add the two mustards to the cream and stir until well combined.

LAMB'S KIDNEYS IN CREAMY MUSTARD SAUCE

Preparation time: 15 minutes
Total cooking time: 25 minutes
Serves 4

8 lamb's kidneys
50 g (1¾ oz) butter
6 French shallots, thinly sliced
1 cup (250 ml/8 fl oz) cream
2 teaspoons wholegrain mustard
2 teaspoons Dijon mustard
⅓ cup (20 g/¾ oz) chopped fresh parsley

1 To prepare the kidneys, slice them in half lengthways. Using a pair of small sharp scissors, carefully snip out the core of each kidney and remove any membrane.

2 Melt half the butter in a small pan. Add the shallots and gently cook for 5 minutes, or until soft and golden. Add the cream and simmer for 10 minutes, or until reduced by one-quarter. Remove from the heat and stir in both mustards, mix well and set aside.

3 Melt the remaining butter in a frying pan over medium heat. When the butter foams, cook the kidney halves for 2 minutes on each side.

4 Pour the creamy mustard sauce over the kidneys and simmer, stirring, for 2 minutes. Stir in the chopped parsley, and serve. Delicious served with mashed potato and steamed green beans.

NUTRITION PER SERVE
Protein 20 g; Fat 40 g; Carbohydrate 2 g; Dietary Fibre 0 g; Cholesterol 455 mg; 1820 kJ (435 cal)

NOTE: When buying kidneys, select those that are firm and have a rich, even color.

Remove the softened leeks and herbs from the pan with a slotted spoon.

Add the chopped eggplant and zucchini to the chicken and leek mixture.

CHICKEN MARSALA

Preparation time: 20 minutes
Total cooking time: 1 hour 10 minutes
Serves 4

¹/₄ cup (60 ml/2 fl oz) olive oil
3 leeks, thinly sliced
1 teaspoon finely chopped fresh rosemary
3 bay leaves, torn
1 kg (2 lb) chicken pieces
seasoned plain flour
1 large eggplant, cut into cubes
2 zucchini, roughly chopped
¹/₂ cup (125 ml/4 fl oz) Marsala
300 ml (10 fl oz) chicken stock
2 cups (500 ml/16 fl oz) tomato purée
200 g (6¹/₂ oz) button mushrooms, halved

1 Heat the oil in a large, heavy-based saucepan. Fry the leek, rosemary and bay leaves over low heat for 5 minutes, or until soft, stirring occasionally. Remove with a slotted spoon, leaving as much oil in the pan as possible.
2 Toss the chicken pieces in the seasoned flour. Add the chicken to the pan and brown well in batches over medium heat. Return all the chicken to the pan with the leek mixture.
3 Add the eggplant and zucchini, and cook, stirring, for 2–3 minutes, or until softened, turning the chicken over. Add the Marsala and stock, and cook for 15 minutes over medium–high heat.
4 Add the tomato purée and season well with salt and pepper. Bring to the boil, turning the chicken pieces in the sauce. Reduce the heat to a very gentle simmer, then cover and cook for 35 minutes. Add the mushrooms and cook, uncovered, for 5 minutes.

NUTRITION PER SERVE
Protein 63 g; Fat 20 g; Carbohydrate 13 g; Dietary Fibre 9 g; Cholesterol 125 mg; 2200 kJ (530 cal)

NOTE: Marsala is a famous Italian fortified wine. It has a smoky, rich flavor and ranges from dry to sweet.

Using a sharp knife, cut the gravy beef into large chunks.

Add the stock, beer, onion and bay leaves to the browned beef.

BEEF IN BEER WITH CAPERS

Preparation time: 25 minutes
Total cooking time: 3 hours 20 minutes
Serves 4–6

1 kg (2 lb) gravy beef
seasoned plain flour
olive oil, for cooking
4 cloves garlic, finely chopped
2 cups (500 ml/16 fl oz) beef stock
1½ cups (375 ml/12 fl oz) beer
2 onions, chopped
3 bay leaves
⅓ cup (55 g/2 oz) stuffed or pitted green
    olives, sliced
6 anchovies
2 tablespoons capers, drained

1 Cut the beef into 4 cm (1½ inch) chunks. Lightly coat in the flour. Heat ¼ cup (60 ml/ 2 fl oz) of oil in a deep heavy-based pan, add the garlic, then brown the beef over high heat.
2 Add the stock, beer, onion and bay leaves, season well and bring to the boil. Reduce the heat and gently simmer, covered, for 2½ hours, stirring about three times during cooking. Remove the lid and simmer for 30 minutes more. Stir, then mix in the olives.
3 Heat 2 teaspoons of oil in a small pan. Add the anchovies and capers, gently breaking up the anchovies. Cook over medium heat for 4 minutes, or until brown and crisp. To serve, place the meat on serving plates, drizzle with the sauce, sprinkle with anchovies and capers, and season with salt and freshly cracked pepper.

NUTRITION PER SERVE (6)
Protein 40 g; Fat 6 g; Carbohydrate 4 g;
Dietary Fibre 1 g; Cholesterol 115 mg;
965 kJ (230 cal)

NOTE: The capers should be squeezed very dry before being added to the pan, or they will spit in the hot oil.

EASY SEAFOOD PAELLA

Preparation time: 25 minutes
Total cooking time: 45 minutes
Serves 6

300 g (10 oz) skinless firm white fish fillets
(see NOTE)
250 g (8 oz) black mussels
500 g (1 lb) raw medium prawns, peeled and
deveined, tails intact
200 g (6½ oz) calamari rings
¼ cup (60 ml/2 fl oz) olive oil
1 large onion, diced
3 cloves garlic, finely chopped
1 small red capsicum, thinly sliced
1 small fresh red chilli, seeded and
chopped (optional)
2 teaspoons paprika
1 teaspoon ground turmeric
2 tomatoes, peeled and diced
1 tablespoon tomato paste
2 cups (400 g/13 oz) long-grain rice
½ cup (125 ml/4 fl oz) white wine
1.25 litres fish stock
¼ cup (7 g/¼ oz) chopped fresh
flat-leaf parsley, for serving
lemon wedges, for serving

1 Cut the fish fillets into 2.5 cm (1 inch) cubes.
Scrub the mussels and pull out the hairy beards.
Discard any broken mussels or those that don't
close when tapped. Refrigerate the seafood,
covered, until ready to use.
2 Heat the oil in a paella pan or a large deep
frying pan with a lid. Add the onion, garlic,
capsicum and chilli to the pan, and cook over
medium heat for 2 minutes, or until the onion
and capsicum are soft. Add the paprika, turmeric
and 1 teaspoon salt, and stir-fry for 1–2 minutes,
or until aromatic.
3 Add the tomato and cook for 5 minutes, or
until softened. Add the tomato paste. Stir in the
rice until it is well coated.

4 Pour in the wine and simmer until almost
absorbed. Add all the fish stock and bring
to the boil. Reduce the heat and simmer for
20 minutes, or until almost all the liquid is
absorbed into the rice. There is no need to stir
the rice, but you may occasionally wish to fluff
it up with a fork to separate the grains.
5 Add the mussels to the pan, poking the shells
into the rice, cover and cook for 2–3 minutes
over low heat. Add the prawns and cook for
2–3 minutes. Add the fish, cover and cook for
3 minutes. Finally, add the calamari rings and
cook for 1–2 minutes. By this time, the mussels
should have opened—discard any unopened
ones. The prawns should be pink and the fish
should flake easily when tested with a fork. The
calamari should be white, moist and tender.
Cook for another 2–3 minutes if the seafood is
not quite cooked, but avoid overcooking as the
seafood will toughen and dry out.
6 Serve with parsley and lemon wedges.
Delicious with a tossed salad.

NUTRITION PER SERVE
Protein 45 g; Fat 15 g; Carbohydrate 59 g;
Dietary Fibre 3.5 g; Cholesterol 217 mg;
2360 kJ (560 cal)

NOTE: You can use just fish, or other seafood
such as scampi, octopus and crabs. If using just
fish, choose one with few bones and chunky
flesh, such as ling, blue-eye or warehou.

Cook the calamari rings for 1–2 minutes. Don't
overcook or they will be tough.

CHINESE BRAISED CHICKEN

Preparation time: 10 minutes
Total cooking time: 1 hour
Serves 4–6

1 cup (250 ml/8 fl oz) soy sauce
1 cinnamon stick
⅓ cup (90 g/3 oz) sugar
⅓ cup (80 ml/2¾ fl oz) balsamic vinegar
2.5 cm (1 inch) piece fresh ginger,
   thinly sliced
4 cloves garlic
¼ teaspoon dried chilli flakes
1.5 kg (3 lb) chicken pieces (skin removed)
1 tablespoon sesame seeds, toasted

1 Combine 1 litre water with the soy sauce, cinnamon stick, sugar, balsamic vinegar, ginger, garlic and chilli flakes in a saucepan. Bring to the boil, then reduce the heat and simmer for 5 minutes.
2 Add the chicken pieces and simmer, covered, for 50 minutes, or until cooked through. Serve the chicken on a bed of steamed greens, drizzled with the poaching liquid and sprinkled with toasted sesame seeds.

Add the chicken to the simmering soy sauce mixture and cook for 50 minutes.

NUTRITION PER SERVE (6)
Protein 45 g; Fat 10 g; Carbohydrate 16 g; Dietary Fibre 0.5 g; Cholesterol 140 mg; 1420 kJ (339 cal)

Cook the chicken pieces in the hot oil until they are golden.

Cook the onion and half the oregano leaves until the onion is soft.

CHICKEN WITH FETA AND OLIVES

Preparation time: 15 minutes
Total cooking time: 1 hour
Serves 4

2 tablespoons oil
8 (1.2 kg/2 lb 6½ oz) chicken pieces
1 onion, chopped
25 g (¾ oz) fresh oregano, leaves picked
2 tablespoons tomato paste
2 x 425 g (14 oz) cans crushed tomatoes
150 g (5 oz) black olives
150 g (5 oz) feta, crumbled

1 Heat half the oil in a saucepan and cook the chicken pieces, in batches, for 3–4 minutes, or until golden. Remove from the pan and set aside.
2 In the same saucepan, heat the reamining oil and cook the onion and half the oregano leaves for 3 minutes, or until the onion is soft. Add the tomato paste to the onion mixture and stir for 2 minutes, then add the tomato and the chicken pieces.
3 Simmer, covered, for 40–50 minutes, or until the chicken is cooked through. Add the olives and remaining oregano leaves. To serve, spoon into bowls and top with the crumbled feta.

NUTRITION PER SERVE
Protein 50 g; Fat 28 g; Carbohydrate 11 g; Dietary Fibre 5 g; Cholesterol 165 mg; 2110 kJ (505 cal)

To peel the tomatoes, score a cross in the base, soak in boiling water, then peel away the skin.

Remove the seeds with a teaspoon, then finely chop the flesh.

CHILLI CON CARNE

Preparation time: 25 minutes + overnight soaking
Total cooking time: 2 hours 15 minutes
Serves 6

185 g (6 oz) dried black-eye beans
1¹⁄₂ tablespoons oil
900 g (1 lb 13 oz) trimmed chuck steak, cut into chunks
3 onions, thinly sliced
2 cloves garlic, chopped
2 teaspoons ground cumin
1 tablespoon paprika
¹⁄₂ teaspoon ground allspice
1–2 teaspoons chilli powder
650 g (1 lb 5 oz) tomatoes, peeled, seeded and finely chopped
1 tablespoon soft brown sugar
1 tablespoon red wine vinegar

1 Put the beans in a bowl, cover with plenty of water and leave overnight to soak. Drain well.
2 Heat 1 tablespoon of the oil in a large heavy-based saucepan and cook the meat in two batches over medium–high heat for 2 minutes, or until well browned. Remove from the pan.
3 Pour the rest of the oil into the saucepan and add the onion. Cook over medium heat for 5 minutes, or until translucent. Add the garlic and spices and cook, stirring, for 1 minute, or until aromatic. Stir in 2 cups (500 ml/16 fl oz) water.
4 Return the meat to the pan with the beans and tomato. Bring to the boil, then reduce the heat to low and simmer, partially covered, for 2 hours, or until the meat is tender and the chilli con carne is thick and dryish, stirring occasionally. Towards the end of the cooking time the mixture may start to catch, so add a little water if necessary. Stir through the sugar and vinegar, and season with salt to taste. This is delicious served with flour tortillas and grated cheese.

NUTRITION PER SERVE
Protein 43 g; Fat 10 g; Carbohydrate 54 g; Dietary Fibre 10 g; Cholesterol 100 mg; 2040 kJ (486 cal)

Remove any excess fat, then cut the veal into 2.5 cm (1 inch) pieces.

Put the veal and flour in a plastic bag and shake to coat.

VEAL GOULASH

Preparation time: 25 minutes
Total cooking time: 2 hours
Serves 4

500 g (1 lb) veal, cut into 2.5 cm
　(1 inch) pieces
2 tablespoons plain flour
2 tablespoons olive oil
2 onions, thinly sliced
2 cloves garlic, finely chopped
1 tablespoon sweet Hungarian paprika
1 teaspoon ground cumin
440 g (14 oz) can diced tomatoes
2 carrots, sliced
$\frac{1}{2}$ red capsicum, chopped
$\frac{1}{2}$ green capsicum, chopped
1 cup (250 ml/8 fl oz) beef stock
$\frac{1}{2}$ cup (125 ml/4 fl oz) red wine
$\frac{1}{2}$ cup (125 g/4 oz) sour cream
chopped fresh parsley, to garnish

1 Put the veal and flour in a plastic bag and shake to coat the veal with flour. Shake off any excess. Heat 1 tablespoon of the oil in a large, deep heavy-based saucepan over medium heat. Brown the meat well in batches, then remove the meat and set aside.

2 Add the remaining oil to the pan. Cook the onion, garlic, paprika and cumin for 5 minutes, stirring frequently. Return the meat and any juices to the pan with the tomato, carrot and capsicum. Cover and cook for 10 minutes.

3 Add the stock and wine, and season with salt and pepper. Stir well, then cover and simmer over very low heat for 1½ hours. Stir in half the sour cream, season with more salt and pepper if needed and serve garnished with parsley and the remaining sour cream. Delicious served with buttered boiled small potatoes or noodles.

NUTRITION PER SERVE

Protein 30 g; Fat 25 g; Carbohydrate 15 g; Dietary Fibre 4.5 g; Cholesterol 144 mg; 1790 kJ (430 cal)

NOTE: If you prefer your sauce to be a little thicker, cook, uncovered, for 5 minutes over high heat before adding the sour cream.

Pour the cider into the saucepan, scraping off any sediment from the bottom of the pan.

Cook until the chicken is tender and the sauce has reduced.

CHICKEN AND CIDER STEW WITH APPLE AND POTATO MASH

Preparation time: 15 minutes
Total cooking time: 55 minutes
Serves 4

1 kg (2 lb) chicken thigh fillets, cut into
   2 cm (³/₄ inch) cubes
1¹/₂ tablespoons finely chopped fresh thyme
1 tablespoon oil
90 g (3 oz) butter
3 French shallots, thinly sliced
1¹/₂ cups (375 ml/12 fl oz) apple cider
1 kg (2 lb) potatoes, cubed
2 large green apples, peeled, cored and
   sliced into eighths
²/₃ cup (170 ml/5¹/₂ fl oz) cream

1 Season the chicken thighs with 2 teaspoons of the thyme and salt and black pepper. Heat the oil and 20 g (³/₄ oz) of the butter in a large saucepan over medium–high heat. Cook the chicken in two batches for 2–3 minutes, or until evenly browned. Remove from the pan.
2 Add the French shallots and the remaining thyme to the pan, and sauté for 2 minutes. Pour in the cider, then bring to the boil, scraping off any sediment that has stuck to the bottom of the pan. Return the chicken to the pan and cover. Reduce the heat to medium–low and cook for 35–40 minutes, or until the chicken is tender and the sauce has reduced (check occasionally to see if any water needs to be added).
3 Meanwhile, cook the potato and apple in a saucepan of boiling water for 15–20 minutes, or until tender. Drain and return to the pan over low heat for 1 minute to allow any water to evaporate. Remove from the heat, and mash with a potato masher. Stir in 2 tablespoons of the cream and the remaining butter with a wooden spoon, then season with salt and pepper.

4 Gently stir the remaining cream into the chicken stew and cook for a further 2–4 minutes, or until the sauce has thickened. Serve at once with the potato and apple mash and a crisp green salad.

NUTRITION PER SERVE

Protein 54 g; Fat 60 g; Carbohydrate 56 g; Dietary Fibre 6 g; Cholesterol 333 mg; 4055 kJ (970 cal)

PORK, PAPRIKA AND POTATO STEW

Preparation time: 15 minutes
Total cooking time: 45 minutes
Serves 4

1 tablespoon paprika
4 thick pork loin cutlets
2 tablespoons olive oil
¹/₄ cup (60 ml/2 fl oz) sherry vinegar
¹/₄ teaspoon cayenne pepper
¹/₂ cup (125 ml/4 fl oz) tomato purée
400 g (13 oz) potatoes, cut into 2 cm
　(³/₄ inch) cubes
8 French shallots, peeled
200 g (6¹/₂ oz) rocket leaves

1 Combine the paprika with ¹/₄ teaspoon each of salt and freshly ground black pepper. Sprinkle over both sides of the pork. Heat the oil over medium heat in a deep frying pan large enough to fit the cutlets in a single layer, and cook the cutlets until brown on both sides.

2 Pour the sherry vinegar into the pan and stir well to scrape up any sediment stuck to the base. Stir in the cayenne pepper, tomato purée and 1 cup (250 ml/8 fl oz) hot water. Bring to the boil, then add the potato and shallots. Reduce the heat and simmer, covered, for 30 minutes, or until the sauce has thickened and reduced by half—check the liquid level once or twice, and add a little more water if necessary. Season.

3 To serve, divide the rocket leaves among four serving plates and place a cutlet on top. Spoon the sauce and potato over the top.

NUTRITION PER SERVE
Protein 41 g; Fat 17 g; Carbohydrate 17 g; Dietary Fibre 3.5 g; Cholesterol 103 mg; 1615 kJ (385 cal)

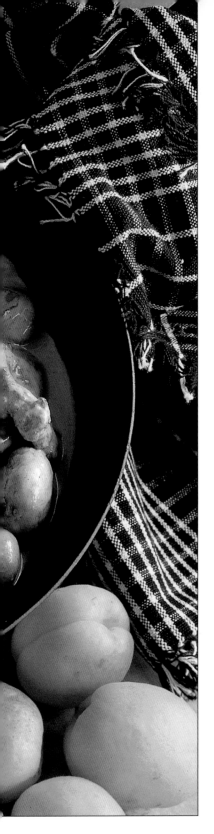

BEEF STROGANOFF

Preparation time: 25 minutes
Total cooking time: 30 minutes
Serves 6

1 kg (2 lb) piece rump steak, trimmed
1/3 cup (40 g/1 1/4 oz) plain flour
1/4 teaspoon ground black pepper
1/4 cup (60 ml/2 fl oz) olive oil
1 large onion, chopped
500 g (1 lb) baby mushrooms
1 tablespoon sweet paprika
1 tablespoon tomato paste
2 teaspoons French mustard
1/2 cup (125 ml/4 fl oz) dry white wine
1/4 cup (60 ml/2 fl oz) chicken stock
3/4 cup (185 g/6 oz) sour cream
1 tablespoon finely chopped fresh parsley

1 Slice the meat across the grain into short, thin pieces. Combine the flour and pepper. Toss the meat in the seasoned flour, shaking off the excess.

2 Heat 2 tablespoons of the oil in a heavy-based saucepan. Cook the meat quickly in small batches over medium–high heat until well browned. Drain on paper towels.

3 Heat the remaining oil in the pan. Cook the onion over medium heat for 3 minutes, or until soft. Add the mushrooms and stir for 5 minutes.

4 Add the paprika, tomato paste, mustard, wine and stock to the pan, and bring to the boil. Reduce the heat and simmer for 5 minutes, uncovered, stirring occasionally. Return the meat to the pan with the sour cream, and stir until combined and just heated through. Sprinkle with the parsley just before serving.

NUTRITION PER SERVE

Protein 42 g; Fat 28 g; Carbohydrate 9.5 g; Dietary Fibre 3.5 g; Cholesterol 147 mg; 1970 kJ (470 cal)

Toss the meat in the seasoned flour, shaking off any excess.

Cook the meat quickly in small batches until it is well browned.

Finely grate a piece of fresh ginger on a wooden ginger grater.

Cook the cubes of beef, in batches, until brown all over.

CHINESE BEEF IN SOY

Preparation time: 20 minutes + overnight marinating
Total cooking time: 1 hour 45 minutes
Serves 4

700 g (1 lb 7 oz) chuck steak, trimmed and
    cut into 2 cm (³/₄ inch) cubes
¹/₃ cup (80 ml/2³/₄ fl oz) dark soy sauce
2 tablespoons honey
1 tablespoon wine vinegar
¹/₄ cup (60 ml/2 fl oz) soy bean oil, or oil
4 cloves garlic, chopped
8 spring onions, thinly sliced
1 tablespoon finely grated fresh ginger
2 star anise
¹/₂ teaspoon ground cloves
1¹/₂ cups (375 ml/12 fl oz) beef stock
¹/₂ cup (125 ml/4 fl oz) red wine
sliced spring onions, extra, to garnish

1 Place the meat in a non-metallic dish. Combine the soy sauce, honey and vinegar in a small bowl, then pour over the meat. Cover with plastic wrap and marinate for at least 2 hours, or preferably overnight. Drain, reserving the marinade, and pat the cubes dry.

2 Place 1 tablespoon of the oil in a saucepan and brown the meat in 3 batches, for 3–4 minutes per batch—add another tablespoon of oil, if necessary. Remove the meat. Add the remaining oil and fry the garlic, spring onion, ginger, star anise and cloves for 1–2 minutes, or until fragrant.

3 Return all the meat to the pan, and add the reserved marinade, stock and wine. Bring to the boil, then reduce the heat and simmer, covered, for 1¹/₄ hours. Cook, uncovered, for a further 15 minutes, or until the sauce is syrupy and the meat is tender.

4 Garnish with the extra sliced spring onion and serve immediately with steamed rice.

NUTRITION PER SERVE
Protein 37 g; Fat 20 g; Carbohydrate 12 g; Dietary Fibre 0.5 g; Cholesterol 117 mg; 1657 kJ (395 cal)

Heat the butter and oil in a pan, then cook the ham, garlic and leek.

Stir in the stock and brandy, then cover and leave to simmer.

HAM, LEEK AND POTATO RAGU

Preparation time: 25 minutes
Total cooking time: 45 minutes
Serves 4–6

50 g (1¾ oz) butter
2 tablespoons olive oil
250 g (8 oz) piece double-smoked ham, cut into cubes (see NOTE)
3 cloves garlic, finely chopped
3 leeks, sliced
1.5 kg (3 lb) potatoes, peeled and cut into large chunks
2 cups (500 ml/16 fl oz) chicken stock
2 tablespoons brandy
½ cup (125 ml/4 fl oz) cream
1 tablespoon each of chopped fresh oregano and parsley

1 Heat the butter and oil in a large heavy-based saucepan. Cook the ham, garlic and leek over low heat for 10 minutes, stirring regularly.
2 Add the potato and cook for 10 minutes, stirring regularly.
3 Slowly stir in the combined stock and brandy. Cover and bring to a gentle simmer. Cook for another 15–20 minutes, or until the potato is very tender but still chunky, and the sauce has thickened. Add the cream and herbs, and season with salt and pepper. Simmer for another 5 minutes. Serve with toast.

NUTRITION PER SERVE (6)
Protein 15 g; Fat 25 g; Carbohydrate 40 g; Dietary Fibre 9 g; Cholesterol 70 mg; 1990 kJ (475 cal)

NOTE: You can use any type of ham for this recipe. A double-smoked ham will give a good flavor.

TOFU, VEGETABLE AND NOODLE HOTPOT

**Preparation time: 10 minutes +
20 minutes soaking**
Total cooking time: 15 minutes
Serves 4

8 dried shiitake mushrooms
500 g (1 lb) fresh round rice noodles
3 litres chicken stock
1 carrot, thinly sliced on the diagonal
100 g (3½ oz) fried tofu puffs, halved
800 g (1 lb 10 oz) bok choy, trimmed
   and quartered
1–1½ tablespoons mushroom soy sauce
6 drops sesame oil
ground white pepper, to season
100 g (3½ oz) enoki mushrooms,
   ends trimmed

1 Place the shiitake mushrooms in a heatproof bowl, cover with boiling water and soak for 20 minutes. Drain and remove the stems, squeezing out any excess water.

2 Meanwhile, place the noodles in a heatproof bowl, cover with boiling water and soak briefly. Gently separate the noodles with your hands and drain well.

3 Place the chicken stock in a large saucepan, cover and slowly bring to a simmer over low heat.

4 Add the noodles to the simmering stock along with the carrot, tofu puffs, shiitake mushrooms and bok choy. Cook for 1–2 minutes, or until the carrot and noodles are tender and the bok choy has wilted slightly. Stir in the soy sauce and sesame oil, and season with white pepper.

5 Divide the noodles, vegetables, tofu puffs and enoki mushrooms among four serving bowls, ladle the broth on top and serve immediately.

NUTRITION PER SERVE
Protein 20 g; Fat 8.5 g; Carbohydrate 69 g; Dietary Fibre 9.5 g; Cholesterol 39 mg; 1825 kJ (435 cal)

SHABU SHABU (JAPANESE BEEF HOTPOT)

Preparation time: 20 minutes +
40 minutes freezing
Total cooking time: 10 minutes
Serves 4

300 g (10 oz) beef fillet, trimmed
1.5 litres chicken stock
2 cm x 6 cm (³/₄ inch x 2¹/₂ inch) piece fresh
   ginger, thinly sliced
¹/₃ cup (80 ml/2³/₄ fl oz) light soy sauce
2 tablespoons mirin
1 teaspoon sesame oil
200 g (6¹/₂ oz) fresh udon noodles
150 g (5 oz) English spinach, stems
   removed, thinly sliced
400 g (13 oz) Chinese cabbage (leaves
   only), finely shredded
100 g (3¹/₂ oz) fresh shiitake mushrooms,
   stems removed and caps thinly sliced

200 g (6¹/₂ oz) firm tofu, cut into 2 cm
   (³/₄ inch) cubes
¹/₃ cup (80 ml/2³/₄ fl oz) ponzu sauce, or
   ¹/₄ cup (60 ml/2 fl oz) soy sauce combined
   with 1 tablespoon lemon juice

1 Wrap the beef fillet in plastic wrap and freeze for 40 minutes, or until it begins to harden. Remove and slice as thinly as possible across the grain.
2 Place the stock, ginger, soy sauce, mirin and sesame oil in a 2.5 litre flameproof casserole dish or hotpot over medium heat, and simmer for 3 minutes. Add the noodles, stir to separate gently with chopsticks and cook for 1–2 minutes. Add the spinach, cabbage, mushrooms and tofu, and simmer for 1 minute, or until the leaves have wilted.
3 Divide the noodles among four serving bowls using tongs, and top with the beef slices, vegetables and tofu. Ladle the hot stock on top and serve the ponzu sauce on the side.

Using a sharp knife, cut the partially frozen beef fillet as thinly as possible.

NUTRITION PER SERVE
Protein 28 g; Fat 11 g; Carbohydrate 41 g;
Dietary Fibre 7.5 g; Cholesterol 50 mg;
1800 kJ (430 cal)

NOTE: Traditionally, raw beef slices are arranged on a plate with the tofu, mushrooms, vegetables and noodles. The stock and seasoning are heated on a portable gas flame at the table. Guests dip the meat and vegetables in the hot stock and eat as they go, dipping into the dipping sauce. The noodles are added at the end and served with the broth.

On the side

ROAST VEGETABLE MASH

Preparation time: 30 minutes
Total cooking time: 1 hour 30 minutes
Serves 4–6

2 large pontiac or sebago potatoes
400 g (13 oz) pumpkin
400 g (13 oz) orange sweet potato
2 large parsnips
1 large onion, chopped
2 tomatoes, quartered
6 cloves garlic
2 tablespoons olive oil
30 g (1 oz) butter, chopped

1 Preheat the oven to moderate 180°C (350°F/Gas 4). Peel the potatoes, pumpkin, sweet potato and parsnips, then cut into large pieces and place in a large baking dish with the onion, tomato and garlic. Drizzle with the oil and sprinkle with salt and freshly cracked black pepper.
2 Roast the vegetables for 1½ hours, or until soft and starting to brown, stirring every 30 minutes.
3 Transfer the vegetables to a bowl, add the butter and mash roughly with a fork. Season to taste with salt and freshly ground pepper, and serve.

NUTRITION PER SERVE (6)
Protein 7.5 g; Fat 10 g; Carbohydrate 40 g; Dietary Fibre 6 g; Cholesterol 13 mg; 1170 kJ (280 cal)

Peel the potatoes, pumpkin, orange sweet potato and parsnip.

Place the cut vegetables in a large baking dish and drizzle with the oil.

Peel the potatoes and parsnips, and chop them into even-sized pieces.

Drain the vegetables well and transfer to a large mixing bowl.

CREAMY POTATO AND PARSNIP MASH

Preparation time: 10 minutes
Total cooking time: 20 minutes
Serves 4–6

2 large potatoes
5 large parsnips
30 g (1 oz) butter
1 tablespoon milk
2 tablespoons sour cream
chopped fresh chives, to garnish

1 Peel the potatoes and parsnips, then chop into even-sized pieces. Cook them in a large saucepan of lightly salted boiling water for about 20 minutes, or until soft.

2 Drain well, then transfer to a bowl and mash with the butter, milk and sour cream until smooth and fluffy. Season generously with salt and freshly ground pepper. Sprinkle with chives and serve at once.

NUTRITION PER SERVE (6)
Protein 5 g; Fat 7 g; Carbohydrate 30 g;
Dietary Fibre 5 g; Cholesterol 25 mg;
800 kJ (190 cal)

NOTE: Sebago, bison, coliban, nicola, pontiac and Kind Edward are some good all-purpose potatoes that give successful results in this recipe.

Fry the finely chopped leek in the butter until soft but not browned.

Stir in the mint, stock cube, peas, lettuce and enough water to cover.

PEA PUREE

Preparation time: 30 minutes
Total cooking time: 15 minutes
Serves 4

30 g (1 oz) butter
1 large leek, finely chopped
1 tablespoon finely chopped fresh mint
1 chicken stock cube, crumbled
1 kg (2 lb) fresh peas, shelled
1 large lettuce leaf, shredded
2 tablespoons sour cream
1 tablespoon chopped fresh chives
1–2 whole fresh chives, to garnish

1 Melt the butter in a saucepan and gently fry the leek for 5 minutes, or until softened but not browned.

2 Stir in the mint, stock cube, peas, lettuce and just enough water to cover the peas. Bring to the boil, then reduce the heat to low and simmer for 8–10 minutes, or until the peas are tender. Do not overcook or the peas will lose their bright color.

3 Drain thoroughly, transfer to a food processor and blend until smooth. Season to taste with salt and white pepper, stir in the sour cream and chopped chives, and serve at once, garnished with whole chives.

NUTRITION PER SERVE
Protein 20 g; Fat 15 g; Carbohydrate 25 g; Dietary Fibre 20 g; Cholesterol 30 mg; 1113 kJ (270 cal)

NOTE: Instead of fresh peas, you could use 3 cups (450 g/14 oz) frozen peas. Reduce the cooking time to 3–4 minutes.

When the roasted walnuts have cooled, chop them roughly.

Place the peeled pumpkin pieces on a baking tray and brush with olive oil.

ROASTED PUMPKIN AND WALNUT MASH

Preparation time: 20 minutes
Total cooking time: 1 hour 5 minutes
Serves 4

12 walnut halves
1.5 kg (3 lb) pumpkin
olive oil, for brushing
$^1/_3$ cup (80 ml/2$^3/_4$ fl oz) cream
90 g (3 oz) butter
1 tablespoon chopped
 fresh parsley

1 Preheat the oven to hot 220°C (425°F/Gas 7). Place the walnuts on a baking tray, transfer to the oven and bake for 3–5 minutes, or until the walnuts are brown. Remove from the oven and leave to cool, then chop the walnuts roughly.
2 Peel the pumpkin and chop into even-sized pieces. Place on a baking tray, brush the pumpkin with olive oil, then roast for 1 hour, or until soft in the centre.
3 Gently warm the cream in a small saucepan. Place the roasted pumpkin in a food processor and blend with the pulse button until smooth. Add the cream, season with salt and pepper, then pulse again until well combined. Do not overprocess.
4 Melt the butter in a small pan and gently cook until nut colored. Add the chopped parsley, then spoon the mixture over the mash. Garnish with the chopped walnuts to serve.

NUTRITION PER SERVE
Protein 10 g; Fat 35 g; Carbohydrate 25 g; Dietary Fibre 5 g; Cholesterol 85 mg; 1826 kJ (436 cal)

Bring the peas, garlic, onion, stock and salt to the boil, skimming off any froth.

Cover and simmer the split pea mixture until thick and of a puréed consistency.

YELLOW SPLIT PEA PUREE

Preparation time: 10 minutes +
15 minutes standing
Total cooking time: 1 hour 15 minutes
Serves 4–6

500 g (1 lb) dried yellow split peas
2–3 cloves garlic, crushed
1 onion, finely diced
1.5 litres chicken stock
1 teaspoon salt
2 tablespoons extra virgin olive oil
2 tablespoons finely chopped fresh parsley

1 Rinse the split peas well, then place them in a large saucepan with the garlic, diced onion, chicken stock and salt. Bring to the boil and skim off any froth. Reduce the heat, then cover and simmer for 1 hour without stirring, or until the split peas are of a thick, puréed consistency.
2 If the mixture is too wet, remove the lid and simmer for 10–15 minutes, or until thick.
3 Remove the pan from the heat and leave the peas to stand for 15 minutes, or until mash-like. Add the olive oil and chopped parsley, and beat with a wooden spoon. Season to taste with salt and freshly ground black pepper, and serve.

NUTRITION PER SERVE (6)
Protein 6 g; Fat 7 g; Carbohydrate 7 g; Dietary Fibre 4 g; Cholesterol 0 mg; 470 kJ (113 cal)

Trim the fennel, reserving the fronds and thin green stems. Chop the bulb finely.

Add the cauliflower florets to the fennel and add enough water to just cover.

CAULIFLOWER AND FENNEL PUREE

Preparation time: 10 minutes
Total cooking time: 25 minutes
Serves 6

1 medium fennel bulb (see NOTE)
1 large cauliflower, trimmed
90 g (3 oz) butter
1 tablespoon cider vinegar or white
  wine vinegar
1 teaspoon salt
1/4 teaspoon sugar

1 Reserving the fronds, trim the fennel and finely chop the bulb and thin green stems. Set the stems aside. Cut the cauliflower into florets.
2 In a large saucepan, melt 60 g (2 oz) of the butter and gently fry the chopped fennel bulb for 5 minutes, stirring occasionally. Add the cauliflower, toss to coat and cook for 1–2 minutes, then add enough water to just cover.
3 Add the vinegar, salt and sugar, and bring to the boil. Reduce the heat and simmer for 15 minutes, or until the cauliflower is very tender. Drain thoroughly, then transfer to a food processor and blend to a smooth purée. Stir in the rest of the butter and the chopped fennel stems. Season to taste and garnish with fennel fronds.

NUTRITION PER SERVE
Protein 6 g; Fat 15 g; Carbohydrate 7 g; Dietary Fibre 6 g; Cholesterol 40 mg; 2015 kJ (480 cal)

NOTE: Fennel bulbs are usually sold already trimmed but, if possible, buy an untrimmed bulb for this recipe, so you can use the stalks to add flavor, and the fronds to garnish.

Cook the potato for about 20 minutes, or until it is tender.

Strain the milk into the mashed potato, discarding the poached spring onion.

CHAMP

Preparation time: 10 minutes
Total cooking time: 25 minutes
Serves 4–6

1 kg (2 lb) floury potatoes, such as sebago
  or pontiac
1 cup (250 ml/8 fl oz) milk
6 spring onions, finely chopped
60 g (2 oz) butter

1 Peel the potatoes, then chop them into even-sized pieces. Cook the potatoes in a saucepan of lightly salted boiling water for about 20 minutes, or until tender. Drain and mash well.

2 Meanwhile, pour the milk into a saucepan. Add two-thirds of the spring onion and poach over low heat for 15 minutes. Strain the milk, discarding the spring onion, and whip it into the mashed potato until creamy.

3 Melt the butter in a small saucepan over low heat. Add the remaining spring onion and gently cook for about 4 minutes, or until softened.

4 Drizzle the melted butter over the potato, spoon the spring onion over the top and serve immediately.

NUTRITION PER SERVE (6)
Protein 6 g; Fat 10 g; Carbohydrate 25 g;
Dietary Fibre 3 g; Cholesterol 30 mg;
890 kJ (215 cal)

Drain the blanched watercress well, then chop finely using a sharp knife.

Drain the potato, then add the garlic, cream and butter, and mash until smooth.

WATERCRESS AND POTATO MASH

Preparation time: 20 minutes
Total cooking time: 25 minutes
Serves 4–6

1.5 kg (3 lb) sebago or pontiac potatoes
250 g (8 oz) watercress, washed
   and trimmed
1 clove garlic, crushed
½ cup (125 ml/4 fl oz) cream
60 g (2 oz) butter

1 Peel and chop the potatoes, then cook in a saucepan of lightly salted boiling water for 20 minutes, or until tender.

2 Blanch the watercress in a saucepan of boiling water for 2 minutes, then rinse with cold water to hold the color. Chop the watercress finely and place in a pan. Warm gently over low heat.

3 Drain the potato, add the crushed garlic, cream and butter, then mash until smooth and creamy. Season to taste with salt and pepper.

4 Stir the warmed watercress into the mashed potato mixture. Serve at once, garnished with roughly ground cracked peppercorns.

NUTRITION PER SERVE (6)
Protein 8 g; Fat 20 g; Carbohydrate 35 g; Dietary Fibre 6 g; Cholesterol 55 mg; 1370 kJ (330 cal)

Remove the husks and silks from the fresh cobs of corn.

Using a sharp knife, cut the kernels from the cooled corn.

CREAMY CORN AND POTATO MASH

Preparation time: 15 minutes
Total cooking time: 15 minutes
Serves 4

6 fresh corn cobs
1 large pontiac potato (about 200 g/6½ oz), peeled and chopped
40 g (1¼ oz) butter
1 onion, chopped
2 tablespoons cream

1 Remove the husks and silks from the corn. Cook the corn cobs in a large saucepan of lightly salted boiling water for about 5 minutes, then drain and allow to cool.

2 Cook the potato in a separate saucepan of lightly salted boiling water until tender, then drain well and mash.

3 Melt the butter in a small pan over low heat. Add the onion and cook, stirring, for about 5–10 minutes, or until very soft but not browned.

4 Cut the kernels from the corn with a sharp knife, then blend them with the cooked onion in a food processor until smooth, adding salt and freshly cracked black pepper to taste. Stir in the mashed potato and cream, and season again with salt.

NUTRITION PER SERVE

Protein 10 g; Fat 15 g; Carbohydrate 60 g; Dietary Fibre 9.5 g; Cholesterol 40 mg; 1760 kJ (420 cal)

NOTE: When removing cobs of corn from their husks, wipe around the cob using a damp cloth. This will help remove the silks that persistently cling to the corn kernels.

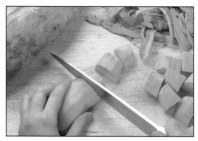

Peel the sweet potatoes, and cut them into even-sized pieces.

Fry the garlic and ginger in the melted butter over low heat.

SWEET POTATO AND CORIANDER MASH

Preparation time: 15 minutes
Total cooking time: 20 minutes
Serves 4

750 g (1½ lb) orange sweet potatoes
45 g (1½ oz) butter, chopped
1 clove garlic, crushed
2 teaspoons grated fresh ginger
1½ tablespoons chopped fresh coriander
2 teaspoons soy sauce
sprigs fresh coriander, to garnish

1 Peel the sweet potatoes and cut them into even-sized pieces. Cook the sweet potato in a saucepan of lightly salted boiling water for 10–15 minutes, or until tender. Drain.
2 Melt the butter in a small pan and add the garlic and ginger. Cook over low heat, stirring, for 1 minute.
3 Mash the hot sweet potato until almost smooth. Stir through the garlic mixture, chopped coriander and soy sauce. Garnish with coriander sprigs and serve immediately.

NUTRITION PER SERVE
Protein 3 g; Fat 10 g; Carbohydrate 30 g; Dietary Fibre 4 g; Cholesterol 30 mg; 935 kJ (220 cal)

NOTE: Orange sweet potato is sweeter than regular potatoes, with a texture between a potato and a pumpkin.

Add the lemon juice to a large bowl of water. Add the peeled, chopped celeriac.

Remove the skins from the cooled cloves of roasted garlic.

CELERIAC, POTATO AND ROASTED GARLIC MASH

Preparation time: 20 minutes
Total cooking time: 30 minutes
Serves 4–6

juice of 1 lemon
1 kg (2 lb) celeriac
500 g (1 lb) sebago or pontiac potatoes,
    peeled and chopped
4 large cloves garlic, unpeeled
50 g (1¾ oz) butter
2 tablespoons cream

1 Preheat the oven to moderately hot 200°C (400°F/Gas 6). Add the lemon juice to a large bowl of water. Peel and chop the celeriac, placing it in the lemon-water to prevent browning.
2 Cook the celeriac and potato in separate saucepans of lightly salted boiling water. Cook the potato for about 15 minutes, or until tender; cook the celeriac for 25 minutes, or until tender. Drain them both well.
3 Meanwhile, place the garlic on a baking tray and bake for 20 minutes, or until softened. Allow to cool a little, then peel away the skins.
4 While the drained potato is still hot, mash it with the butter and cream using a potato masher—do not use a food processor, or the mixture will become gluggy.
5 Process the drained celeriac with the roasted garlic in a food processor until smooth, then beat it into the potato mixture using a wooden spoon. Season to taste with salt and freshly ground black pepper, and serve hot.

NUTRITION PER SERVE (6)
Protein 5 g; Fat 10 g; Carbohydrate 20 g;
Dietary Fibre 9 g; Cholesterol 30 mg;
815 kJ (195 cal)

Stir the drained potato over medium heat until the moisture has evaporated.

Fry the cabbage in a third of the butter until softened, then stir in the spring onion.

COLCANNON

Preparation time: 15 minutes
Total cooking time: 20 minutes
Serves 4

800 g (1 lb 10 oz) floury potatoes
   (see NOTE)
90 g (3 oz) butter, chopped
3 cups (225 g/7 oz) finely shredded green
   cabbage
8 spring onions, finely chopped
²/₃ cup (170 ml/5¹/₂ fl oz) milk
pinch ground nutmeg
chopped fresh parsley, to garnish

1 Peel the potatoes and cut them into even-sized pieces. Cook the potato in a saucepan of lightly salted boiling water for about 15 minutes, or until tender. Drain the potato, return it to the pan and stir over low heat until all the moisture has evaporated, then mash well.
2 Melt 30 g (1 oz) of the butter in a frying pan, add the shredded cabbage and stir-fry over high heat until softened and lightly browned. Stir in the spring onion.
3 Add the remaining butter and the milk to the mashed potato. Stir the cabbage mixture into the potato with the nutmeg, and season with salt and freshly ground pepper. Sprinkle with chopped parsley to serve.

NUTRITION PER SERVE
Protein 8 g; Fat 20 g; Carbohydrate 30 g;
Dietary Fibre 6 g; Cholesterol 60 mg;
1412 kJ (340 cal)

NOTE: King Edward, russet and spunta are some floury potatoes. You could also use pontiac or sebago.

Peel and slice the artichokes, placing them in the lemon-water to stop browning.

In a food processor, purée the artichokes, butter, and some lemon juice and rind.

JERUSALEM ARTICHOKE PUREE

Preparation time: 20 minutes
Total cooking time: 15 minutes
Serve 4–6

rind and juice of 1 lemon
1 kg (2 lb) Jerusalem artichokes
20 g (³/₄ oz) butter
2 tablespoons olive oil

1 Add half the lemon juice to a large bowl of water. Peel and slice the artichokes, placing them in the lemon-water as you work to prevent them discoloring. Cook them in a large saucepan of boiling salted water for 12 minutes, or until tender. Drain well.

2 In a food processor, purée the artichokes, butter, 1 tablespoon of the reserved lemon juice and 1 teaspoon of the lemon rind, adding more juice and rind to taste. With the motor still running, gradually pour in the oil, mixing until it is incorporated. Season to taste, and serve hot.

NUTRITION PER SERVE (6)
Protein 4 g; Fat 9 g; Carbohydrate 6 g;
Dietary Fibre 5 g; Cholesterol 9 mg;
515 kJ (125 cal)

NOTE: Jerusalem artichokes have a white, sweet, nutty flesh. Buy tubers that look firm and fresh.

Pour the polenta into the boiling water, stirring well with a wooden spoon.

Add half the cream to the polenta and cook for 2–3 minutes, or until thick.

CREAMY POLENTA WITH PARMESAN

Preparation time: 10 minutes
Total cooking time: 10 minutes
Serves 4

1 teaspoon salt
2 cloves garlic, crushed
1 cup (150 g/5 oz) instant polenta
¹/₂ cup (125 ml/4 fl oz) cream
40 g (1¹/₄ oz) butter, chopped
¹/₃ cup (35 g/1¹/₄ oz) grated fresh Parmesan
¹/₄ teaspoon paprika, and extra to garnish
Parmesan shavings, to garnish

1 Bring 3¹/₂ cups (875 ml/28 fl oz) water to the boil in a large, heavy-based saucepan. Add the salt and crushed garlic. Stir in the polenta with a wooden spoon, breaking up any lumps. Cook over medium heat for 4–5 minutes, or until smooth, stirring often.
2 Add half the cream and cook for 2–3 minutes, or until the polenta is thick and comes away from the pan. Stir in the butter. Remove from the heat and stir in the Parmesan, paprika and remaining cream. Transfer to a warm serving bowl and sprinkle with paprika. Garnish with Parmesan shavings and serve at once.

NUTRITION PER SERVE
Protein 7 g; Fat 25 g; Carbohydrate 30 g; Dietary Fibre 1 g; Cholesterol 80 mg; 1510 kJ (360 cal)

NOTE: Polenta must be served hot to keep its creamy, light consistency.

Place the couscous and mint in a large heatproof bowl. Pour in the boiling stock.

Remove the salty flesh from the preserved lemon using a sharp knife.

PRESERVED LEMON COUSCOUS

Preparation time: 10 minutes
Total cooking time: Nil
Serves 4

1¹/₂ cups (280 g/9 oz) instant couscous
1¹/₂ cups (375 ml/12 fl oz) boiling
  chicken stock
1¹/₂ tablespoons finely chopped
  fresh mint
¹/₂ preserved lemon
45 g (1¹/₂ oz) butter

1 Place the couscous in a large heatproof bowl. Add the chicken stock and mint, and stir to combine. Leave the couscous to stand for 3–4 minutes.

2 Remove and discard the salty flesh from the preserved lemon and rinse the rind thoroughly under running water. Chop the rind finely: you will need 1–2 tablespoons, to taste.

3 Stir the butter and preserved lemon through the couscous with a fork to fluff up the grains. Serve hot.

NUTRITION PER SERVE
Protein 4.5 g; Fat 10 g; Carbohydrate 40 g; Dietary Fibre 1 g; Cholesterol 30 mg; 1030 kJ (245 cal)

NOTES: If possible, use a low-salt chicken stock or a home-made stock, as preserved lemons are very salty.

Preserved lemons are sold in some speciality shops. You can make your own by cutting fresh lemons into quarters, then firmly packing them in a jar with salt and lemon juice and leaving them to stand for 4 weeks.

Working on a lightly floured surface, flatten the dough into discs.

Spoon the filling onto one disc and top with another, pressing down firmly.

CHEESE AND HERB PULL-APART LOAF

**Preparation time: 25 minutes +
  1 hour 40 minutes rising**
Total cooking time: 30 minutes
Serves 6–8

7 g (¼ oz) dried yeast
1 teaspoon sugar
4 cups (500 g/1 lb) plain flour
1½ teaspoons salt
2 tablespoons chopped fresh parsley
2 tablespoons chopped fresh chives
1 tablespoon chopped fresh thyme
½ cup (60 g/2 oz) grated Cheddar
milk, to glaze

1 Combine the yeast, sugar and ½ cup (125 ml/4 fl oz) warm water in a small bowl. Cover and set aside in a warm place for 10 minutes, or until the mixture is frothy.
2 Sift the flour and salt into a bowl. Make a well in the centre and pour in 1 cup (250 ml/8 fl oz) warm water and the frothy yeast. Mix to a soft dough. Knead on a lightly floured surface for 10 minutes, or until smooth. Put the dough in an oiled bowl, cover loosely with greased plastic wrap and leave for 1 hour, or until doubled in size.
3 Punch down the dough and knead for 1 minute. Divide the dough in half and shape each half into 10 flat discs, 6 cm (2½ inches) in diameter. Mix the fresh herbs with the Cheddar and put 2 teaspoons on a disc. Press another disc on top. Repeat with the remaining discs and herb mixture.

4 Grease a 21 x 10.5 x 6.5 cm (8½ x 4¼ x 2½ inch) loaf tin. Stand the filled discs upright in the prepared tin, squashing them together. Cover the tin with a damp tea towel and set aside in a warm place for 30 minutes, or until well risen. Preheat the oven to hot 210°C (415°F/Gas 6–7).
5 Glaze the loaf with a little milk and bake for 30 minutes, or until brown and crusty.

NUTRITION PER SERVE (8)

Protein 10 g; Fat 4 g; Carbohydrate 60 g; Dietary Fibre 3 g; Cholesterol 8 mg; 1255 kJ (300 cal)

Generously grease the loaf tin with melted butter or oil.

Squeeze the excess moisture from the zucchini over a bowl or the kitchen sink.

ZUCCHINI AND OLIVE BREAD

Preparation time: 10 minutes
Total cooking time: 40 minutes
Serves 6–8

1 cup (135 g/4¹/₂ oz) finely grated zucchini
2 cups (250 g/8 oz) self-raising flour
1 teaspoon baking powder
1 teaspoon salt
1 teaspoon caster sugar
1 cup (125 g/4 oz) grated Cheddar
2 tablespoons chopped fresh chives
12 pitted black olives, sliced
2 eggs
1 cup (250 ml/8 fl oz) milk
¹/₄ cup (60 ml/2 fl oz) olive oil

1 Preheat the oven to moderately hot 200°C (400°F/Gas 6). Generously grease a 20 x 10 cm (8 x 4 inch) loaf tin.

2 Squeeze as much moisture from the zucchini as possible and set aside.

3 In a large bowl, sift the flour, baking powder, salt and sugar. Add the Cheddar, chives and olives. Beat the eggs and add the milk, oil and the zucchini, and combine. Make a well in the centre of the dry ingredients and add the zucchini mixture. Stir for 30 seconds, or until well combined.

4 Pour into the prepared tin and bake for 35–40 minutes, or until a skewer inserted comes out clean. Leave to rest for 5 minutes, then turn out onto a wire rack to cool.

NUTRITION PER SERVE (8)
Protein 10 g; Fat 15 g; Carbohydrate 25 g; Dietary Fibre 2 g; Cholesterol 65 mg; 1160 kJ (280 cal)

HINT: The best olives to use are Spanish, as Kalamata olives taste a little bitter when cooked.

Mix the fresh yeast, sugar and milk in a small bowl until smooth.

Gather the dough into a ball and turn out onto a lightly floured surface.

MINI WHOLEMEAL LOAVES

Preparation time: 40 minutes +
   2 hours rising
Total cooking time: 45 minutes
Serves 8

15 g (¹/₂ oz) fresh yeast (or 7 g/¹/₄ oz
   dried yeast)
1 tablespoon caster sugar
¹/₂ cup (125 ml/4 fl oz) warm milk
4 cups (600 g/1¹/₄ lb) wholemeal
   plain flour
1 teaspoon salt
¹/₄ cup (60 ml/2 fl oz) oil
1 egg, lightly beaten

1 Grease four 13 x 6.5 x 5 cm (5 x 2¹/₂ x 2 inch) baking tins. Mix the yeast, sugar and milk in a small bowl. Cover and set aside in a warm place until frothy.

2 Combine the flour and salt in a large bowl. Make a well in the centre and pour the oil, 1 cup (250 ml/8 fl oz) warm water and the frothy yeast into the well. Mix to a soft dough and gather into a ball; turn out onto a floured surface and knead for 10 minutes. Add a little extra flour if the dough is too sticky. Put the dough in a large oiled bowl, cover loosely with greased plastic wrap and leave in a warm place for 1 hour, or until well risen.

3 Punch down the dough, turn out onto a floured surface and knead for 1 minute, or until smooth. Divide the dough into four pieces; knead into shape and put in the tins. Cover the dough with a damp tea towel and leave in a warm place for 45 minutes, or until risen. Preheat the oven to hot 210°C (415°F/Gas 6–7).

4 Brush the loaf tops with the beaten egg. Bake for 10 minutes, then reduce the oven temperature to moderate 180°C (350°F/Gas 4) and bake for a further 30–35 minutes, or until the base sounds hollow when tapped. Cover with foil if the tops become too brown.

NUTRITION PER SERVE
Protein 10 g; Fat 10 g; Carbohydrate 40 g; Dietary Fibre 9 g; Cholesterol 25 mg; 1270 kJ (305 cal)

Sprinkle the prosciutto and Parmesan on the dough, leaving a clear border.

Lightly roll up the dough lengthways to form a log shape.

PARMESAN AND PROSCIUTTO LOAF

Preparation time: 30 minutes +
**   2 hours rising**
Total cooking time: 25 minutes
Serves 6

7 g (¹/₄ oz) dried yeast
1 teaspoon caster sugar
¹/₂ cup (125 ml/4 fl oz) warm milk
2 cups (250 g/8 oz) plain flour
1 teaspoon salt
1 egg, lightly beaten
30 g (1 oz) butter, melted and cooled slightly
1 tablespoon milk, extra
60 g (2 oz) sliced prosciutto, finely chopped
¹/₂ cup (50 g/1³/₄ oz) grated fresh Parmesan

1 Grease a baking tray. Mix the dried yeast, sugar and milk in a bowl. Cover and set aside in a warm place for 10 minutes, or until frothy.
2 Mix the flour and salt in a bowl. Make a well in the centre and add the egg, butter and frothy yeast. Mix to a soft dough and gather into a ball; turn out onto a floured surface and knead for 8 minutes, or until elastic.
3 Put in an oiled bowl, cover loosely with greased plastic wrap and leave in a warm place for 1¹/₄ hours, or until doubled in size.
4 Punch down the dough, turn out onto a floured surface and knead for 30 seconds, or until smooth. Roll out to a rectangle, 30 x 20 cm (12 x 8 inches), and brush with some extra milk. Sprinkle with the prosciutto and Parmesan, leaving a border. Roll lengthways into a log shape.
5 Place the loaf on the baking tray and brush with the remaining milk. Using a sharp knife, slash the loaf diagonally at regular intervals. Leave to rise in a warm place for 30 minutes. Preheat the oven to hot 220°C (425°F/Gas 7). Bake the loaf for 25 minutes, or until golden.

NUTRITION PER SERVE
Protein 10 g; Fat 9 g; Carbohydrate 30 g; Dietary Fibre 2 g; Cholesterol 60 mg; 1060 kJ (250 cal)

Combine the dry ingredients in a large bowl and mix with a wooden spoon.

Add the combined egg, milk, sour cream and oil, and mix until combined.

SOUR CREAM POLENTA BREAD

Preparation time: 15 minutes
Total cooking time: 50 minutes
Serves 6–8

1½ cups (225 g/7 oz) fine polenta
½ cup (60 g/2 oz) plain flour
2 tablespoons soft brown sugar
1 teaspoon baking powder
½ teaspoon bicarbonate of soda
½ teaspoon salt
1 egg
⅓ cup (80 ml/2¾ fl oz) milk
1¼ cups (310 g/10 oz) sour cream
2 tablespoons oil
½ teaspoon poppy seeds

1 Preheat the oven to moderately hot 200°C (400°F/Gas 6) and grease an 11 x 18 cm (4½ x 7 inch) loaf tin.

2 Combine the polenta, flour, sugar, baking powder, bicarbonate of soda and salt in a large bowl.

3 Whisk together the egg, milk, sour cream and oil, and add them to the dry ingredients, mixing just long enough for them to be evenly combined. Pour the mixture into the tin and sprinkle with the poppy seeds.

4 Bake for 30 minutes, reduce the temperature to moderate 180°C (350°F/Gas 4) and continue baking for a further 15–20 minutes, or until the loaf is golden.

NUTRITION PER SERVE (8)
Protein 5 g; Fat 20 g; Carbohydrate 30 g; Dietary Fibre 1 g; Cholesterol 70 mg; 1400 kJ (335 cal)

NOTE: There are different grades of polenta; some are finer than others. Compare different brands before purchasing. The fine-textured polenta is best for this recipe as it produces a finer bread.

Add the onion mixture and some of the Cheddar to the flour and butter mixture.

On a lightly floured surface, knead gently until the mixture forms a ball.

BACON, CHEESE AND ONION BREAD

Preparation time: 25 minutes
Total cooking time: 1 hour 10 minutes
Serves 6–8

1 tablespoon oil
3 onions, thinly sliced into rings
2 teaspoons soft brown sugar
4 rashers bacon, trimmed and finely
    chopped
3 cups (375 g/12 oz) self-raising flour
100 g (3½ oz) butter, chilled
¾ cup (90 g/3 oz) grated Cheddar
½ cup (125 ml/4 fl oz) milk

1 Heat half of the oil in a large, heavy-based frying pan. Add the sliced onion and cook over medium heat for 10 minutes, stirring occasionally. Add the brown sugar and continue to cook for a further 10–15 minutes, or until the onion is golden brown. Set aside to cool. Heat the remaining oil in a small frying pan, add the bacon and cook over moderately high heat until the bacon is crisp. Drain on paper towels and add to the onion mixture.

2 Lightly grease a baking tray. Sift the flour into a large bowl, cut the butter into small cubes and rub into the flour with your fingertips until the mixture resembles breadcrumbs.

3 Add three-quarters of the onion mixture and ½ cup (60 g/2 oz) of the Cheddar to the flour mixture, and mix well. Make a well in the centre and add the milk with about ½ cup (125 ml/4 fl oz) water (add enough water to bring the dough together). Using a flat-bladed knife, mix to a soft dough. Gently knead together to form a ball. Preheat the oven to hot 210°C (415°F/Gas 6–7).

4 Lay the dough on the tray and press out to form a 22 cm (8¾ inch) circle. Using a sharp knife, mark the dough into quarters, cutting two-thirds of the way through. Sprinkle with the rest of the onion mixture and the remaining Cheddar. Bake for 15 minutes, then reduce the oven temperature to moderate 180°C (350°F/Gas 4). Cover the top loosely with foil if it starts getting too brown. Bake for a further 20–25 minutes, or until the base sounds hollow when tapped.

NUTRITION PER SERVE (8)

Protein 10 g; Fat 20 g; Carbohydrate 40 g; Dietary Fibre 2 g; Cholesterol 55 mg; 1525 kJ (365 cal)

Mix all the ingredients together with enough milk to form a soft dough.

Knead the dough on a well-floured surface for 2–3 minutes, or until smooth.

NAAN

Preparation time: 15 minutes +
   2 hours resting
Total cooking time: 10 minutes
Makes 8

4 cups (500 g/1 lb) plain flour
1 teaspoon baking powder
1/2 teaspoon bicarbonate of soda
1 egg, beaten
1 tablespoon ghee or butter, melted
1/2 cup (125 g/4 oz) plain yoghurt
1 cup (250 ml/8 fl oz) milk
2–3 tablespoons ghee or butter, melted,
   extra

1 Preheat the oven to moderately hot 200°C (400°F/Gas 6). Lightly grease two 28 x 32 cm (11 x 13 inch) baking trays. Sift together the flour, baking powder, bicarbonate of soda and 1 teaspoon salt. Mix in the egg, ghee and yoghurt, and gradually add enough of the milk to form a soft dough. Cover with a damp cloth and leave in a warm place for 2 hours.

2 Knead the dough on a well-floured surface for 2–3 minutes, or until smooth. Divide into 8 portions and roll each one into an oval 15 cm (6 inches) long. Brush with water and place, wet-side down, on the prepared baking trays. Brush with the extra ghee and bake for 8–10 minutes, or until golden brown. Serve with Indian curries.

NUTRITION PER NAAN
Protein 9.5 g; Fat 12 g; Carbohydrate 48 g; Dietary Fibre 2.5 g; Cholesterol 55 mg; 1418 kJ (340 cal)

VARIATION: To make garlic naan, crush 6 garlic cloves and sprinkle evenly over the dough prior to baking.

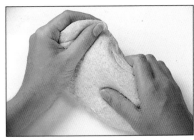

Add enough water to the flour mixture to form a firm dough.

Knead the dough on a lightly floured surface until smooth.

CHAPATIS

**Preparation time: 40 minutes +
50 minutes standing**
Total cooking time: 1 hour 10 minutes
Makes 14

2¼ cups (280 g/9 oz) atta flour
(see NOTE)
melted ghee or oil, for brushing

1 Place the flour in a large bowl with a pinch of salt. Slowly add 1 cup (250 ml/8 fl oz) water, or enough to form a firm dough. Place on a lightly floured surface and knead until smooth. Cover with plastic wrap and leave for 50 minutes.
2 Divide into 14 portions and roll into 14 cm (5½ inch) circles. Heat a frying pan over medium heat and brush with the ghee or oil. Cook the chapatis one at a time over medium heat, flattening the surface, for 2–3 minutes on each side, or until golden brown and bubbles appear. Serve with Indian curries.

NUTRITION PER CHAPATI
Protein 2.5 g; Fat 3 g; Carbohydrate 10 g;
Dietary Fibre 2 g; Cholesterol 0 mg;
335 kJ (80 cal)

NOTE: Atta flour is also known as chapati flour and is a finely milled, low-gluten, soft-textured, wholemeal wheat flour used to make Indian flatbreads. If unavailable, use plain wholemeal flour—sift it first and discard the husks. This may result in heavier, coarser bread.

Cook the bay leaves and rice in the butter until all the moisture has evaporated.

Soak the saffron threads in 2 tablespoons of hot water.

SAFFRON RICE

**Preparation time: 10 minutes +
    30 minutes soaking**
Total cooking time: 25 minutes
Serves 6

2 cups (400 g/13 oz) basmati rice
25 g (³/₄ oz) butter
3 bay leaves
¹/₄ teaspoon saffron threads (see NOTE)
2 cups (500 ml/16 fl oz) boiling vegetable
    stock

1 Wash the basmati rice thoroughly, cover with cold water and soak for 30 minutes. Drain.
2 Heat the butter gently in a frying pan until it melts. Add the bay leaves and washed rice, and cook, stirring, for 6 minutes, or until all the moisture has evaporated.
3 Meanwhile, soak the saffron in 2 tablespoons hot water for a few minutes. Add the saffron, and its soaking liquid, to the rice with the vegetable stock, 1¹/₂ cups (375 ml/12 fl oz) boiling water and salt, to taste. Bring to the boil, then reduce the heat and cook, covered, for 12–15 minutes, or until all the water is absorbed and the rice is cooked. Serve with Indian curries.

NUTRITION PER SERVE
Protein 4.5 g; Fat 4 g; Carbohydrate 53 g; Dietary Fibre 1.5 g; Cholesterol 10 mg; 1115 kJ (266 cal)

NOTE: Saffron threads are the dried stigmas of the crocus flower. While available in powdered form, it is generally inferior.

Cook the onion and spices together until the onion is soft and the spices are fragrant.

Stir gently with a fork until all the excess moisture has evaporated.

KITCHEREE

Preparation time: 15 minutes
Total cooking time: 30 minutes
Serves 6

1¹/₂ cups (300 g/10 oz) basmati rice
1¹/₂ cups (300 g/10 oz) split mung beans
  (mung lentils)
2 tablespoons oil
1 onion, sliced
3 bay leaves
1 teaspoon cumin seeds
2 pieces cassia bark
1 tablespoon cardamom seeds
6 cloves
¹/₄ teaspoon black peppercorns

1 Wash the rice and lentils, then drain and set aside.
2 Heat the oil in a frying pan, add the onion, bay leaves and spices, and cook over low heat for 5 minutes, or until the onion is softened and the spices are fragrant. Add the rice and lentils, and cook, stirring, for 2 minutes. Pour in 1.25 litres water, and season with salt. Bring to the boil, then reduce the heat to low and cook, covered, for 15 minutes. Stir gently to avoid breaking the grains and cook, uncovered, for 3 minutes, or until all the moisture has evaporated. Serve hot with Indian curries.

NUTRITION PER SERVE
Protein 6 g; Fat 10 g; Carbohydrate 44 g; Dietary Fibre 3 g; Cholesterol 0 mg; 1217 kJ (290 cal)

NOTE: To avoid serving with the whole spices left intact, tie the spices in a piece of muslin and add it to the pan along with the water. Discard when the dish is cooked.

Gently tie the pandan leaf in a knot, being careful not to tear it.

Place the pandan leaf in the saucepan with the soaked rice.

COCONUT RICE

**Preparation time: 35 minutes +
40 minutes standing
Total cooking time: 15 minutes
Serves 6**

2 cups (400 g/13 oz) long-grain rice
1 pandan leaf, tied in a knot
  (see NOTES)
³/₄ cup (185 ml/6 fl oz) coconut cream

1 Rinse the rice and cover with 1 litre water. Set aside for 30 minutes. Drain. Bring 3 cups (750 ml/24 fl oz) water to the boil. Add the rice and pandan leaf, and season with salt. Reduce the heat and cook, covered, for 12 minutes, or until the rice is just cooked.
2 Remove from the heat and add the coconut cream. Stir gently to avoid breaking the grains. Cover and set aside for 10 minutes, or until the rice absorbs the coconut cream in the residual heat. Discard the pandan leaf before serving.

NUTRITION PER SERVE
Protein 5 g; Fat 6.5 g; Carbohydrate 54 g; Dietary Fibre 2 g; Cholesterol 0 mg; 1240 kJ (295 cal)

NOTES: Pandan leaves, also known as pandanus or screw pine leaves, are used both to wrap food and to flavor rice or curries. They are available in Asian grocery stores.
  Coconut rice (nasi lemak) is a Malaysian dish and goes very well with Malaysian, Indonesian or Singaporean curries.

Reduce the heat and simmer until the water has been absorbed.

Form the rice into a log shape along the long side of the oiled calico.

LONTONG (RICE DUMPLINGS)

**Preparation time: 15 minutes +
  refrigeration**
Total cooking time: 2 hours 10 minutes
Serves 4

2 cups (400 g/13 oz) long-grain rice
4 pieces unbleached calico,
    15 x 25 cm (6 x 10 inches)
oil, to spread on calico

1 Rinse the rice under cold running water and drain. Place the rice in a saucepan with 2 cups (500 ml/16 fl oz) water and bring to the boil. Reduce the heat and simmer for 5 minutes, or until the water has been absorbed. Cool.
2 Oil the calico and divide the cooled rice among the pieces. Form the rice into a log shape along the long side of the calico and roll up to enclose. Tie with string.
3 Bring a large saucepan of water to the boil and add the rice packages. Reduce the heat and simmer over medium heat for 2 hours. Top up with boiling water, if necessary, to keep the packages afloat. Remove the packages and refrigerate until cold and firm. Unwrap and serve sliced or cubed with Indonesian or Malaysian curries.

NUTRITION PER SERVE
Protein 6.5 g; Fat 0 g; Carbohydrate 80 g;
Dietary Fibre 2.5 g; Cholesterol 0 mg;
1470 kJ (350 cal)

NOTE: Steamed rice dumplings are traditionally cooked in blanched banana leaves. Packaged banana leaves can be found in Asian speciality stores and some supermarkets.

Add the ginger and turmeric to the lentils, and cook until the lentils are tender.

Cook the garlic, onion and mustard seeds until the onion is golden.

DHAL

Preparation time: 15 minutes
Total cooking time: 35 minutes
Serves 4–6

200 g (6¹/₂ oz) red lentils
4 cm (1¹/₂ inch) piece fresh ginger,
    cut into 3 slices
¹/₂ teaspoon ground turmeric
1 tablespoon ghee or oil
2 cloves garlic, crushed
1 onion, finely chopped
¹/₂ teaspoon yellow mustard seeds
pinch asafoetida (optional)
1 teaspoon cumin seeds
1 teaspoon ground coriander
2 fresh green chillies, halved lengthways
2 tablespoons lemon juice
1 tablespoon chopped fresh coriander leaves

1 Place the lentils and 3 cups (750 ml/24 fl oz) water in a saucepan, and bring to the boil. Reduce the heat, add the ginger and turmeric, and simmer, covered, for 20 minutes, or until the lentils are tender. Stir occasionally to prevent the lentils sticking to the pan. Remove the ginger and stir in ¹/₂ teaspoon salt.

2 Heat the ghee in a frying pan, add the garlic, onion and mustard seeds, and cook over medium heat for 5 minutes, or until the onion is golden. Add the asafoetida, cumin seeds, ground coriander and chilli, and cook for 2 minutes.

3 Add the onion mixture to the lentils and stir gently to combine. Add ¹/₂ cup (125 ml/4 fl oz) water, reduce the heat to low and cook for 5 minutes. Stir in the lemon juice, and season. Sprinkle with the coriander. Serve as a side dish with Indian curries.

NUTRITION PER SERVE (6)
Protein 8.5 g; Fat 3.5 g; Carbohydrate 13 g;
Dietary Fibre 5 g; Cholesterol 8 mg;
505 kJ (120 cal)

Slice the onion into paper-thin slices, and place on paper towels to drain.

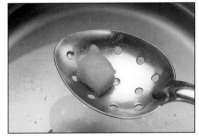

Heat the oil until a cube of bread dropped in it browns in 30–35 seconds.

CRISPY FRIED ONIONS

Preparation time: 15 minutes +
**   10 minutes standing**
Total cooking time: 10 minutes
Makes 1 cup (serves 12)

1 onion, sliced paper-thin
oil, for deep-frying

1 Place the onion on paper towels and leave for 10 minutes to drain off any excess moisture.
2 Fill a deep, heavy-based saucepan one-third full of oil and heat to 160°C (315°F), or until a cube of bread dropped into the oil browns in 30–35 seconds. Cook the onion in batches for up to 1 minute, or until brown and crispy. Drain on paper towels. Cool and store in an airtight container for up to 2 weeks. Use as a garnish and flavor enhancer in Indonesian rice and noodle dishes.

NUTRITION PER SERVE
Protein 0.2 g; Fat 3 g; Carbohydrate 0.5 g; Dietary Fibre 0 g; Cholesterol 0 mg; 128 kJ (30 cal)

NOTE: It is very important to have the oil at the correct heat to cook the onion. If possible, use a deep-fry thermometer.

Use a large metal spoon to scoop out the mango flesh.

Simmer the mixture for 1 hour, or until the mango is tender.

MANGO CHUTNEY

Preparation time: 20 minutes
Total cooking time: 1 hour 10 minutes
Makes 3 cups (serves 36)

3 large green mangoes
¹/₂ teaspoon garam masala
1¹/₂ cups (375 g/12 oz) sugar
1 cup (250 ml/8 fl oz) white vinegar
2 small fresh red chillies, seeded and finely
   chopped
1 tablespoon finely grated fresh ginger
¹/₂ cup (95 g/3 oz) finely chopped dates

1 Cut the cheeks from the rounded side of each mango and use a large spoon to scoop out the flesh. Cut the remaining flesh from around the sides of the seed and chop all the flesh into large slices. Sprinkle with salt.
2 Place the garam masala and sugar in a bowl, and mix together well. Place in a large saucepan with the vinegar. Bring to the boil, then reduce the heat and simmer for 5 minutes.
3 Add the mango slices, chilli, ginger and dates, and simmer for 1 hour, or until the mango is tender. Stir often during cooking to prevent the chutney from sticking and burning on the bottom, especially towards the end of the cooking time.
4 Spoon immediately into very clean, warm jars and seal. Turn the jars upside down for 2 minutes, then invert and leave to cool. Label and date. Store for up to six months.

NUTRITION PER SERVE
Protein 0.2 g; Fat 0 g; Carbohydrate 12.5 g; Dietary Fibre 0.5 g; Cholesterol 0 mg; 212 kJ (50 cal)

NOTES: To make sure the jars are very clean, preheat the oven to very slow 120°C (250°F/ Gas ¹/₂). Thoroughly wash the jars and lids in hot, soapy water (or preferably in a dishwasher) and rinse well with hot water. Put the jars on baking trays and place them in the oven for 20 minutes, or until they are fully dried and you are ready to use them. Do not dry the jars, or the lids, with a tea towel.

Sweet mango chutney is great with almost any Indian curry, especially the hotter ones. It also tastes delicious on sandwiches with roast lamb or beef.

Place the cucumber and yoghurt in a bowl, and mix together.

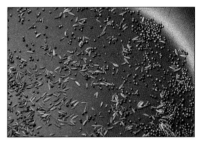

Dry-fry the ground cumin and mustard seeds until fragrant and lightly browned.

CUCUMBER RAITA

Preparation time: 5 minutes
Total cooking time: 1 minute
Makes 11/3 cups (serves 10)

2 Lebanese cucumbers, peeled, seeded and finely chopped (see NOTES)
1 cup (250 g/8 oz) plain yoghurt
1 teaspoon ground cumin
1 teaspoon mustard seeds
$^1/_2$ teaspoon grated fresh ginger
paprika, to garnish

1 Place the cucumber and yoghurt in a bowl, and mix together well.
2 Dry-fry the ground cumin and mustard seeds in a small frying pan over medium heat for 1 minute, or until fragrant and lightly browned, then add to the yoghurt mixture. Stir in the ginger, season to taste with salt and pepper, and mix together well. Garnish with the paprika. Serve chilled. Will keep in an airtight container in the refrigerator for up to 3 days.

NUTRITION PER SERVE
Protein 1 g; Fat 0.5 g; Carbohydrate 1 g; Dietary Fibre 0 g; Cholesterol 4.5 mg; 54 kJ (13 cal)

NOTES: If Lebanese cucumbers are not available, use seeded regular cucumbers. To seed a cucumber, cut it in half lengthways and scrape out the seeds with a teaspoon.

Raitas are deliciously soothing and cooling Indian yoghurt-based side dishes that cool the palate when eating hot curries.

VARIATIONS: Add 2 tablespoons chopped fresh coriander or mint leaves to the cucumber raita. Or, replace the cucumber with 1 bunch (500 g/1 lb) English spinach. Bring a large saucepan of water to the boil, add the spinach and cook for 1–2 minutes. Drain the spinach, squeezing out any excess water. Chop finely and combine with the yoghurt.

To make a tomato raita, replace the cucumber with 2 medium, seeded, diced tomatoes. Add 1 tablespoon very finely chopped onion as well.

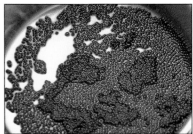

Heat the mustard seeds and vinegar over low heat until the vinegar reduces.

Place the mustard seeds, ginger and garlic in a blender, and blend to a paste.

TOMATO PICKLE

Preparation time: 15 minutes
Total cooking time: 1 hour
Makes 11/2 cups (serves 18)

2 teaspoons black or brown mustard seeds
1/3 cup (80 ml/2³/4 fl oz) cider vinegar
1 tablespoon grated fresh ginger
5 cloves garlic, chopped
1/4 cup (60 ml/2 fl oz) oil
3 teaspoons ground cumin
2 teaspoons ground turmeric
1 teaspoon chilli powder
1 kg (2 lb) firm, ripe tomatoes, peeled,
    seeded and chopped
1/4 cup (60 g/2 oz) sugar
1 tablespoon cider vinegar, extra

1 Place the mustard seeds and vinegar in a small saucepan, and heat over low heat for 12 minutes, or until the seeds just start to pop. The vinegar will be nearly evaporated. Cool. Place the seeds, ginger and garlic in a blender, and blend to a paste.

2 Heat the oil in a saucepan, add the cumin and turmeric, and cook, stirring gently, over low heat for 4 minutes, or until fragrant.

3 Add the mustard seed mixture, chilli powder, tomato, sugar and 1 teaspoon salt. Reduce the heat and simmer, stirring occasionally, for 45 minutes, or until quite thick. Stir through the extra vinegar. Spoon into clean, warm jars, seal and cool. Refrigerate for up to 1 month. Serve with Indian curries.

NUTRITION PER SERVE
Protein 1 g; Fat 3 g; Carbohydrate 4.5 g;
Dietary Fibre 1 g; Cholesterol 0 mg;
208 kJ (50 cal)

Roughly chop the fresh coriander leaves, stems and roots.

Place all the ingredients in a food processor and process until finely chopped.

CORIANDER CHUTNEY

Preparation time: 10 minutes
Total cooking time: Nil
Makes 11/4 cups (serves 9)

90 g (3 oz) fresh coriander, including the
    roots, roughly chopped
1/4 cup (25 g/3/4 oz) desiccated coconut
1 tablespoon soft brown sugar
1 tablespoon grated fresh ginger
1 small onion, chopped
2 tablespoons lemon juice
1–2 small fresh green chillies, seeded

1 Place all the ingredients, and 1 teaspoon salt, in a food processor and process for 1 minute, or until finely chopped. Refrigerate until ready to serve. Serve chilled.

NUTRITION PER SERVE
Protein 0.2 g; Fat 1 g; Carbohydrate 2 g;
Dietary Fibre 0.5 g; Cholesterol 0.5 mg;
75 kJ (18 cal)

NOTE: Chutneys are spicy, vegetarian Indian relishes eaten as side dishes. They are generally used to perk up blander dishes such as dhal or rice. They are traditionally made fresh for each meal, although ready-made varieties are commonly available in supermarkets and speciality stores. Traditional Indian chutneys are quite sour in taste, however the popular British adaptations are often sweet and jam-like in consistency.

VARIATIONS: There are numerous variations, depending on region and tastes. Try substituting 1 bunch of roughly chopped fresh mint leaves for the coriander in this recipe, or add 5 roughly chopped spring onions (including the green part) instead of the onion.

If you prefer more fire in your chutney, do not remove the seeds from the chillies. It is the seeds and white fibrous tissue inside the chillies that contain most of the heat.

MADRAS CURRY PASTE

Preparation time: 5 minutes
Total cooking time: Nil
Makes ¹/₂ cup

2¹/₂ tablespoons coriander seeds, dry-
  roasted and ground
1 tablespoon cumin seeds,
  dry-roasted and ground
1 teaspoon brown mustard seeds
¹/₂ teaspoon cracked black peppercorns
1 teaspoon chilli powder
1 teaspoon ground turmeric
2 cloves garlic, crushed
2 teaspoons grated fresh ginger
3–4 tablespoons white vinegar

1 Place the ground coriander, ground cumin,
mustard seeds, cracked black peppercorns,
chilli powder, ground turmeric, garlic, ginger
and 1 teaspoon salt in a small bowl, and mix
together well. Add the vinegar and mix to a
smooth paste. Store in a clean airtight container
jar in the refrigerator for up to a month.

INDIAN CURRY POWDER

Preparation time: 5 minutes
Total cooking time: 3 minutes
Makes ¹/₃ cup

2 teaspoons cumin seeds
2 teaspoons coriander seeds
2 teaspoons fenugreek seeds
1 teaspoon yellow mustard seeds
1 teaspoon black peppercorns
1 teaspoon cloves
1 teaspoon chilli powder
2 teaspoons ground turmeric
¹/₂ teaspoon ground cinnamon
¹/₂ teaspoon ground cardamom

1 Dry-fry the whole spices separately in a small
frying pan over medium heat for 2–3 minutes, or
until fragrant. Place in a spice grinder, mortar
and pestle or small food processor with a fine
blade, and grind to a fine powder.
2 Place in a bowl with the pre-ground spices
and mix well. Store in an airtight container in a
cool, dark place.

SRI LANKAN CURRY POWDER

Preparation time: 5 minutes
Total cooking time: 20 minutes
Makes ¹/₃ cup

3 tablespoons coriander seeds
1¹/₂ tablespoons cumin seeds
1 teaspoon fennel seeds
¹/₄ teaspoon fenugreek seeds
2 cm (³/₄ inch) cinnamon stick
6 cloves
¹/₄ teaspoon cardamom seeds
2 teaspoons dried curry leaves
2 small dried red chillies

1 Dry-fry the coriander, cumin, fennel and
fenugreek seeds separately over low heat until
fragrant. It is important to do this separately, as
all spices brown at different rates. Make sure the
spices are well browned, not burnt.
2 Place the browned seeds in a food processor,
blender, or mortar and pestle, add the remaining
ingredients and process or grind to a powder.
Store in an airtight container in a cool, dry place.

1 Separately dry-fry the coriander seeds, cumin seeds, cinnamon sticks, fennel seeds, black mustard seeds, cardamom seeds, fenugreek seeds and cloves in a small frying pan over medium heat for 2–3 minutes, or until each of the spices just start to become fragrant.

2 Transfer all the spices to a food processor or mortar and pestle, allow to cool and process or grind to a powder. Add the bay leaves, curry leaves, ground turmeric, garlic, ginger, chilli powder and ³/₄ cup (185 ml/6 fl oz) vinegar, and mix together well.

3 Heat the oil in the pan, add the paste and cook, stirring, for 5 minutes. Stir in the remaining vinegar. Pour into clean, warm jars and seal. Store in the refrigerator for up to a month.

GARAM MASALA

Preparation time: 7 minutes
Total cooking time: 3 minutes
Makes ¹/₂ cup

2 tablespoons coriander seeds
1¹/₂ tablespoons cardamom pods
1 tablespoon cumin seeds
2 teaspoons whole black peppercorns
1 teaspoon cloves
3 cinnamon sticks
1 nutmeg, grated

1 Dry-fry all the ingredients, except the nutmeg, separately in a frying pan over medium heat for 2–3 minutes, or until fragrant.

2 Remove the cardamom pods, crush with the handle of a heavy knife and remove the seeds. Discard the pods.

3 Place the fried spices, cardamom seeds and grated nutmeg in a food processor, blender, or mortar and pestle, and process or grind to a powder. Store in an airtight container in a cool, dark place.

VINDALOO PASTE

Preparation time: 10 minutes
Total cooking time: Nil
Makes ¹/₂ cup

2 tablespoons grated fresh ginger
4 cloves garlic, chopped
4 fresh red chillies, chopped
2 teaspoons ground turmeric
2 teaspoons ground cardamom
4 cloves
6 peppercorns
1 teaspoon ground cinnamon
1 tablespoon ground coriander
1 tablespoon cumin seeds
¹/₂ cup (125 ml/4 fl oz) cider vinegar

1 Place all the ingredients in a food processor and process for 20 seconds, or until well combined and smooth. Refrigerate for up to a month.

BALTI MASALA PASTE

Preparation time: 5 minutes
Total cooking time: 30 minutes
Makes 1 cup

4 tablespoons coriander seeds
2 tablespoons cumin seeds
2 cinnamon sticks, crumbled
2 teaspoons fennel seeds
2 teaspoons black mustard seeds
2 teaspoons cardamom seeds
1 teaspoon fenugreek seeds
6 cloves
4 fresh bay leaves
20 fresh curry leaves
1 tablespoon ground turmeric
2 cloves garlic, crushed
1 tablespoon grated fresh ginger
1¹/₂ teaspoons chilli powder
1 cup (250 ml/8 fl oz) malt vinegar
¹/₂ cup (125 ml/4 fl oz) oil

YELLOW CURRY PASTE

Preparation time: 20 minutes
Total cooking time: Nil
Makes ¹/₂ cup

8 small fresh green chillies
5 red Asian shallots, roughly chopped
2 cloves garlic, chopped
1 tablespoon finely chopped coriander stems
  and roots
1 stem lemon grass (white part only),
  chopped
2 tablespoons finely chopped fresh galangal
1 teaspoon ground coriander
1 teaspoon ground cumin
¹/₂ teaspoon ground turmeric
¹/₂ teaspoon black peppercorns
1 tablespoon lime juice

1 Place all the ingredients in a food processor,
blender, or mortar and pestle and process or
grind to a smooth paste. Store in an airtight
container in the refrigerator for up to a month.

GREEN CURRY PASTE

Preparation time: 30 minutes
Total cooking time: 10 minutes
Makes 1 cup

1 teaspoon white peppercorns
1 teaspoon cumin seeds
2 tablespoons coriander seeds
2 teaspoons shrimp paste (wrapped
  in foil)
1 teaspoon sea salt
4 stems lemon grass (white part only), finely
  chopped
2 teaspoons chopped fresh galangal
2 teaspoons finely shredded kaffir lime leaves
1 tablespoon chopped fresh coriander roots
5 red Asian shallots, chopped
10 cloves garlic, chopped
16 large fresh green chillies, seeded and
  chopped

1 Preheat the oven to moderate 180°C
(350°F/Gas 4). Place the peppercorns, cumin
and coriander seeds, and shrimp paste in a
baking dish, and bake for 5–10 minutes, or until
fragrant. Remove the foil.

2 Place the shrimp paste mixture and the
remaining ingredients in a food processor or
mortar and pestle, and process or grind to a
smooth paste. Store in an airtight container in
the refrigerator for up to a month.

RED CURRY PASTE

Preparation time: 20 minutes +
** 10 minutes soaking**
Total cooking time: 10 minutes
Makes 1 cup

15 large dried red chillies
1 teaspoon white peppercorns
2 teaspoons coriander seeds
1 teaspoon cumin seeds
2 teaspoons shrimp paste (wrapped in foil)
5 red Asian shallots, chopped
10 cloves garlic
2 stems lemon grass (white part only), thinly
  sliced
1 tablespoon chopped fresh galangal
2 tablespoons chopped fresh coriander roots
1 teaspoon finely grated kaffir lime rind

CHU CHEE CURRY PASTE

Preparation time: 20 minutes +
10 minutes soaking
Total cooking time: 5 minutes
Makes ¹/₂ cup

10 large dried red chillies
1 teaspoon coriander seeds
1 tablespoon shrimp paste (wrapped in foil)
1 tablespoon white peppercorns
10 kaffir lime leaves, finely shredded
10 red Asian shallots, chopped
2 teaspoons finely grated kaffir lime rind
1 tablespoon chopped fresh coriander stems
   and roots
1 stem lemon grass (white part only), finely
   chopped
3 tablespoons chopped fresh galangal
1 tablespoon chopped Krachai (optional—
   see NOTE)
6 cloves garlic, chopped

1 Preheat the oven to moderate 180°C
(350°F/Gas 4). Soak the dried chillies in boiling
water for 10 minutes. Drain, remove the seeds
and roughly chop.
2 Place the coriander seeds, shrimp paste and
peppercorns on a foil-lined baking tray, and
bake for 5 minutes, or until fragrant. Remove
the foil.
3 Place the roasted shrimp paste mixture, chilli
and the remaining ingredients in a food
processor or mortar and pestle, and process or
grind to a smooth paste. You may need to use a
little lemon juice if the paste is too thick. Store
the paste in an airtight container in the
refrigerator for up to a month.

NOTE: Krachai (bottled lesser galangal) is
available from Asian grocery stores. It can be
omitted if it is unavailable.

---

1 Preheat the oven to moderate 180°C
(350°F/Gas 4). Soak the chillies in boiling
water for 10 minutes. Remove the seeds and
roughly chop the flesh.
2 Place the spices and shrimp paste in a
baking dish. Bake for 5–10 minutes, or until
fragrant. Remove the foil.
3 Place all the ingredients in a food processor
or mortar and pestle, and process or grind to a
smooth paste. Store in an airtight container in
the refrigerator for up to a month.

MUSAMAN CURRY PASTE

Preparation time: 20 minutes +
10 minutes soaking
Total cooking time: 5 minutes
Makes ¹/₂ cup

10 large dried red chillies
3 cardamom pods
1 teaspoon cumin seeds
1 tablespoon coriander seeds
¹/₄ teaspoon black peppercorns
1 teaspoon shrimp paste (wrapped in foil)
5 red Asian shallots, chopped
1 stem lemon grass (white part only), finely
   chopped
1 tablespoon chopped fresh galangal
10 cloves garlic, chopped
¹/₄ teaspoon ground cinnamon
¹/₂ teaspoon ground nutmeg
¹/₄ teaspoon ground cloves

1 Preheat the oven to moderate
180°C (350°F/Gas 4). Soak the dried chillies in
boiling water for 10 minutes, then drain, remove
the seeds and roughly chop.
2 Place the whole spices, shrimp paste,
shallots, lemon grass, galangal and garlic in a
baking dish, and bake for 5 minutes, or until
fragrant. Remove the foil.
3 Place the chilli, roasted ingredients, ground
cinnamon, ground nutmeg and ground cloves in
a food processor, mortar and pestle or spice
grinder, and process or grind to a smooth paste.
If the mixture is too dry, add a little vinegar to
moisten it. Store in an airtight container in the
refrigerator for up to a month.

A

apple and potato mash, Chicken and cider stew with, 206
Apricot chicken, 74
apricot chicken, Spicy, 185
apricots, Chicken curry with, 131
artichoke and broad bean stew, Chicken, 194
artichoke casserole, Beef and, 64
Asian chicken noodle soup, 30
Autumn vegetable stew, 180
Avgolemono with chicken, 20

B

Bacon, cheese and onion bread, 235
bacon stew, Lamb's liver and, 146
baked beans, Boston, 58
Balinese seafood curry, 112
balsamic vinegar, Chicken with, 173
Balti chicken, 111
Balti masala paste, 249
Barley soup with golden parsnips, 28
beans
    Boston baked, 58
    and capsicum stew, 143
    casserole, Lamb and, 71
    casserole, Pork sausage and soy, 84
    casserole, Tuna and white, 40
    chowder, Mexican, 36
    Lamb with borlotti, 45
    soup, Pasta and, 12
    stew, Chicken, artichoke and broad, 194
    stew, Pork sausage and white, 166
beef
    and artichoke casserole, 64
    in beer with capers, 199
    borscht, Hot, 8
    bourguignonne, 148
    carbonnade, 56
    casserole with caraway dumplings, 46
    Corned, 196
    curry, Madras, 104
    curry, Musaman, 130
    and eggplant curry, Red, 117
    hotpot, Japanese, 213
    and lentil curry, 128
    Panang, 100
    and peanut curry, Thai, 100
    and peppercorn stew, 187
    pho, 17
    pot roast, 175
    pot roast with eggplant, 192
    pot roast Provençale, 168
    potato and capsicum casserole, 51

and potatoes, Spiced, 133
and pumpkin curry, Thai, 92
in red wine, Braised, 168
and red wine stew, 193
rendang, 120
in soy, Chinese, 210
Spiced, 76
stew, Mexican, 158
stroganoff, 208
and vegetable casserole, 72
beer with capers, Beef in, 199
beer and chickpea stew, Pork, 179
bhujia stew, Lentil, 137
borlotti beans, Lamb with, 45
borscht, Hot beef, 8
Boston baked beans, 58
Bouillabaisse, 18
bourguignonne, Beef, 148
Braised beef in red wine, 168
braised chicken, Chinese, 202
Braised chicken and leek in wine, 184
Braised oxtail casserole, 89
Braised pork with prunes, 147
bread, Bacon, cheese and onion, 235
bread, Sour cream polenta, 234
bread, Zucchini and olive, 231
broad bean stew, Chicken, artichoke and, 194
broccoli casserole, Chicken and, 70
broth, Roast duck and noodle, 10
broth with rice, Portuguese chicken, 31

C

Cabbage rolls, 155
Canja, 31
caper casserole, Veal, lemon and, 65
capers, Beef in beer with, 199
capsicum casserole, Beef, potato and, 51
capsicum stew, Bean and, 143
Caramel pork with Shanghai noodles, 42
caraway dumplings, Beef casserole with, 46
caraway noodles, Paprika veal with, 195
carbonnade, Beef, 56
Cassoulet, 50
Catalan fish stew, 141
Cauliflower and fennel purée, 220
Celeriac, potato and roasted garlic mash, 224
Champ, 221
Channa masala, 118
Chapatis, 237
Cheese and herb pull-apart loaf, 230
cheese and onion bread, Bacon, 235
Cheese and pea curry, 99
chicken
    Apricot, 74

artichoke and broad bean stew, 194
Avgolemono with, 20
with balsamic vinegar, 173
Balti, 111
and broccoli casserole, 70
broth with rice, Portuguese, 31
casserole, Mexican, 85
casserole, Tomato, 74
Chinese braised, 202
and cider stew with apple and potato mash, 206
and coconut milk soup, 14
curry with apricots, 131
curry, Green, 103
curry, Nonya, 115
curry, Vietnamese, 119
with feta and olives, 203
kapitan, 95
laksa, 7
leek and sweet potato one-pot, 43
and leek in wine, Braised, 184
Madrid, 149
Marsala, 198
Moroccan, 189
and mushroom casserole, 81
and noodle hotpot, Ponzu, 139
noodle soup, Asian, 30
and pasta casseroles, Individual, 79
and red wine casserole, 66
and rice stew, Spanish, 161
Sichuan, 188
Spicy apricot, 185
stew, Creamy tomato and, 176
stew, Lemon and rosemary, 165
Chickpea curry, 118
Chickpea and herb dumpling soup, 25
chickpea stew, Italian sausage and, 174
chickpea stew, Pork, beer and, 179
Chilli con carne, 204
Chilli con pollo, 160
chilli, Vegetarian, 159
Chinese beef in soy, 210
Chinese braised chicken, 202
Chinese pork and noodle soup, 11
chowder, Clam, 37
chowder, Mexican bean, 36
chowder, Smoked haddock, 29
Chu chee curry paste, 251
Chu chee seafood, 116
Chu chee tofu, 105
Chunky vegetable soup, 27
chutney, Coriander, 247
chutney, Mango, 244

cider stew with apple and potato mash, Chicken and, 206
Cioppino, 186
Clam chowder, 37
Cocino madrileno, 183
coconut curry, Duck and, 124
coconut curry, Indonesian vegetable and, 125
coconut milk soup, Chicken and, 14
Coconut rice, 240
Coconut seafood and tofu curry, 96
Colcannon, 226
Coriander chutney, 247
coriander mash, Sweet potato and, 224
coriander, Moroccan seafood with, 156
coriander stew, Pork and, 134
corn and noodle soup, Pork, 22
corn and potato mash, Creamy, 223
Corned beef, 196
couscous, Preserved lemon, 229
Crab curry, 101
Creamy corn and potato mash, 223
Creamy fish casserole, 60
Creamy garlic seafood stew, 150
Creamy polenta with Parmesan, 228
Creamy potato casserole, 68
Creamy potato and parsnip mash, 216
Creamy tomato and chicken stew, 176
Creamy veal and mushroom stew, 164
Crispy fried onions, 243
Cucumber raita, 245
curry paste
    Chu chee, 251
    Green, 250
    Madras, 248
    Musaman, 251
    Red, 250
    Yellow, 250
curry powder, Indian, 248
curry powder, Sri Lankan, 248

D
Dhal, 242
dhal, Spicy vegetable stew with, 170
duck
    and coconut curry, 124
    with juniper berries, 80
    and noodle broth, Roast, 10
    with pears, 167
    and pineapple curry, Thai, 98
Dum alu, 122
dumpling soup, Chickpea and herb, 25
dumplings, Beef casserole with caraway, 46
dumplings, Chicken paprika with, 88
dumplings, Rice, 241

E
Easy seafood paella, 200
eggplant, Beef pot roast with, 192
eggplant curry, Red beef and, 117
eggplant hotpot, Pork and, 153
Eggplant parmigiana, 63
Eight-treasure noodle soup, 32

F
fennel casserole, Veal and, 86
fennel purée, Cauliflower and, 220
fennel stew, Seafood and, 136
feta and olives, Chicken with, 203
feta and olives, Seafood casserole with, 59
fish
    ball and noodle soup, 33
    casserole, Creamy, 60
    casserole, Whole, 67
    curry, Goan, 129
    ginger and tomato hotpot, 78
    koftas in tomato curry sauce, 110
    and lemon grass casserole, 48
    and macaroni casserole, 44
    and noodle soup, Vietnamese, 23
    stew, Catalan, 141

G
Garam masala, 249
garlic, Lamb shanks with, 87
garlic mash, Celeriac, potato and roasted, 224
garlic seafood stew, Creamy, 150
ginger and tomato hotpot, Fish, 78
Goan fish curry, 129
goulash, Veal, 205
Greek octopus stew, 151
Green chicken curry, 103
Green curry paste, 250
Green tofu curry, 93

H
Ham, leek and potato ragu, 211
herb dumpling soup, Chickpea and, 25
herb pull-apart loaf, Cheese and, 230
Hot beef borscht, 8
Hot and sour soup, 16
hotpot, Fish, ginger and tomato, 78
hotpot, Japanese beef, 213
hotpot, Lamb, 9
hotpot, Lancashire, 57
hotpot, Mongolian lamb, 172
hotpot, Ponzu chicken and noodle, 139
hotpot, Pork and eggplant, 153
hotpot with rice noodles, Lamb, 144
hotpot, Tofu, vegetable and noodle, 212

I
Indian curry powder, 248
Individual chicken and pasta casseroles, 79
Indonesian vegetable and coconut curry, 125
Italian sausage and chickpea stew, 174

J
Japanese beef hotpot, 213
Jerusalem artichoke purée, 227
Jungle curry prawns, 121
juniper berries, Duck with, 80

K
kapitan, Chicken, 95
kefta, Lamb, 135
kidney stew, Steak and, 152
kidneys in creamy mustard sauce, Lamb's, 197
Kitcheree, 239
koftas in tomato curry sauce, Fish, 110
korma, Lamb, 106

L
laksa, Chicken, 7
laksa, Prawn, 24
lamb
    and bean casserole, 71
    with borlotti beans, 45
    hotpot, 9
    hotpot, Mongolian, 172
    hotpot with rice noodles, 144
    kefta, 135
    kidneys in creamy mustard sauce, 197
    korma, 106
    liver and bacon stew, 146
    and mustard stew, 177
    Navarin of, 39
    neck curry, 114
    with quince and lemon, Tagine of, 49
    rogan josh, 97
    shanks with garlic, 87
    shanks with Puy lentils, 82
    shanks in tomato sauce on polenta, 55
    and spinach curry, 127
    tagine, 154
Lancashire hotpot, 57
leek and potato ragu, Ham, 211
leek and sweet potato one-pot, Chicken, 43
leek in wine, Braised chicken and, 184
lemon and caper casserole, Veal, 65
lemon couscous, Preserved, 229
lemon grass casserole, Fish and, 48
Lemon and rosemary chicken stew, 165
lemon, Tagine of lamb with quince and, 49
lentil

bhujia stew, 137
curry, Beef and, 128
Lamb shanks with Puy, 82
and silverbeet soup, 21
soup, Spiced, 34
stew, Pork and, 178
Lion's head meatballs, 61
liver and bacon stew, Lamb's, 146
loaf, Cheese and herb pull-apart, 230
loaf, Parmesan and prosciutto, 233
loaves, Mini wholemeal, 232
Lontong, 241

M
macaroni casserole, Fish and, 44
Madras beef curry, 104
Madras curry paste, 248
Madrid chicken, 149
Mango chutney, 244
Marsala, Chicken, 198
mash
    Celeriac, potato and   roasted garlic, 224
    Chicken and cider stew with
    apple and potato, 206
    Creamy corn and potato, 223
    Creamy potato and parsnip, 216
    Roast vegetable, 215
    Roasted pumpkin and walnut, 218
    Sweet potato and coriander, 224
    Watercress and potato, 222
Mattar paneer, 99
meatballs, Lion's head, 61
meatballs, Sweet and sour, 73
Mexican bean chowder, 36
Mexican beef stew, 158
Mexican chicken casserole, 85
Mexican tomato casserole, 77
Minestrone, 13
Mini wholemeal loaves, 232
Miso with ramen, 35
Mongolian lamb hotpot, 172
mornay casserole, Seafood, 41
Moroccan chicken, 189
Moroccan seafood with coriander, 156
Mulligatawny, 15
Musaman beef curry, 130
Musaman curry paste, 251
Musaman vegetable curry, 102
mushroom casserole, Chicken and, 81
mushroom stew, Creamy veal and, 164
Mussel and tomato stew, 171
mustard sauce, Lamb's kidneys in creamy, 197
mustard stew, Lamb and, 177

N
Naan, 236
Navarin of lamb, 39
Nonya chicken curry, 115
noodles
    broth, Roast duck and, 10
    Caramel pork with Shanghai, 42
    hotpot, Ponzu chicken and, 139
    hotpot, Tofu, vegetable and, 212
    Lamb hotpot with rice, 144
    Paprika veal with caraway, 195
    soup, Asian chicken, 30
    soup, Chinese pork and, 11
    soup, Eight-treasure, 32
    soup, Fish ball and, 33
    soup, Pork, corn and, 22
    soup, Vietnamese fish and, 23
    and vegetable soup, Soba, 26

O
octopus, Provençale, 182
octopus stew, Greek, 151
olive bread, Zucchini and, 231
olives, Chicken with feta and, 203
olives, Seafood casserole with feta and, 59
one-pot, Chicken, leek and sweet potato, 43
onion bread, Bacon, cheese and, 235
onions, Crispy fried, 243
Osso buco, 140
osso buco, Turkey, 190
oxtail casserole, Braised, 89

P
paella, Easy seafood, 200
Panang beef, 100
paprika with dumplings, Chicken, 88
paprika and potato stew, Pork, 207
Paprika veal with caraway noodles, 195
Parmesan, Creamy polenta with, 228
Parmesan and prosciutto loaf, 233
parmigiana, Eggplant, 63
parsnip mash, Creamy potato and, 216
parsnips, Barley soup with golden, 28
Pasta and bean soup, 12
pasta casseroles, Individual chicken and, 79
Pasta and vegetable casserole, 53
pea curry, Cheese and, 99
Pea purée, 217
peanut curry, Thai beef and, 100
pears, Duck with, 167
peppercorn stew, Beef and, 187
pho, Beef, 17
pickle, Tomato, 246
pineapple curry, Thai duck and, 98

polenta bread, Sour cream, 234
polenta, Lamb shanks in tomato sauce on, 55
polenta with Parmesan,   Creamy, 228
Ponzu chicken and noodle hotpot, 139
pork
    beer and chickpea stew, 179
    and coriander stew, 134
    corn and noodle soup, 22
    and eggplant hotpot, 153
    and lentil stew, 178
    and noodle soup, Chinese, 11
    paprika and potato stew, 207
    with prunes, Braised, 147
    sausage and soy bean casserole, 84
    sausage and white bean stew, 166
    with Shanghai noodles, Caramel, 42
    and tamarind curry, 108
    vindaloo, 94
Portuguese chicken broth with rice, 31
pot roast, Beef, 175
pot roast with eggplant, Beef, 192
pot roast Provençale, Beef, 168
pot roast, Turkey, 52
potato
    and capsicum casserole, Beef, 51
    casserole, Creamy, 68
    mash, Chicken and cider stew
    with apple and, 206
    mash, Creamy corn and, 223
    mash, Watercress and, 222
    and parsnip mash, Creamy, 216
    ragu, Ham, leek and, 211
    and roasted garlic mash, Celeriac, 224
    Smothered, 122
    Spiced beef and, 133
    stew, Pork, paprika and, 207
Prawn laksa, 24
prawns, Jungle curry, 121
prawns, Spicy, 91
Preserved lemon couscous, 229
prosciutto loaf, Parmesan and, 233
Provençale octopus, 182
prunes, Braised pork with, 147
pull-apart loaf, Cheese and herb, 230
pumpkin curry, Thai beef and, 92
pumpkin and walnut mash, Roasted, 218
purée, Cauliflower and fennel, 220
purée, Jerusalem artichoke, 227
purée, Pea, 217
purée, Yellow split pea, 218
Puy lentils, Lamb shanks with, 82

Q
quince and lemon, Tagine of lamb with, 49

R

ragu, Ham, leek and potato, 211
raita, Cucumber, 245
ramen, Miso with, 35
Ratatouille, 162
Red beef and eggplant curry, 117
Red curry paste, 250
red wine, Braised beef in, 168
red wine casserole, Chicken and, 66
red wine stew, Beef and, 193
rendang, Beef, 120
rice
    Coconut, 240
    dumplings, 241
    Portuguese chicken broth with, 31
    Saffron, 238
    stew, Spanish chicken and, 161
Roast duck and noodle broth, 10
Roast vegetable mash, 215
Roasted pumpkin and walnut mash, 218
rogan josh, Lamb, 97
rosemary chicken stew, Lemon and, 165

S

Saffron rice, 238
sausage and chickpea stew, Italian, 174
sausage and soy bean casserole, Pork, 84
sausage and white bean stew, Pork, 166
seafood
    casserole with feta and olives, 59
    Chu chee, 116
    with coriander, Moroccan, 156
    curry, Balinese, 112
    and fennel stew, 136
    mornay casserole, 41
    paella, Easy, 200
    stew, 186
    stew, Creamy garlic, 150
    and tofu curry, Coconut, 96
Shabu shabu, 213
Sichuan chicken, 188
silverbeet soup, Lentil and, 21
Smoked haddock chowder, 29
Smothered potatoes, 122
Soba noodle and vegetable soup, 26
Sour cream polenta bread, 234
sour soup, Hot and, 16
soy bean casserole, Pork sausage and, 84
soy, Chinese beef in, 210
Spanish chicken and rice stew, 161
Spiced beef, 76
Spiced beef and potatoes, 133
Spiced lentil soup, 34
Spicy apricot chicken, 185

Spicy prawns, 91
Spicy vegetable stew with dhal, 170
spinach curry, Lamb and, 127
split pea purée, Yellow, 218
squid stew, Stuffed, 163
Sri Lankan curry powder, 248
Steak and kidney stew, 152
stroganoff, Beef, 208
Stuffed squid stew, 163
Sukiyaki, 138
Sweet potato and coriander mash, 224
sweet potato one-pot, Chicken, leek and, 43
Sweet and sour meatballs, 73

T

tagine, Lamb, 154
Tagine of lamb with quince and lemon, 49
tagine, Vegetable, 142
tamarind curry, Pork and, 108
Thai beef and peanut curry, 100
Thai beef and pumpkin curry, 92
Thai duck and pineapple curry, 98
tofu, Chu chee, 105
tofu curry, Coconut seafood and, 96
tofu curry, Green, 93
Tofu, vegetable and noodle hotpot, 212
tomato
    casserole, Mexican, 77
    chicken casserole, 74
    and chicken stew, Creamy, 176
    curry sauce, Fish koftas in, 110
    hotpot, Fish, ginger and, 78
    pickle, 246
    sauce on polenta, Lamb shanks in, 55
    stew, Mussel and, 171
Tuna and white bean casserole, 40
Turkey osso buco, 190
Turkey pot roast, 52

V

veal
    with caraway noodles, Paprika, 195
    and fennel casserole, 86
    goulash, 205
    lemon and caper casserole, 65
    and mushroom stew, Creamy, 164
vegetable
    casserole, Beef and, 72
    casserole, Pasta and, 53
    and coconut curry, Indonesian, 125
    curry, 109
    curry, Musaman, 102
    curry, Yellow, 126
    mash, Roast, 215

    and noodle hotpot, Tofu, 212
    soup, Chunky, 27
    soup, Soba noodle and, 26
    stew, Autumn, 180
    stew with dhal, Spicy, 170
    tagine, 142
Vegetarian chilli, 159
Vietnamese chicken curry, 119
Vietnamese fish and noodle soup, 23
Vindaloo paste, 249
vindaloo, Pork, 94

W

walnut mash, Roasted pumpkin and, 218
Watercress and potato mash, 222
white bean casserole, Tuna and, 40
white bean stew, Pork sausage and, 166
Whole fish casserole, 67
wholemeal loaves, Mini, 232
wine, Braised beef in red, 168
wine, Braised chicken and leek in, 184
wine casserole, Chicken and red, 66
wine stew, Beef and red, 193

Y

Yellow curry paste, 250
Yellow split pea purée, 218
Yellow vegetable curry, 126

Z

Zucchini and olive bread, 231

USEFUL INFORMATION

The recipes in this book were developed using a tablespoon measure of 20 ml. In some other countries the tablespoon is 15 ml. For most recipes this difference will not be noticeable but, for recipes using baking powder, gelatine, bicarbonate of soda, small amounts of flour and cornflour, we suggest that, if you are using the smaller tablespoon, you add an extra teaspoon for each tablespoon.

The recipes in this book are written using convenient cup measurements. You can buy special measuring cups in the supermarket or use an ordinary household cup: first you need to check it holds 250 ml (8 fl oz) by filling it with water and measuring the water (pour it into a measuring jug or even an empty yoghurt carton). This cup can then be used for both liquid and dry cup measurements.

Liquid cup measures

1/4 cup	60 ml	2 fluid oz
1/3 cup	80 ml	2 1/2 fluid oz
1/2 cup	125 ml	4 fluid oz
3/4 cup	180 ml	6 fluid oz
1 cup	250 ml	8 fluid oz

Spoon measures

1/4 teaspoon	1.25 ml
1/2 teaspoon	2.5 ml
1 teaspoon	5 ml
1 tablespoon	20 ml

Nutritional information

The nutritional information given for each recipe does not include any garnishes or accompaniments, such as rice or pasta, unless they are included in specific quantities in the ingredients list. The nutritional values are approximations and can be affected by biological and seasonal variations in foods, the unknown composition of some manufactured foods and uncertainty in the dietary database. Nutrient data given are derived primarily from the NUTTAB95 database produced by the Australian New Zealand Food Authority.

Oven Temperatures

You may find cooking times vary depending on the oven you are using. For fan-forced ovens, as a general rule, set oven temperature to 20°C lower than indicated in the recipe.

Note: Those who might be at risk from the effects of salmonella food poisoning (the elderly, pregnant women, young children and those suffering from immune deficiency diseases) should consult their GP with any concerns about eating raw eggs.

Weight

10 g	1/4 oz	220 g	7 oz	425 g	14 oz
30 g	1 oz	250 g	8 oz	475 g	15 oz
60 g	2 oz	275 g	9 oz	500 g	1 lb
90 g	3 oz	300 g	10 oz	600 g	1 1/4 lb
125 g	4 oz	330 g	11 oz	650 g	1 lb 5 oz
150 g	5 oz	375 g	12 oz	750 g	1 1/2 lb
185 g	6 oz	400 g	13 oz	1 kg	2 lb

Alternative names

bicarbonate of soda	—	baking soda
capsicum	—	red or green (bell) pepper
chickpeas	—	garbanzo beans
cornflour	—	cornstarch
fresh coriander	—	cilantro
cream	—	single cream
eggplant	—	aubergine
flat-leaf parsley	—	Italian parsley
hazelnut	—	filbert
jaffle	—	toasted sandwich
plain flour	—	all-purpose flour
prawns	—	shrimp
rocket	—	arugula
sambal oelek	—	chilli paste
snow pea	—	mange tout
spring onion	—	scallion
thick cream	—	double/heavy cream
tomato paste (US/Aus.)	—	tomato purée (UK)
kettle barbecue	—	Kettle grill/Covered barbecue
zucchini	—	courgette

2006 Barnes & Noble Publishing

ISBN-13: 978-0-7607-8295-8
ISBN-10: 0-7607-8295-4

Printed and bound in China by Toppan Printing Co. Ltd.

10 9 8 7 6 5 4 3 2 1